The Law that Changed the Face
of America

The Law that Changed the Face of America

The Immigration and Nationality Act of 1965

Margaret Sands Orchowski

ROWMAN & LITTLEFIELD
Lanham • Boulder • New York • London

Published by Rowman & Littlefield
A wholly owned subsidary of The Rowman & Littlefield Publishing Group, Inc.
4501 Forbes Boulevard, Suite 200, Lanham, Maryland 20706
www.rowman.com

Unit A, Whitacre Mews, 26-34 Stannary Street, London SE11 4AB

British Library Cataloguing in Publication Information Available

Library of Congress Cataloging-in-Publication Data

Orchowski, Margaret Sands, 1941-- author.
The law that changed the face of America : The Immigration and Nationality Act of 1965 / by Margaret Sands Orchowski.
pages cm.
Includes bibliographical references and index.
ISBN 978-1-4422-5136-6 (cloth : alk. paper) -- ISBN 978-1-4422-5137-3 (electronic)
1. United States. Immigration and Nationality Act. 2. Emigration and immigration law--United States--History. 3. Aliens--United States. 4. Citizenship--United States. 5. Naturalization--United States. I. Title.
KF4806.61965073 2015
342.7308'2--dc23
2015015413

♾ ™ The paper used in this publication meets the minimum requirements of American National Standard for Information Sciences Permanence of Paper for Printed Library Materials, ANSI/NISO Z39.48-1992.

Printed in the United States of America

Contents

Foreword

There is hardly a day that goes by that some congressman, political activist, pundit, or media anchor doesn't say "Our immigration system is broken and needs to be fixed! It is in urgent need of reform!" It's the one statement in all the contentious debates about immigration reform—perhaps the hottest political issue in Congress today and said to impinge on President Obama's legacy—about which almost everyone seems to agree.

I have been covering immigration and immigration reform in Congress the past ten years for a national Hispanic magazine. For me, as a senior journalist, the highly active story about changing immigration laws provokes the essential questions of my craft: why, how, and who? Why and how did the present immigration law become so broken? How did it come into being in the first place and by whom? Are those same characters and issues still around in trying to fix it? What is similar and what is different?

Problem is, these questions regarding immigration law require a historical perspective. But many people think that is boring! Or . . . ?

Turns out, I discovered, that our history of evolving immigration laws is not boring! Not boring at all. In fact, it's highly enlightening!

It turns out that the immigration law that is so maligned today was a product of one of the most transformational periods in American history: the civil rights era. Turns out that the Immigration and Nationality Act (the INA) that was voted in and signed on October 3, 1965, was (and arguably is still) the most liberal national immigration law in the world. It was created by Ted Kennedy in the "fabulous 89th Congress"—a large majority Democratic House and Senate that was voted in along with President Lyndon B Johnson after the shocking assassination of the Camelot President John F. Kennedy. JFK was the first Catholic ever to be president, the grandson of Irish immigrants, a liberal Democrat from the Northeast at a time (the 1960s) when Southern Democrats, many of them openly racists, ruled Congress.

Today's INA, the law that is so often dismissed as draconian, was part of the wave of Johnson's "Great Society" liberal laws passed in 1965 following the almost miraculous passage in 1964 of the Civil Rights Act. That act committed the United States to end discrimination everywhere in the country based on race, creed, religion, and *national origin*. Yet national origin was the very core of the U.S. immigration law at the time, the National Origins Act of 1924, which established *quota*s for immigrant entry based on their nationality.

Bingo! Aha! Lightbulb!

There is so much more! This is just the beginning of the history of the INA and how it evolved over the past 50 years. This is just the beginning of the "lightbulb" moments that occur when understanding how immigration laws evolved in the United States, what were the key movements, who were the people involved in developing, passing, and implementing them, and what were the impacts and consequences. It's about how the two great masters of bipartisan compromise and respect—President Johnson and the young brother of JFK, Senator Edward M. Kennedy—worked to pass laws that transformed America. The history of the INA puts into perspective how times have changed or haven't: what is similar and what is different today in dealing with the demands to reform immigration laws.

But the dilemma for a writer, and especially a journalist, is how to present all this complex history in as comprehensive but readable and easy-to-capture way as possible?

There are so many good stories about the people involved that are natural for a journalist to include. But what about the history of the legislation itself? How is the best way for a journalist to show how the legislation evolved?

For me, the most readable and visual way to trace how it happened is with narrative timelines. I believe especially in narrative timelines because on February 23, 1970, students at the bucolic University of California, with surfboards leaning against classroom walls near the beachside, leisurely, Hispanic-heritage town of Santa Barbara, burned down the Bank of America in a rampage of protest.

Santa Barbara is my hometown and even though I was intimately involved with the university (my father was a professor there and in 1970 I had just finished an MA degree at UCSB in political science and international relations), I was stunned by the violence of the protests and police reaction. Hundreds were arrested and hauled off to jail (including my brother-in-law who had gone out in the courtyard to check the student apartment complex he lived in and managed in Isla Vista, the student village next to the UCSB campus where the Bank of America was located).

The city's citizens, many of them well-off, well-educated, and active in civic affairs, were equally shocked. Within days, they formed the Santa Barbara Citizens Commission on Civil Disorders to find out why and exactly what propelled the quiet campus to explode and to write a report on recommended actions to make sure it never happened again. For the commission, 23 Democrats and 23 Republicans were appointed as commissioners from all backgrounds and walks of life. The co-chairpersons (a woman and a man) were well-known active partisan leaders in the city and the state. Two hearings, three times a week, were held for two months with hundreds of witnesses including students, police, university administrators, shopkeepers, everyone who was involved. The hearings were taped, transcribed, and printed out each day for the commissioners and the public. I was the one and only full-time commission staff person.

The report took two months to write by committee and was approved by consensus of the whole—every word. It was printed on newsprint, available to everyone for free after being published verbatim in the *Santa Barbara News-Press*. There were more than 100 recommendations and almost all were implemented and many still exist (such as the "IV" police foot and bicycle patrols). The report included sections about personal stories and analysis of the issues. But its most enlightening section according to almost everyone, was a historical timeline of events—national, state, and local—that had come up in hearings and investigations as being significant in politicizing (some called it "radicalizing") the students.

(NOTE: For the record, only a few students were involved in the evening bank-burning plot. The bank had been warned and had installed a mobile bank nearby just in case. The massive student protests and arrests that followed were due to the overreaction of the police department that then escalated into a vicious cycle of student/official reactions-to-the-reactions to fast-moving events. In the end, most of the arrested students were released, without a record, after a night in jail.)

But it was the timeline that made the citizens of Santa Barbara and the city and university officials realize that even students at a bucolic beach campus could be and would be involved in the issues of their day. The timeline gave perspective to the changing environment in the United States above and beyond the politics of the day. That new environment was comprised of the culmination of things that had happened over the years—such as the assassinations of the Kennedys—President JFK in 1963 and Robert in 1968; the highly unpopular war in Vietnam throughout the 1960s and the big oil spill in Santa Barbara in 1969 that is said to have started the environmental movement. Those events affected everyone and their attitude toward government and American society.

So it is with immigration and immigration reform, immigrants and citizens of every nation-state. No one lives in a vacuum. I try to show in this book how ever-changing global and national conditions, including economic, demographic, technological, and political factors, drive not only immigration but also the national laws that manage it. Seeing those changes in a time-line—even with a quick perusal down the dates and action—allows greater understanding of the whys and whos of the reform of immigration laws.

I have no illusions that I have told the whole story, however. There is a lot of history presented here and much that I had to leave out. There are bound to be errors of omission and details. As a journalist I hope to follow up on many of these stories and hope to see others added to what is here with new and/or corrected details.

What I have tried to do is to honestly present the information in a factual nonpartisan way. I truly do not have an agenda on immigration reform and there is no intention on my part to push any particular immigration policy. I am a credentialed congressional journalist and eagerly interview, cover, try to understand, and report the positions of all congressional representatives no matter what their party affiliation and ideology, as well as the members of interest groups that lobby Congress on all sides of the immigration issue.

This nonpartisan, non–agenda-driven, non-advocative approach is especially relevant in writing for a magazine oriented to the interests of the Hispanic-heritage population in the United States. As I point out several times in the book, Hispanic-heritage Americans, especially the young, are as diverse as America itself—as multinational, multiethnic, multilingual, multi-religious, multisocioeconomic, multi-everything as the amazing new millennial generation growing up now in America. Like all Americans today, Hispanics are a part of the significant impact of the Immigration and Nationality Act of 1965 that opened immigration to everyone no matter their race, creed, religion, or national origin. The act truly changed the face of America.

Introduction

Why This Book?

The year 2015 marks the 50th anniversary of the passage of "the law that changed the face of America"—the Immigration and Nationality Act (INA), the Hart-Celler Immigration Act of 1965. At the Statue of Liberty on October 3, 1965, President Lyndon B. Johnson with Senator Ted Kennedy, the brother of the slain president, at his side, signed this historic law that made the United States the highly diverse nation of immigrants that it is today.

The Immigration and Nationality Act of 1965 completely replaced the nation's first comprehensive immigration law of 1924 that had set specific quotas against and preferences for immigrants of particular nationalities. The INA did away with the codified quotas and discrimination of immigrants based on national origin; it opened the front gate of America to immigrants from every race, creed, religion, and nationality. It gave a legal priority for permanent immigration to extended family "unification" for the first time. Its importance and impact on the country equals that of the Civil and Voting Rights Acts of 1964 that have been celebrated, analyzed, and extolled by books and events throughout the country the past two years. The Immigration and Nationality Act of 1965 was responsible for the United States becoming the world model of what a successful "Nation of Immigrants" can be.

Now is a critical time for the public and immigration policy makers to understand how and why the historic 1965 INA passed and how it evolved over five decades. Americans and our leaders need to understand the profound and dramatic impact that the nationality-diversity and family-first principles of the INA had and continue to have on immigration policy in the country. Efforts to reform it the past eight years have become an increasingly invective gotcha political battle. The so-called immigration reform debate

1

between advocates has become increasingly shrill, narrow, polarized, coarsened, less civil, less sensible, and less to do with the core issues of immigration itself. If continued, the abusive tones and narrowing points of view of the discourse in public forums over immigration reform will debilitate the chances for our once successful "Nation of Immigrants" to remain so.

What is needed today is a universal understanding about what immigration is, and why there are immigration laws. That includes what crucial roles immigration laws have in a nation, how they evolve, and what are the major factors in the political and economic environment that affect global immigration and national immigration regulations. What is needed is a civil debate that shows that the proponents of different options for immigration reform understand what comprise the major factors in the global, national, political, and economic environment that affect immigration and immigration laws. A more productive debate about U.S. immigration reform can begin by understanding how our own immigration laws, especially the INA of 1965, developed and evolved, putting its passage into perspective with the expectations of today, and learning lessons from its 50 years of existence.

That is the goal of this book. Chapter 1 has been written with the intent to understand why immigration laws exist. It describes the romanticized view of immigration and then outlines the true basics. It lays out what are the four main factors, events, and drivers that cause immigration and immigration laws to change.

Chapter 2 traces the evolution of how we managed immigrants from our earliest colonial days in the 1600s, until after the Civil War from the 1880s to the 1920s. That was when the first national immigration laws were established (in 1882) and the first national attempts to manage them including the opening of Ellis Island as an official port of entry and the development of the first national immigration bureaucracy. It describes the reasons behind the largest surge of immigrants into the country in our history—between 1880 and 1920, the post-World War I isolationist era, and the wild prosperity of the Roaring Twenties. It reports how all that led to the passage of the first comprehensive immigration law in the country—the highly restrictive National Origins Act of 1924 that dictated strict quotas for immigrants from anywhere but Northern Europe.

Chapter 3 describes the tumultuous years after the 1924 National Origins Act that led to the historical passage of the 1924 law's opposite: the 1965 Immigration and Nationality Act that prioritized immigration diversity and family unification. It's a journey through the Depression and the progressive New Deal, and then a second world war that projected a reluctant United States into a position of world leadership. It shows how a totally new era of prosperity and revolution developed with increasing demands for activism against discrimination coming from the growing awareness and repugnance of the Holocaust and the Jim Crow laws. It was the beginning of the civil rights movement propelled by the assassination of President Kennedy and the ascension of President Johnson, a liberal Democrat inside the racist, Democratic-dominated South who was a master of bipartisan negotiation. It drove a new era of Great Society legislation, of growing demands for ethnic rights and growing internationalism reflected in the popularity of the Peace Corps and budding international corporations.

The story of the passage of the INA also is imbedded in the legacy of President Johnson and the "fabulous 89th"—arguably the most liberal democratic Congress in our history. The story profoundly involves the Kennedys—President John and Attorney General Robert, but especially Senator Ted Kennedy for whom the Immigration and Nationality Act of 1965 became his proudest legacy of diversity and fairness. Immigration was an issue he was passionate about until his death in 2009.

There is a mystery as well. Why was the (rather obvious with hindsight) potential of the INA to rapidly increase the number of immigrants into the country and to powerfully change the nation's demographic composition, completely understated and underplayed by Ted Kennedy and the Johnson administration? How much did they understand and know about what profound impact on American culture the INA would have? Who else drove its passage in 1965 other than Ted Kennedy? Why did they do it and why were they successful? How much did Kennedy's Catholicism and the election of his brother as the first Catholic president have to do with it? What impact did World War II and especially the Holocaust have on specific reformers of 1965? And why was the archaic Congressional Committee Reorganization Act of 1947 such a vital player in the passage of the INA almost 20 years later?

Chapter 4 reveals the multitude of unexpected consequences and impacts that the INA of 1965 inflicted on the country. Those include, first and foremost, the continual rise in the diversity of immigrants from all over the world and the rapid multiplication of the numbers of new immigrants and immigrant statuses: permanent, temporary, and illegal.

This chapter particularly describes the significant growth in the illegal immigrant population as well as the increase in actions, official and not, to protect illegal immigrants from sanctions, especially deportation and the denial of national and state benefits. The chapter also traces how new ethnic, identity, and immigrant rights groups were invented over the decades, such as the ethnic group most associated (unfairly as it turns out) with illegal immigration—"Latinos."

Chapter 4 also depicts an increasing confusion about immigration by the general public and lawmakers. Why was immigration—especially illegal immigration—being treated like a civil right when it inherently isn't? Is the very act of managing and enforcing laws that codify a sovereign nation state's core responsibility to protect its borders and to choose who can come in, stay, work, and become a citizen and who can't, really unfair discrimination? Are immigration laws per se inhumane? Is deportation a crime against humanity? Should only the "free market" decide who can immigrate and work in a country?

Even the core raison d'etre of the INA is being challenged. How important is national diversity, or its opposite, to oppose nationality preferences? Should exceptions be allowed? What about codifying special deals for Cubans fleeing Communism? Or Mexican neighbors seeking a better life? Or Irish descendants who are from an original American founding nationality? Or Chinese and Indian IT workers and scientists—"the best and brightest" in the world? Or Ethiopian taxi drivers? Or El Salvadorian construction workers? What about nationality clustering; should it be allowed? Should the INA be reformed completely to change back to nationality preferences and caps?

All of these challenges, questions, and consequences described in chapter 4, were neither expected nor intended by the enthusiastic liberal idealists who created the Immigration and Nationality Act of 1965. They fought for it with the goal of ending immigration discrimination based on national origins.

Chapter 5 tracks the evolving focus of immigration law and enforcement now in the twenty-first century after the terrorist attack of 9/11. Among other things, it describes the impetus behind the creation of the Department of Homeland Security and for the first time in American history, an agency charged with internal enforcement of immigration laws—the Immigration and Customs Enforcement bureau. It shows how changes in the structure of immigration administration reflect a new national focus on immigration as a matter of national security—including the security of work opportunities in the nation for Americans first.

The chapter also covers how in the twenty-first century, immigration reform is taking place in a changing globalized competitive world, where while some see immigration as a threat to national security (including jobs for Americans), others see globalization as the freeing of a global labor force to get work in any country they choose. Some question if nation-states' borders and immigration laws might be obsolete altogether. Chapter 5 describes how in the past ten years, the 1965 Immigration and Nationality Act has been increasingly attacked in Congress as being "broken," even draconian, and in urgent need of reform. It examines what are the principal drivers and who are the key players for immigration reform in the twenty-first century. It describes how the rhetoric of comprehensive immigration reform used by its twentieth-century advocates and opponents has been transformed into a savage game of "gotcha" politics.

The chapter also shows how some of the successes of the INA seem to have left some core twentieth-century issues and advocates stuck in time. There is the startling development of a whole new and unique twenty-first-century generation: the "Millennials," the "whatever" generation of hypertolerant, multi-everything, totally global–social media–connected, 18–30-some thing-year-olds. They not only "get" diversity; they "are" diversity itself. They are the product of the 1965 Immigration and Nationality Act—a growing percentage are American-born Hispanic and mixed-heritage second and third generation immigrants. They are the result of civil rights and twenty-first-century technology. They are the model of the post-racial future and they look at the diversity of immigrants and American culture as absolutely normal.

Underlying all of this is the changing politics of political parties toward immigration issues. The chapter describes how both parties are split from within by competing interests. They include free market and civil libertarians who want more unrestricted immigration and the legalization of all illegal immigrants. They are countered by restrictionist-environmentalists, national security and law enforcement officials, and "American Firsters" who want to be sure the American environment and American workers are protected from massive unregulated waves of "cheaper labor" immigrants of all occupational levels, by having better enforcement of immigration laws and fewer immigration visas given out.

It's all part of the dynamics of immigration. In many ways they are the same challenges that faced the proponents of the liberal 1965 INA as well as those who enabled the passage of the harsh, 1924, restrictionist policy based on national origins.

There are many lessons to be learned from the history of the INA and the evolution of national immigration laws in the United States. Chapter 6 picks out seven major "lessons," as well as the prospects for immigration reform in 2016 and beyond, based on the past history of immigration law. The first lesson is that immigration laws are a constant work in progress that must change with the changing times. They will always need tweaking and updating, culling, adding onto, modernizing—call it "reforming" if you will. Immigration laws and policies can never be set in stone as a poem may be. They never will be changed "once and for all."

It is the intention of this book that knowing the story of the passage of the "fabulous" Immigration and Nationality Act of 1965, those interested in immigration and immigration reform today will use its lessons. More specifically, the goal is that with the perspective of immigration history in our country and the achievements, impacts, and consequences of the INA, the politics of immigration reform today can become more civil and productive. It hopefully can teach that some aspects of past immigration laws become obsolete, while some new changes will better fit the changing times and be reflective of a successful Nation of (diverse) Immigrants in the twenty-first century.

Chapter One

Why Immigration Laws?

THE IDEALISTIC VIEW OF U.S. IMMIGRATION

Immigration is a very personal, very emotional topic especially in the United States. Almost every resident of the United States today has an interesting and compelling family immigrant history, some more recent than others. Immigration touches almost every basic belief we have about our country and ourselves—especially our belief in our uniqueness as a Nation of Immigrants, and our belief in human equality and democracy. Often we tend to romanticize those histories. We almost always view immigration through our personal experiences with immigrants in our lives.

There are many surprisingly enduring myths about immigration in the United States. They are often cited as truths by today's immigrant advocates and pundits who criticize current law—the historic 1965 Immigration and Naturalization Act—for not following the ideals of the past. The myths cited usually include the following:

- From its beginning, the United States was a Nation of Immigrants, a unique nation made by and for immigrants with no restrictions. It's part of America's exceptionalism.
- From the beginning, America was the place to where anyone seeking freedom could come, work, settle down, and freely practice one's religion.
- Immigrant families including extended families were always welcome.
- Anyone wanting to, could just come in. They just had to get here. There were no visas, no immigration statuses like "permanent" or "temporary," or even "illegal" (except for the tired joke that "pilgrims were the first illegal immigrants who settled illegally on Indian lands"). There were no laws and no enforcement.

- America always welcomed the poor, the tired, the "huddled masses yearning to be free"; that is America's immigration policy and it is written literally in stone.
- Almost everyone in the world, especially those who suffer in their attempt(s) to immigrate to the United States, dream of and intend to become U.S. citizens—to become "Americans"—the only word we have for a U.S. citizen. In our eagerness to help immigrants fulfill their dream of becoming like us, we tend to accept them as being American almost as soon as they get here. We expect all immigrants to become enthusiastic, involved, voting (mainly democratic) citizens as soon as they can. Many people (who certainly don't know how it is in most other countries) believe our requirements for citizenship are too harsh, too long, and draconian.
- Immigration is a human right and therefore all immigrants are equal; it is discriminatory and inhumane to label immigrants by their actual status: permanent, temporary, or illegal.

Of course the truth about immigration to the United States is quite different. Even the idea that the United States is unique in being a Nation of Immigrants is not really true. Almost all the "new" nations of the world including those in South America, Australia, New Zealand, and even Africa were settled, developed, and proclaimed as nations in the eighteenth and nineteenth centuries by mostly immigrants (mostly from Western Europe), not by the native populations.

BASICS ABOUT IMMIGRATION AND IMMIGRATION LAW

Perhaps the biggest reason that the myths about immigration are so strong is because the basics of immigration are largely unrecognized. To better understand immigration and the laws that have evolved to manage it in the United States, to better have perspective on the historic 1965 "immigration law that changed the face of America," consider first the cold, basic facts that underlie immigration and immigration law.

Basic Fact One: The Paradox

There is a paradox about migration and immigration that greatly confuses, even emotionalizes, the debate. On one hand, it is a human right that is even codified in the United Nations Declaration of Human Rights,[1] that every citizen of any country in the world can leave their country—for any reason and often forever—without being impeded (with very few exceptions). Of course many countries have tried to rule that their citizens cannot leave and have enforced that ruling harshly—the Soviet Union and Cuba are two that are particularly well-known. But their citizens resist—often dramatically and usually bravely. Most of the nations of the world recognize every citizens' human right to leave their homeland.

The paradox is that there is no human, international, or civil right for any human being to just simply come into any country they choose, stay indefinitely, work, and become a citizen—to immigrate. The permission to do so (whether as a refugee, asylee, temporary worker, permanent visa immigrant, student, whatever) is the sole right of every sovereign nation-state to decide. It is one of the core responsibilities and right of every nation-state to protect their borders and to decide who can enter, stay, and become a citizen (even everyone holding a European Union passport has to be a citizen of one of the 23 independent EU member nation-states; each of those have their own rules and regulations as to whom and how immigrants can become citizens including to what extent the applicant must be fluent in the nation's language, such as Dutch or Danish).

Who can be a legal immigrant in a country is reflected in a nation-state's immigration laws, which also spell out how those laws are to be enforced.

Basic Fact Two: Immigration and Sovereign Nation-States

Every sovereign nation-state in the world with defined borders and national laws has immigration laws. It's how they define the immigration requirements they have chosen (usually through the legislative process in democratic states) of who can come in, stay, work, and become a citizen. No nation-state can sustain open borders. Even their international agreements to host refugees who come to their borders come with the caveat that the refugee must apply to the nation-state and qualify for that status.

Every nation-state sets for itself the qualifications for and the number of refugees, asylees, and legal immigrants (permanent and temporary) they will accept—with the possibility (rather high in most Western countries actually) that many if not most applicants will not qualify for the status. Of course there are many nation-states that neighbor countries at war where the refugees flood into the country in great numbers; but even they try to have order, set up limits, cooperate with refugee organizations such as the UNHCR to help vet and take care of the refugees in separate camps. These refugees are not regarded as documented immigrants until they have met requirements set by the host country.

It is clear that immigration and immigration laws are national affairs. The legislative jurisdiction for immigration in the United States (nor in most countries that I know about) has never been in the foreign affairs committee (although that committee, like others, have some specific interests on immigration—consular, visa-granting operations; vetting universities for foreign students; and so forth, over which they can have some legislative say).

While to immigrate is not a civil right, all immigrants have basic civil rights, but some countries consider "basic" differently than others. In the United States everyone regardless of immigration status has a right to habeas corpus, for instance, and the right to a defense attorney if they are innocent of a crime for which they are arrested. Not all countries grant that.

But all immigrants in a country, even those in the country legally, don't have equal rights. That depends on the kind of permit they have. In the United States, Legal Permanent Residents (immigrants who have been granted "green cards") have almost all the rights of a citizen except the vote. They also have the right to apply for citizenship after a certain period of time (usually five years); holding the green card is the only immigration status that is allowed to apply for citizenship. Some 1.2 million green cards are granted every year in the United States.

Citizens of other countries who are living in the United States on a wide alphabet soup of temporary permits (H-1Bs, student Fs and Js, investor visas, etc.) do not have the same rights as those on green cards. In all cases the permits are temporary, time limited, and often have working restrictions—especially for the spouses and children of the actual visa holder. Over two million temporary visas are issued every year.

Foreign nationals who are living in the United States without a valid permit (whether they came in illegally or overstayed a temporary visa) are illegal immigrants and have very few rights except the basics. In the United States however they are allowed free emergency medical care and their children have the right to attend public schools without question.

Almost all foreign nationals living in the United States regardless of their immigration status are expected to obey the laws of the land and be held responsible if they violate them—in other words with a few exceptions, all foreign nationals in the United States are considered to be under its jurisdiction. Under federal law, any immigrant can be deported by federal authorities for violation of U.S. laws.

That being said, until the 1880s in the United States, the responsibility to register and decide if an immigrant could stay fell under the jurisdiction of towns and states. Some were quite strict about the religious and ethnic backgrounds of immigrants in their local areas. Some early colonies and states forbade Jews or Catholics or even different kinds of Protestants to settle and work and raise families in their communities. The states even determined their own qualifications for naturalization, even though the Oath of Allegiance for Naturalization has been administered since the beginning of the Republic. It was understood that any immigrant who was naturalized in any state became a citizen of the entire United States.

After the Civil War, immigration was one of many issues that had been controlled by the states, but which then came under federal jurisdiction. Nationally, the legislative jurisdiction for immigration was assigned to the commerce committee; when that committee split up, jurisdiction went primarily to the labor committee; then became a standing committee. After World War II, immigration came under the jurisdiction of the Justice Department and the Judiciary Committees of both Houses, where each have subcommittees on immigration. Today, the Judiciary Committees have the principal responsibility for proposing and passing immigration law, although many other committees can contribute and hold hearings and suggest proposals on pieces of immigration proposals as well—from education to labor to homeland security and more.

In 2007 the White House initiated comprehensive immigration legislation and sent it directly to the Senate, without going through the committee hearing process at all. It can be done legally with the sponsorship of a major senator or congressman. But it does not assure success—even with (or perhaps despite) strong presidential support. The 2007 comprehensive bills developed by the Bush White House and strongly whipped by Senators Ted Kennedy and John McCain failed on the Senate floor—twice.

States do not have the jurisdiction to make immigration law since that is a national responsibility. However, states are not prohibited from making laws within their jurisdictions that affect immigrants. They do all the time. Examples include deciding to grant in-state tuition subsidies to college students who are illegally in the country under certain conditions that each state may determine (i.e., commonly states require that the unauthorized immigrant have graduated or earned a GED from a high school in that state); giving driving permits (or not) to illegal immigrants; prohibiting all but legal permanent immigrants from getting state welfare benefits; mandating that in order to get a state business license a business must use E-Verify to check if all employees are either citizens or have a legal permit to work. Most states and cities do not allow immigrants (legal or illegal) to vote, but not all state registration forms contain affidavits of citizenship and there is no single federal voting registration form to date. Some cities allow all residents no matter what their immigration status to vote in a local election.

Under national immigration law, those who qualify for immigration status in a nation-state are given documentation of that status, either as a temporary or permanent immigrant. Those who do not qualify and who are already residing in the country are legally required to voluntarily leave or face deportation, as are all foreign nationals who enter the country illegally or overstay a temporary permit and therefore are residing in the country illegally. In every immigration decision, it is the nation-state, not the immigrant, who decides the official and legal status and the enforcement of the laws.

Immigration laws of every country in the world contain deportation as an enforcement measure. It can be said that immigration laws would have no validity without forcible deportation and withdrawal of any future permits as the ultimate enforcement. In the United States, that enforcement can only be implemented by a national enforcement agency within the Department of Homeland Security, although other state and local agencies have been granted permission in federal law to help.

Basic Fact Three: Immigration is Mainly about Work

While there are many compelling reasons that drive world as well as intranational migration, at their core—both for the immigrant and for the nation-state—migration and immigration are about the ability and opportunity to get a good job, to work.

For the Immigrant

The main reason immigrants leave their homelands is because they want to improve their (or a family member's) opportunity to work, to earn or get an income, to provide for one's self and one's family. No matter what the reason, for the lack of sufficient income-generating opportunities in their homeland (be it discrimination or economic depression, competition, or ambition) most immigrants decide to leave because of income opportunities. Even the most activist of immigrant advocates will say that all immigrants and their families, including those who stay illegally, "come to work," come to "make a better life for their families."

It is a huge decision—maybe the biggest any individual or family makes—to leave their homeland; it has significant consequences. The decision to immigrate permanently will not only affect the immigrant but also all his family—those left behind and those who immigrate, too. It will greatly affect the lives of the immigrants' descendants who will be raised in another culture, with other customs, and often another language. By the third generation, most families of immigrants in the United States have little if any contact with the original homeland's customs and language, especially when there are the expected intermarriages of the next generations with America's great diversity of people. Parents and grandparents may not be able to speak the primary language of their children and grandchildren. That is just one of the significant but expected consequences of an immigrant's decision to immigrate.

For the Host Nation

Sovereign nation-states that welcome and host immigrants such as the United States strongly recognize the value of the immigrant worker. They like them, want them, appreciate their desire to work hard to make a better life for themselves and their families—even if it's a lower wage than Americans earn, that is usually better for many immigrants than in their homelands. It is usual for immigration laws in the United States and in most countries, to encourage specific immigrant workers to settle in their nation-states. New laws spell out in increasing detail exactly what kind of workers (and investors) can come into the country as a legal immigrant (temporary or permanent). Nation-states historically welcome immigrants because of their need for productive workers who will contribute to the prosperity of the country. Usually, the visas include the immediate family of the permit holder: spouse and minor children.

Increasingly, many of the new skilled immigrants and former foreign students are highly educated. Many completed secondary school educations more focused than ours in math and science. These young immigrants are thought to think in different ways. Some can be innovative. They also can create businesses with jobs for others—a few actually create big jobs in big companies based on Nobel prize–winning ideas that they may have developed in America's top global universities. That is the reason that President Obama and even many Republican legislators want to change the visa status of foreign students who have graduated with advanced degrees (MAs, PhDs) in the science, technology, engineering, and math fields from the temporary, nonimmigrant student permit it has always been, to a permanent residency green card leading to citizenship if they so choose

Yet, there are common conflicts between an immigrants' desire for income and a nation-state's desire for good workers. Obviously, no nation-state in the world can or does allow any and every immigrant who wants to come, to enter legally and especially illegally, solely on the basis of "wanting income, work, a job." No country recognizes "economic refugees"—those who leave their homelands solely because they can't make a living or have a precarious life there. Increasingly, in countries such as France and others that have strong labor unions, few good jobs are open to immigrants—legal or illegal—especially to those without a valid permit, a good education, and who have not assimilated into the culture. Increasingly, in countries with generous welfare systems open to all residents (like many social democratic states of Europe), a growing number of new immigrants and children of immigrants derive their basic income and living needs not from work but from government welfare programs and community outreach organizations. [2]

Employers in the United States on the other hand, where there are weaker private unions and government benefit programs, tend to have a high regard for immigrant workers and welcome them, even those without work permits. Most first-generation immigrants after all are usually exceedingly grateful to have work at and even below the normal wage of U.S. citizens; many are willing to work extremely hard, live stringently, and save money so that their children may have an American lifestyle that they never had. Many create small businesses that provide work usually at first for family members, then for other immigrants, and eventually for Americans. And while often much of the money that the first-generation immigrant earns is "repatriated," still their new, American-born families help the economy by spending and add to schools' full-time student count and income. Their children, especially American-born, usually quickly assimilate into the American educational system and culture.

But unlimited access to good, cheap, first-generation temporary and illegal immigrant labor—high skilled and low—cannot be an excuse for undermining a nation's immigration and labor laws.

Basic Fact Four: Two Roles of Immigration Laws

While the news media and advocates for illegal immigrants tend to portray immigration laws as being something restrictive, intolerant, and discriminatory, in fact immigration laws really are by definition positive. They define who can immigrate: who and how many are welcomed.

Assuming that no nation-state can sustain open borders for all the workers and their families who are eager to come, and that every nation-state is therefore obliged to choose who can be an immigrant, immigration laws are positive advocates for that choice. They set the limits that legislators believe will maintain the nation-state as a productive prosperous country for its citizens and new immigrants alike. The two roles for immigration laws are:

1. Legally bring in new immigrant workers that are needed and can contribute the most.
2. Protect national working standards that already exist for citizen and immigrant workers already working legally.

Obviously, these two roles have conflicting proponents. There are many commercial interests in the country (such as Chambers of Commerce) that want as productive (read: hardworking and inexpensive, high- and low-skilled) unregulated labor as possible. Many believe that willing foreign labor and the jobs they want are more numerous than there are American workers to fill them. They believe that within a few parameters, the free market will match these workers to the jobs available. Many are adamant: "The fewer restrictions the better."

Other interests (economic nationalists and some environmentalists especially) are concerned about the impact of lower-paid immigrant workers (especially those working illegally) on the environment and on America's resources—physical and economic, local and national. They are concerned how hundreds of thousands of new immigrants—legal and illegal, high tech and low—will continue the trend of declining wages, work standards, benefits, working hours, and living standards of long-time, native workers and legal immigrants.

Still others see only the humanitarian side of immigration—a chance for the bravest, most entrepreneurial people throughout the world to move and make a better life for themselves and their family. There are some globalist humanitarians who believe there should be no borders to human mobility.

These are historic economic, social, and political areas of tension and disagreement regarding immigration in the United States. They are the stuff of immigration politics.

Basic Fact Five: A Successful Nation of Immigrants Is Balanced: The Interests of the Nation and the Interests of Immigrants

This is easier said than done, but the United States has had long periods of being particularly successful and being a model for the balancing of the interests of our nation-state and those of immigrants. We have particularly congratulated ourselves for having successfully assimilated our immigrants into the American way of life. Immigrants have diversified our culture, enriched and made the country prosperous economically. In varying degrees, throughout our history, immigrants have been welcomed to come, to assimilate, and, over time, to be successful in the American culture, especially its commercial culture.

THE DRIVERS OF IMMIGRATION

So what drives immigrants to come? And why do nations welcome, accept, and even compete for immigrants sometimes, and why are they at times less welcoming? What drives immigrants to make the life-changing, family heritage–changing decision to leave their homelands? What drives countries to host them? Similarly, on what demands to change immigration laws based?

There seems to be four main drivers of immigration that affect both why immigrants leave their homelands and want to immigrate (in this case to the United States) and the changing needs of host countries (the United States in this case) for new immigrants:

1. Economic conditions
2. National demographics and culture
3. New technology
4. National politics—especially congressional politics and interest groups

These elements can be clearly seen in a brief look at how immigration laws and the management of immigrants and immigration laws evolved from the earliest days of our republic to the enactment of America's first "comprehensive" immigration law of 1924—the Nationality Origins Act , and then 40 years later, the historic Immigration and Nationality Act of 1965.

The following chapters review immigration history as seen through the eyes of the nation-state since national immigration laws were established. It gives perspective to understanding how and why the management of immigrants has changed throughout our history in the United States—from local and state and eventually (after the Civil War) to national jurisdiction. This view also explains the great changes in the country after 1924 that resulted in the passage of the historic Immigration and Nationality Act of 1965 and even civil rights and the Great Society legislation itself. Knowing the historical drivers of immigration explains the unintended consequences of those laws and why the intense demands for "reforming" it.

It is clear that the history of U.S. immigration isn't just about immigrant inflows. It's also about our nation's economic conditions and the attitude of various influential interest groups—particularly business and labor interest groups—toward the workforce at particular points in time. It reflects the historic and ongoing tensions in the United States between political philosophies favoring free market economies and unregulated labor flows versus the support for government regulation and benefits for labor. It's about the attitude toward immigration itself.

Chapter Two

From States to Feds

America's Evolving Immigration Laws

It may surprise some to learn that the flow of immigrants—that is, people who come with the intention of staying, working, and perhaps becoming citizens—into the United States, even when we were just colonies, has always been managed in some way. We never really had open borders when it came to immigration. Management throughout our history has varied between formal and informal; done by townships, states, and eventually through national law (1880s). There have been basically five periods of immigration management and laws:

- 1600s–1880s: Colonial and early American period of strict township management (none but orthodox Calvinists in colonial Boston thank you very much) that gradually evolved into highly varied, tight and loose, state management of diverse immigrants with a focus on building up the economic viability and cultural identity of the local areas;
- 1880s–1920s: Post-Civil War period when historic waves of new immigrants were met by new laissez faire federal management for all but immigrant workers from China, with the focus on building the booming postwar American economy;
- 1920s–1964: The first strict comprehensive immigration national law adhered to quotas based on national origin with a focus on protecting American jobs and the Protestant American culture;
- 1965–2005: Liberal national laws that opened the doors to immigrants of all backgrounds were enacted with increasingly little enforcement, with the focus on family unification and nondiscrimination of national origins, race, and creed;

- 2006–present: Since the 9/11 terrorist attack on the United States, immigration management has been seen as vital as ever to national security; increased focus on enforcement leads to increasing fervor to reform the 1965 immigration law amid widely disparate views on how to do it: More immigrants? Fewer? More enforcement or less?

These distinct periods in immigration management and laws throughout the history of the United States evolved in reaction to world and national economic and social events that affected the ebb and flow of new immigrants into the country and the political climate to welcome them or not. Understanding the dynamics behind these changes, puts into perspective the historic passage of the Immigration and Nationality Act of 1965—the law that changed the face of America—and, now 50 years later, the fervent politics to reform it.

Since one of the basics about immigration is that it is, at its core, about work opportunities, both for the immigrant and for the nation-state, it is interesting to see what the sources of labor were for the growing American republic in its first two centuries.

SOURCES OF LABOR IN EARLY AMERICA

From early on, the colonies and motherlands of England, France, and Spain had strict regulations about who could come in and who couldn't. Even the Pilgrims and the early colonists were given land grants from colonial authorities in the Old Country to work and claim parcels of land in the New World (although Nathaniel Philbrick, author of the 2006 book *Mayflower*, said at the 2007 Library of Congress Book Fair in Washington, D.C., that the settlers of the Mayflower compact missed their original destination up the Hudson River and were dumped off at Plymouth Rock at the last minute before the return crossing would be impossible, hence "becoming the first illegal settlers" (at least in the eyes of English officials) "until their new location was documented and made official."[1] So it was that most all the colonials were well documented in the motherland, establishing themselves in small towns, small farms, and small businesses—all legal. Even the slave trade was legal and the slaves who were brought to America were documented for the most part—as "legal cargo."[2]

Of course there was much need for labor in the developing villages and towns of the colonies. Each area sought to employ newcomers according to their own standards. Briefly, labor sources during the colonial period were:

- 1560–1600s Native American labor: In the early days of colonization of America, the early settlers (especially in Jamestown, Virginia) assumed that the native indigenous population would supply the manual labor needed for construction and survival of the early townships. But that was a tragic assumption. "Some 90 percent of the natives died in the early colonial period because of disease, warfare, and social disorganization brought on by European immigration—a virtual if unintended genocide."[3]

- 1700s Indentured Servants: The next major source of colonial labor was bonded "indentured" immigrants. For a while they fit the bill perfectly, being mostly white, English-speaking, voluntary labor with a good work ethic. They worked basically unpaid for the length of their agreed-to bond, when they would then be free to establish their own businesses and hire indentured servants of their own. Many colonies granted 50 acres of land to the newly freed servant—and land ownership was a prerequisite for citizenship in many colonies. According to Deanna Barker of the National Center for Cultural Interpretation, "One half to two thirds of all immigrants to Colonial America arrived as indentured servants."[4] At times, as many as 75 percent of the population of some colonies were under terms of indenture. This was a labor system, not a system of apprenticeship. While there were abuses, it was a dream opportunity for many in England who could only look forward to a lifetime of servitude in the Old World; many came eagerly to the new America for the opportunity to work themselves out of bondage in a relatively short time, to become landowners and citizens.[5]

- 1760s–1870s Slavery: But indentured servants could not fill the needs of the new nation's thriving economy driven by Southern plantation productive potential and profit, if labor costs could be kept low. Eventually in the South, "slavery replaced entirely the indentured servant labor," writes Otis Graham. It became "a philosophical problem that was set aside, in the 1780s in order to form the union. But slavery continued into the 1800s to split the country"[6] —even as England passed its absolution of the slave trade laws in 1807. But as the South developed an agricultural economy dependent on labor intensive commodity crops such as cotton and tobacco, its planters rapidly acquired a significantly higher number and proportion of slaves to the population overall. The number of people imported mainly from Africa to the Southern United States peaked in 1701–1760: 189,000. By the end of the Civil War and the Emancipation Proclamation, close to 600,000 slaves had been imported into the country. It is not clear exactly how many slaves were freed in 1865: estimates vary between one to four million. Slaves were never considered to be "immigrants"; they were actually registered and counted as "cargo" in slave ships ladle documents. But by 1868, their emancipation and the 12th, 13th and 14th Amendments to the U.S. Constitution assured that freed slaves and their families would be considered to be full citizens before the law. In truth, it can be said that the slaves of those days were "involuntary immigrants."

- 1800–1880 Immigrants: Immigration of people who were not indentured servants or involuntary slaves, was not high during the colonial period and early days of the United States. In fact, some of the founding fathers were very ambiguous about opening the nation to immigrants at all, believing, as did Thomas Jefferson, that Virginia's (and the rest of the states') population would be adequately replenished by natural births.[7] No national records of immigrants were kept until the 1820s, but they numbered less than 10,000 a year during the first three decades of the Republic and consisted almost entirely of single males from England. They were recruited and employed for their skills as professionals, trained workers, and apprentices of varying degrees in various states.

THE DRIVERS OF IMMIGRATION IN THE EARLY REPUBLIC 1800–1880

Economics

It is obvious that the developing economies of the colonies and then federal states made them open in various ways to immigrant labor, the only one of the four labor resources outside of citizen workers that endured. While the "right kind" of immigrants who came during the first 100 years barely filled the jobs available, they were welcome. During the 1860s and the Civil War, immigrant numbers declined; but then came the world depression of the 1870s. America was about to see an explosion of immigrants especially from Eastern and Southern Europe, especially Jews and Catholics, seeking work and refuge in unprecedented numbers. America after the Civil War was in the throes of high unemployment, labor unrest, and the growth of labor organization.

Demographics

On the East Coast during the early years of the nation, immigrants were almost all from Western Europe. A surge of mainly Catholic immigrants from Germany starting in the 1830s and from Ireland in the 1840s reached some 120,000 by the 1850s. This was augmented at that time by previously rare immigrant populations from Eastern and Southern Europe—Catholics, orthodox Christians, and Jews. They all came to the United States propelled to migrate by chronic unemployment in the Old World due to exploding population growth, wars, famine, and religious persecution of ethnic subsets (especially of Armenians and Eastern European Jews).

There were clear social prejudices and restrictions in many of the colonies and early states about accepting various nationalities and religions (such as Southern Catholics and East European Jews) than the dominant Protestant or even secular cultures of most of America, but most immigrants knew in which areas they would be welcomed and which not; they tended to go where family and friends had gone before them and from there, their now-Americanized descendants spread out. For instance, Rhode Island from its founding had been open to Jews and free thinkers; the commercially oriented shipping centers of New York and Charleston were likewise open to trade and settlement to all.

By the mid-1800s, over 50 percent of the population of the seven "Lower South" states were black slaves, according to William Freehling.[8] Slaves by the mid-1800s were almost all from Africa; about 30 percent of them were of the Muslim faith.[9]

The new state of California (1850) saw an exponential increase of migrants, especially from Asia—most especially China—seeking their fortunes in the gold fields, in manual labor, and in retail enterprises—especially in gold miners' camps. There were no labor or immigration laws, nor laws of any kind that were enforceable. Chinese workers became the prime day laborer —the equivalent of bonded indentured servants of the colonial days in the mines, railroad construction crews, and lawless goldrush towns of the new chaotic state of California.

Immigration rates diminished significantly because of the Civil War and the consequent economic depression. But many of those who did come looked westward for a new life. A growing homestead movement was developing to make it easier for settlers to acquire unclaimed government land to develop and live on. The deal was especially attractive to Irish and German immigrant farmers. The United States welcomed them to settle the vast prairies of the Midwest and the north. According to documents about homesteading in the National Archives,

> In 1862, the Homestead Act established a three-fold homestead acquisition process in the United States (at the time 11 states had seceded from the union). It provided that any U.S. citizen, or intended citizen, who had never borne arms against the U.S. Government could file an application and lay claim to 160 acres of surveyed Government land. For the next 5 years, the homesteader had to live on the land and improve it by building a 12-by-14 dwelling and growing crops. After 5 years, the homesteader could file for his patent (or deed of title) by submitting proof of residency and the required improvements to a local land office. (By 1934, over 1.6 million homestead applications were processed and more than 270 million acres—10 percent of all U.S. lands—passed into the hands of individuals.) The Homestead Act also led to the Morill Act of 1862 which established the first state land-grant colleges; this was the beginning of the uniquely American public college system that benefited citizens and immigrants alike with free vocational and post-secondary education.[10]

Gradually, the growing need for labor along with the growing number and assimilation of new diverse immigrant populations created a visible diversity of immigrants in various states: for instance Catholics in Protestant New England and Jews in Catholic Maryland.

Technology

The building of the transcontinental railroad mainly by immigrants—Chinese in the Western Rockies and Volga Germans in the northern Midwest, among others—was probably the single biggest technological innovation that united the highly diverse states of the developing United States.

After the war with Mexico (1846–1848), new canals and roadways reduced Western dependence on the harbor in New Orleans and England's repeal of its corn laws opened new markets to American agriculture that needed more crosscountry rail transportation and ships out of the Great Lakes. By1869, Duluth, Minnesota, on the western tip of Lake Superior, was the fastest growing city in America. It was and still is the most furthest west port city in the Americas that a seagoing freighter can reach from the Atlantic Ocean, providing a direct route for Midwestern farmers to markets in Europe and beyond.

Politics

The growing number of Chinese immigrant workers was beginning to be of concern, especially as they spread east after the gold rush, especially among the growing and powerful unions and associations of American workers. By the 1870s, feelings toward Chinese "coolie" labor turned hostile when the gold rush waned, the Union Pacific Railroad was completed, and Asian immigration continued—reaching 10 percent of the state's population and one-quarter of its labor force in 1879. Chinese labor was seen as a low-wage labor pool competing with American labor. Organized opposition to Chinese labor came from coalitions of workers (many of them Irish immigrants), small farmers, and shop owners energized by the harsh worldwide depression of the mid-1870s. The pushback in California to surging numbers of Chinese laborers and their reluctance to naturalize them (make them citizens) became the pivotal issue for the nationalization of immigration law in 1882.

The Civil War was the unifying event that made the collection of semi-sovereign states in the federation become a unitary one. Labor concerns became national and so did social concerns. Economic strains merged with a set of political and social worries such as political corruption, urban congestion and vice, child labor, alcohol and tobacco abuse, and the degradation of natural environments. As a result, a broad progressive reform movement began to build, and with that, the jurisdiction for various responsibilities that had been done by the developing states, now became federal.

This included both the functions of immigration management and the naturalization of new citizens. Until the 1880s, the naturalization of immigrants was administered by state officials, although it was under national jurisdiction—the only one in the Constitution that dealt with immigration (Article 1, Section 8: "The Congress shall have Power to establish an uniform Rule of Naturalization"). The rule was not specified, however, and state standards differed on citizenship. In most states five years of residency and good character were the basic qualifications. Throughout the Union, it was a state official who vetted the new citizens and administered the citizenship pledge (basically the same one used today) that emphasizes allegiance and fidelity to the United States.

1868. The 14th Amendment and Birthrights Citizenship

After the Civil War, the 14th Amendment was voted in along with the 13th Amendment to assure that former slaves and their descendants would be considered citizens. The first sentence of the amendment states, "All persons born or naturalized in the United States, and subject to the jurisdiction thereof, are citizens of the United States and of the State wherein they reside." That has been interpreted to mean that anyone born in the United States is automatically a U.S. citizen.

IMMIGRATION LAWS BECOMES NATIONAL BY 1882

All this led to the establishment of immigration laws and management as a national jurisdiction in a number of court and legislative actions between 1875 and 1882:

- In 1875, the U.S. Supreme Court ruled that the federal government had the exclusive right to regulate immigration.
- Congress began enacting immigration laws in the1880s, including the Immigration Act of 1882 that charged a tax on every immigrant and prevented the entry of convicts, idiots, lunatics, and persons likely to become a public charge. The list of persons who were excluded expanded quickly and immigration law became increasingly complex.
- The Chinese Exclusion Act of 1882 excluded Chinese laborers but not Chinese professionals (doctors, scholars); but it prohibited any Chinese national in the country legally from being naturalized.

IMMIGRATION MANAGEMENT IS NATIONALIZED — A NEW BUREAUCRACY IS CREATED

The nationalization of laws quickly brought about the establishment of a national agency and bureaucracy to implement, manage, and enforce national immigration law. This included the important decision of which department of the executive branch would house the agencies and which committees of the legislature would have jurisdiction. The immigration bureaucratic and legislative jurisdictions evolved rapidly.

- 1891: The Immigration Act established an Office of the Superintendent of Immigration within the Department of the Treasury and was responsible for implementing the admission (or rejection) process of immigrants and collecting a tax at every port of entry.
- 1892: All immigrants to the United States now had to be screened through Ellis Island where they were either granted entry or not. (The museum at Ellis Island has poignant exhibits of the immigrants who were not allowed in.)
- 1893: Both houses of Congress for the first time had standing committees on immigration. "The national government was taking the first halting steps toward equipping itself to make immigration policy."[11]
- 1898: In *U.S. v. Wong Kim Ark*, the Supreme Court ruled that the son of Chinese immigrants—who were legally in the country but because of the Chinese Exclusionary Act were not allowed to naturalize—was a citizen under the 14th Amendment. But the Supreme Court has not reexamined this issue since the concept of illegal alien entered the language.
- 1903: The legislative jurisdiction for immigration and labor was placed under the new Department of Commerce and Labor and its legislative committees.
- 1906: The Immigration and Naturalization Service was established to take over immigrant admission/rejection duties and focus on record keeping and standardized forms, fees, and taxes required for immigrant naturalization. Committee jurisdiction was in Commerce and Labor.

AMERICA'S FIRST COMPREHENSIVE IMMIGRATION LAW: THE NATIONAL ORIGINS ACT OF 1924

The turn of the century and World War I brought on epic changes in the numbers of immigrants coming to the United States and the attitude toward immigration among the public and its leaders. In the booming American manufacturing industry and the advent of the gilded age of extreme income disparity, eager, cheap, immigrant labor was welcomed. Unregulated corporate employers and unregulated immigration worked to leverage the growing restlessness of American union members who, many feared, were taking their inspiration from the Bolshevik revolution in Russia (1917). But the cities teeming with immigrants, often living in wretched conditions, also stoked a growing humanitarian and Progressive movement.

In this mixed environment, the first comprehensive and highly restrictive immigration law was passed with many of the same conflicts and arguments heard today for comprehensive immigration reform. They are worth noting.

Immigration Drivers 1880s–1920s

Between 1880 and 1920, America experienced the largest wave of immigrants to its shores in its history. Reaction to it was both positive and negative. Immigration issues brought on and strengthened the social Progressive movement in the United States for the next century. But the massive immigration wave also brought on increased regulation and by 1924 the first comprehensive immigration reform act in the United States that focused on highly restricting who could immigrate and who could not—the National Origins Act. The four general drivers that led to the first federal immigration law are described below:

Economic

From the era of Reconstruction to the end of the nineteenth century, the United States underwent an economic transformation marked by the maturing of the industrial economy, the rapid expansion of big business, the development of large-scale agriculture, and the rise of national labor unions and industrial conflict. American industry had found itself and was a pull for labor from rural America and Europe.

Over 100 American cities in the East and Midwest doubled in size in the 1880s. From 1880–1910 the American urban population tripled. During the early part of the 1900s, relaxed regulation allowed corporations and investment houses to expand and consolidate into monolithic corporations. This resulted in a concentration of the nation's productive capacities in fewer and fewer hands with few regulations, protections, and safety nets for the workers, including many immigrants new to the country. Economic dynamism drove the growth and wealth of American cities but at the price of degradation of much of the individual American urban populace's wealth.

Real GNP growth during the 1920s was relatively rapid: 4.2 percent per year from 1920 to 1929 according to the most widely used estimates of historical statistics. Real GNP per capita grew 2.7 percent per year between 1920 and 1929. By both nineteenth- and twentieth-century standards these were relatively rapid rates of real economic growth and they would be considered rapid even today. There were several interruptions to this growth.

- In the mid-1920s, the American economy began to contract and the 1920–1921 depression lasted about a year. The Federal Reserve System's monetary policy was a major factor in initiating the 1920–1921 depression.
- A rapid recovery reestablished full employment by 1923.
- There was a very mild recession in 1924 and another mild recession in 1927 both of which may be related to oil price shocks. The 1927 recession was also associated with Henry Ford's shutdown of all his factories for six months in order to changeover from the Model T to the new Model A automobile. Though the Model T's market share was declining after 1924, in 1926 Ford's Model T still made up nearly 40 percent of all the new cars produced and sold in the United States.
- The Great Depression began in the summer of 1929, possibly as early as June. The initial downturn was relatively mild but the contraction accelerated after the crash of the stock market at the end of October. Real total GNP fell 10.2 percent from 1929 to 1930, while real GNP per capita fell 11.5 percent from 1929 to 1930.

Earnings for laborers varied during the 1902s. For 25 manufacturing industries, male skilled and semiskilled laborers generally commanded a premium of 35 percent over the average weekly earnings of unskilled male laborers in the 1920s. Unskilled males received on average 35 percent more than females during the 1920s. Real average weekly earnings for these 25 manufacturing industries rose somewhat during the 1920s. For skilled and semiskilled male workers real average weekly earnings rose 5.3 percent between 1923 and 1929, while real average weekly earnings for unskilled males rose 8.7 percent between 1923 and 1929. Real average weekly earnings for females rose 1.7 percent between 1923 and 1929. Real weekly earnings for bituminous and lignite coal miners fell as the coal industry encountered difficult times in the late 1920s and the real daily wage rate for farmworkers, reflecting the ongoing difficulties in agriculture, fell after the recovery from the 1920–1921 depression.

Employment rates for males who were 65 or older fell from 60.1 percent in 1920 to 58.0 percent in 1930. During the depression of 1920–1921 the unemployment rate rose rapidly from 5.2 to 8.7 percent. The recovery reduced unemployment to an average rate of 4.8 percent in 1923. The unemployment rate rose to 5.8 percent in the recession of 1924 and to 5.0 percent with the slowdown in 1927. Otherwise unemployment remained relatively low. The onset of the Great Depression from the summer of 1929 on brought the unemployment rate from 4.6 percent in 1929 to 8.9 percent in 1930.

Demographics

While most of America's population growth came from citizen births, the problems of the cities were greatly intensified and shaped by the long relentless tide of the Great Wave out of Europe. They were mostly "displaced peasants" from southern and Eastern Europe. They clustered in ethnic neighborhoods rich in immigrant culture but incredibly dense (more than Bombay) and defiled by unsanitary conditions—two qualities that came to be attributed to immigrants in general. "The new immigrants crowd into any available employment . . . into unskilled calling and work at starving wages they undermine standards and labor organizations," said the new American Federation of Labor president Samuel Gompers. [12] The exceptions to the concept that most immigrants were uneducated peasants, were Jewish immigrants who were "classified by port officials as nearly 70 percent skilled workers." [13]

The nation's urban population was 41 percent foreign born by 1920, but because major northeastern cities were the primary destination of most new immigrants in the 1920s, their proportion of foreign born was closer to two-thirds.

After a short but severe two-year depression in 1921–1922, however, the population picture changed in the next decade. At the same time that overall production was growing, population growth was declining from an annual rate of increase of 1.85 and 1.93 percent in 1920 and 1921, respectively; population growth rates fell to 1.23 percent in 1928 and 1.04 percent in 1929. These changes in the overall growth rate were linked to the birth and death rates of the resident population and a decrease in foreign immigration.

Although the crude death rate changed little during the period, the crude birth rate fell sharply into the early 1930s. There are a couple explanations for the decline in the birthrate during this period.

- First, there was an accelerated rural-to-urban migration. Urban families have tended to have fewer children than rural families because urban children do not augment family incomes through their work as unpaid workers as rural children do.
- Second, the period also saw continued improvement in women's job opportunities and a rise in their labor force participation rates.

Immigration also fell sharply. This was largely because of the impact of the new immigration laws enacted in 1917, 1921, and 1924 (see below). The exception was large numbers of Latin American workers, especially from Mexico, who had entered the United States to supplement the labor force related to war industries or farming, especially in the sparsely populated Southwest. Immigrants from Latin America represented approximately 30 percent of total immigration between approximately 1910 and 1940; they were exempted from the quota system of 1924. [14]

The American population also continued to move during the interwar period. Two regions experienced the largest losses in population shares: New England and the Plains. For New England this was a continuation of a long-term trend. The population share for the Plains region had been rising through the nineteenth century. In the interwar period its agricultural base, combined with the continuing shift from agriculture to industry, led to a sharp decline in its share. The regions gaining population were the Southwest and, particularly, the far West. California began its rapid growth at this time.

During the 1920s, the labor force grew at a more rapid rate than population. This somewhat more rapid growth came from the declining share of the population less than 14 years old and therefore not in the labor force. In contrast, the labor force participation rates, or fraction of the population aged 14 and over that was in the labor force, declined during the 1920s from 57.7 percent to 56.3 percent. This was entirely due to a fall in the male labor force participation rate from 89.6 percent to 86.8 percent as the female labor force participation rate rose from 24.3 percent to 25.1 percent. The primary source of the fall in male labor force participation rates was a rising retirement rate.

Technology

An outburst of technological innovation in the late nineteenth century fueled the headlong economic growth of the Gilded Age. During this period, the Wright Brothers demonstrated their new flying machine on December 17, 1903, at Kitty Hawk, North Carolina; America opened the Panama Canal; a world war was fought and won utilizing air power that had been invented just a decade earlier.

Mechanization brought farming into the realm of big business as well, making the United States the world's premier food producer. Modernization made agriculture vastly more efficient, but it disrupted family farms and small rural businesses, provoking the country's farmers to organize protest movements as never before.

During this period there also is a rapid adoption of the automobile, to the detriment of passenger rail travel. Though suburbs had been growing since the late nineteenth century, their growth had been tied to rail or trolley access and this was limited to the largest cities. The flexibility of car access changed this and the growth of suburbs began to accelerate. The demands of trucks and cars led to a rapid growth in the construction of all-weather-surface roads to facilitate their movement.

The rapidly expanding electric utility networks led to new consumer appliances and new types of lighting and heating for homes and businesses. The introduction of the radio, radio stations, and commercial radio networks began to break up rural isolation, as did the expansion of local and long-distance telephone communications. Recreational activities such as traveling, going to movies, and attending professional sporting events became major businesses.

The period also saw major innovations in business organization and manufacturing technology. The Federal Reserve System first tested its powers and the United States moved to a dominant position in international trade and global business. These things make the 1920s a period of considerable importance independent of what happened in the 1930s.

Politics

The Progressive presidential leadership of Theodore Roosevelt who seemed able to stride the lines easily between the elite, the workers, and the press, was to be sorely missed after he died. "President Warren Harding was incompetent and Calvin Coolidge was a disengaged man of few words and no passion for change, although he did agree it was time for immigration to be limited. Teddy, on the other hand, who died in 1919, had a remarkable gift for urging immigration restriction even while appearing to have confidence in assimilation and deliver a decisive immigrant-embracing message. But no such message came from the White House in the 1920s."[15]

The 1920s were not kind to labor unions even though World War I had solidified the dominance of the American Federation of Labor (AFL) among labor unions in the United States. The rapid growth in union membership fostered by federal government policies during the war ended in 1919. A committee of AFL craft unions undertook a successful membership drive in the steel industry in that year. When U.S. Steel refused to bargain, the committee called a strike which failed. In the same year, the United Mine Workers undertook a large strike and also lost. These two lost strikes and the 1920–1921 depression took the impetus out of the union movement and led to severe membership losses that continued through the 1920s.

Under Samuel Gompers's leadership, the AFL's "business unionism" had attempted to promote the union and collective bargaining as the primary answer to the workers' concerns with wages, hours, and working conditions. The AFL officially opposed any government actions that would have diminished worker attachment to unions by providing competing benefits, such as government-sponsored unemployment insurance, minimum wage proposals, maximum hours proposals, and social security programs although Gompers' direction differentiated from the official one on the basis of whether the statute would or would not aid collective bargaining. After Gompers's death, William Green led the AFL in a policy change as the AFL promoted the idea of union-management cooperation to improve output and promote greater employer acceptance of unions. But on the whole it can be concluded that union-management cooperation in the 1920s was a failure.

To combat the appeal of unions in the 1920s, firms used the "yellow-dog" contract requiring employees to swear they were not union members and would not join one; the "American Plan" promoting the open shop and contending that the closed shop was un-American; and welfare capitalism. The most common aspects of welfare capitalism included personnel management to handle employment issues and problems, the doctrine of "high wages," company group life insurance, old-age pension plans, stock-purchase plans, and more. Some firms formed company unions to thwart independent unionization and the number of company-controlled unions grew from 145 to 432 between 1919 and 1926.

Until the late 1930s the AFL was a voluntary association of independent national craft unions. Craft unions relied upon the particular skills the workers had acquired (their craft) to distinguish among the workers and provide barriers to the entry of other workers. Most craft unions required a period of apprenticeship before a worker was fully accepted as a journeyman worker. The skills, and often lengthy apprenticeship, constituted the entry barrier that gave the union its bargaining power. [16]

Even so, social problems that accompanied the nation's industrial development fueled the unprecedented clashes between capital and labor. This discontent captured the attention of reformers and politicians who began to challenge traditional party politics through third-party movements. Concern over social worries created a broad, progressive, labor, and social reform movement that in the first two decades of the twentieth century became the main theme of multifaceted interventions.

American society was in transition. Immigrants arriving from southern and eastern Europe, from Asia, Mexico, and Central America, were creating a new American mosaic. And the power of Anglo-Saxon Protestants—once so dominant—began to wane. By 1896, the platforms of both major political parties recognized large-scale immigration as a problem, in language that would be considered highly unacceptable today. [17]

There was a backlash against non-English-speaking immigrants as well. The literacy requirement for new immigrants became a central issue of dispute in the presidential race of 1917. "Taft and Wilson had virtually promised ethnic politicians that they would reject a literacy requirement and any other plan to limit immigration, thus pandering to the immigrant vote," according to Graham. [18] But in the end it was an issue that was deeply supported by the public deep in the fears of war and depression.

The progressive reform impulse was now confronted with immigration "reformers" or "restrictionists" who wanted to severely limit immigration. They were "erratically searching for a national immigration policy to replace the laissez-faire stance toward the uncontrolled Great Wave of immigrants sweeping into America from war ravaged Europe and work-hungry Asia—a stance now so inappropriate to the modern era. [19]

Passage of the National Origins Quota Act

By the 1920s America was experiencing the largest immigration wave in its history with few laws or infrastructure that could manage its impact. Immigrants entering American ports in 1920–1921 alone numbered 500,000, with only 1,500 rejected by the literacy test and others were disqualified including those whose "presence deemed contrary to public safety," which included those with "radical beliefs."

This, after, all was the peak of the Red Scare sparked by the success of the Bolshevik Revolution in Russia that in the United States led to increasingly widespread labor unrest, strikes in major industries, and even some terrorist bombings traced to anarchists. These war measures did not supply the systematic control of immigration that had been debated so long. [20] A deluge of immigrants from war-torn and instable Europe was seen as pending toward the United States. "More than ten million [immigrants] are now waiting in various war-stricken Europe to swarm to the United States as soon as they can obtain transportation," said the Commissioner of Immigration at the port of New York. And an officer of the Hebrew Sheltering and Aid Society of America stated that "if there were in existence a ship that could hold 3 million human beings, the 3 million Jews of Poland would board it to escape to America." [21]

In Congress, the American Federation of Labor appealed for a prohibition on all immigration for four years. The 65th Congress (1917–1919) responded with a number of pieces of legislation that tried to limit immigration:

- In 1907 President Theodore Roosevelt appointed a commission to study immigration and come up with a plan for a "definite solution of this immigration business." He signed the Immigration Act of 1907 on February 27 which introduced and reformed a number of restrictions on immigrants who could be admitted into the United States, most notably ones regarding disability and disease. [22]
- In 1910 the Dillingham Commission came out with a 42-volume report on the economic and social impacts of immigration. It affirmed that "further general legislation concerning admission of aliens should be based primarily upon economic or business considerations—especially restricting unskilled laborers of which there was already an oversupply." [23] It also recommended a much disputed literacy test requirement for potential immigrants.
- In 1917 a law was passed in the midst of World War I to limit immigration, based primarily on concerns about national security. It contained a

literacy requirement for immigrants that was politically controversial and was vetoed three times by President Woodrow Wilson and overridden each time; as presidential candidates Taft and Wilson both rejected the requirement in their presidential campaigns.

- In 1920 the House overwhelmingly (296–42) passed a bill suspending immigration for two years, but the Senate, feeling more pressure from employers, pushed for a bill with a longer-term strategy.
- Also in 1920, a nationwide prohibition against the public sale, distribution, importation, and drinking of alcohol was passed in a constitutional amendment (the 18th); anti-prohibitionists (known as wets) criticized the alcohol ban as an intrusion of mainly rural Protestant ideals on a central aspect of urban, immigrant, and Catholic life.
- In 1921 Congress passed the Emergency Quota Act, limiting the number of new incoming immigrants to about 365,500: 198,081 from northern and western Europe and about 158,367 from other countries, principally southern and eastern Europe. This represented a 3 percent reduction overall of immigrants and a drastic reduction in immigration from southern and eastern Europe, mainly Italian Catholics and East European Jews.
- In 1922 the percentage level was again dropped—to 2 percent. This dropped immigration levels to 140,999 from Northern and Western Europe, and 21,847 from other countries, principally Southern and Eastern Europe. No numerical limits were placed on Western Hemisphere immigration.

The Dillingham Commission of 1910 had predicted that immigration would be cut to approximately 360,000 "quota" per year. But they were wrong.

1. Immigrants admitted in 1921: 800,000
2. Immigrants admitted in 1922: 310,000
3. Immigrants admitted in 1923: 523,000
4. Immigrants admitted in 1924: 707,000—mostly from Mexico and Canada (nonquota countries) although quota-country immigrants from non-English-speaking Southern and Eastern Europe still predominated.

The national immigration bureaucracy also continued to grow during this period:

- In 1913 the Department of Labor is created and both the Bureau of Immigration and the Naturalization Service are placed under its jurisdiction.
- In 1924 the Border Patrol is created.

With some 50,000 immigrants a month pouring into the United States, it was clear that a broad, more systematic, nationally recognized immigration law must be established. More "comprehensive" if you will. But America's first comprehensive immigration law faced head-on the grueling question that all immigration reformers must answer: Who to choose and how? If immigration is to be limited in number—as it must be, for no nation or its workers can sustain open borders—then how are the lucky, chosen immigrants to be determined? And how many? It's not unlike top universities having to choose among thousands of qualified applicants—except they usually make the choices secretly, privately. Nation-states spell out their choices in immigration law that is driven by economic conditions, demographic concerns, technological changes, and politics.

For the next few years, Congress tinkered with the formulas. There was a mixed bag of argument and counterargument as Graham describes it. The basic politics of immigration was already clear among the 1919/1920 political players: labor unions wanted restrictions on masses of eager working immigrants who would challenge the status quo of labor politics at the time; and large employers (particularly manufacturers) insisted on fewer restrictions on the number of incoming immigrant workers.

But there was another element surfacing that growing nation-states were struggling with—expanding manufacturing (postwar and prewar) and increasing changes in technology that made it easier and faster for peoples from all over the world to come into the United States seeking jobs.

The new immigration law that was being conceived was to be openly and frankly framed around the concept of national origins and based on preference for immigrants from nations (and cultures) that had formed the United States, mainly British, Irish, and German. This would limit immigration from the rest of Europe, Asia, and Africa. Latin America was not seen as a problem as there was an informal but regular system of immigrant inflow and outflow based pretty much on a laissez-faire free market system of employment of seasonal farm workers—most of them known for generations. In general, the workers came without their families as they were often extended over many generations with a solid identity in their local culture; the workers crossed the border to earn money and then to return home.

Even so, at the time (and remember this is pre-Hitler, pre-Mein Kampf, and pre-civil rights legislation) the idea of basing immigration on national origins was troublesome to some—particularly politicians from New York and other Northeastern cities where the surge of new, especially Catholic and Jewish, immigrants were particularly strong, claimed that immigration based on natural origin was morally wrong, "despite the decade's reputation for unchecked bigotry."[24]

- "It's the worst kind of discrimination against a large class of individuals and absolutely opposed to our American ideas of equality and justice," said Congressman Richard Aldrich (R-Rhode Island).[25]
- Such legislation smacks of Nordic superiority.
- Such legislation is an abandonment of American ideals.

Racist rhetoric (that is now universally rejected throughout the Western world) was all too commonly used in those pre-civil rights era days by those wanting to restrict immigration numbers and backgrounds for fear that American jobs and culture were being negatively impacted. Such rhetoric strengthened the objections by laissez-faire immigration advocates that re-formist/restrictionist arguments were basically immoral.

Opponents to the national origins quota bill would argue that assimilation had worked so far. Examples were the numerous Catholics who had immigrated from Ireland and Germany. The worry had been that since they were devoted to the hierarchical order of the Catholic Church, these new Catholic immigrants would not be attuned to the protestant Anglo-Saxon ideal of "republican (as in Republic) self-governance." But as it turned out, "American Catholics proved more American than Catholic, defying the energetic efforts of the clerical hierarchy to hold them to older European ways."[26]

It also helped that immigration numbers had abated greatly during the Civil War, which found New England Catholics fighting loyally for the Union cause, and allowing some space to assimilate (and erasing bad memories when some Catholics joined the Mexicans to fight Americans in the Mexican-American War of 1845).

But reformers (or restrictionists) objected. They argued that the idea of American Ideals—those essential ideas about human equality, fairness to all, and social tolerance—was unique to Americans.

"Immigration reformers in the 1920s were at pains to not only avoid invidious enthnoracial language but also to vigorously deny that their preference for an immigration stream composed mostly of the older nationalities that has founded and developed the nation, represented discrimination in the derogatory sense."[27] Congressman Albert Johnson suggested that "All these charges of discrimination and the talk of "Nordic superiority" was injected by the opponents of restriction to make them look bad."[28]

Reformers preferred another line of argument based on the fact that "All nations concede to each other the right to decide who could make a home within their boundaries"[29] (i.e., to immigrate). It was based on concerns to continue building a national unity, cohesion, and common culture into which immigrants would assimilate. Today one might call that a "national identity."

- Nations come of slow growth and long travail that they depend on like-mindedness and . . . if the United States becomes a hodge-podge of a score of races, no one of which is dominant it will lose its unity and become like Metternich's idea of Italy—a geographical expression," wrote Edward Lewis, a Chicago lawyer, in his 1928 book *America, Nation or Confusion?*[30]

- *"Like-mindedness"* was an idea also explored by John Dewey, a well-known contemporary philosopher who wrote that "the term expressed the importance of no-racial, cultural principles of selection in order to maintain national unity."[31]
- "Spiritual unity of the nation depended on the continued cultural and ethnic homogeneity of a nation founded by mostly British settlers," wrote an American of Italian descent Gino Speranza in a series of articles in *World's Work* in 1923–1924.
- "Who could object to a policy then that replicated the nation, rather than weakened it with new elements who were unassimilable?" said Johnson.[32]
- "Others have come to this country and greatly enriched it, but they didn't make it (inherently different) and they have not yet greatly changed it."[33]
- (The United States) was made as an Anglo-Saxon commonwealth and it's a good country. We are not going to allow other people no matter what their merits to make it something different.[34]
- "If there is any changing (in basic U.S. culture and character) to be done, we will do it ourselves," said Rep William Vaile of Colorado.[35]

There is no doubt that these concerns were aimed mainly at the surge of Jewish immigrants coming from Eastern Europe —those "huddled wretched masses" that was the reference point of Emma Lazarus, an American-born, Jewish poet from New York City. She wrote her poem "The New Colossus" in 1883 as a fund-raiser for the base of the French Statue of Liberty, fourteen lines of which was permanently engraved on the base in 1945.

As for African Americans, it may be surprising to some that some prominent black leaders of the time also supported a more restrictive immigration policy. In fact even before and after the Civil War, black leaders had expressed concern about the increasing numbers of immigrants coming to America to work: "Every hour sees the black man (in the North) elbowed out of employment by some newly arrived immigrant whose hunger and whose color are thought to give him a better title to the place," said Frederick Douglas in 1853.[36]

Booker T. Washington at the Atlanta Exposition in 1895 agreed in a passionate speech that included an appeal to white employers of the South "who look to the incoming of those of foreign birth and strange tongue and habit for the prosperity of the South. Cast down your bucket . . . among the eight millions of Negroes whose habits you know, who without strikes and labor wars tilled your fields, cleared our forests, built our railroads and cities."[37]

According to Graham, a trickle of northward migrating Southern blacks had begun but Booker T. Washington knew that the ready availability of cheap foreign labor at the gates of Northeastern industries left no incentive among employers to welcome or recruit black labor. The Great Wave was not only happening, it was preventing something else from happening in the nation's labor markets: a labor shortage that would have opened opportunities for American blacks, requiring only a short migration up the Eastern Seaboard.

Driving the need for a new law restricting immigration certainly was a deep, even passionate, concern by some (especially labor unions) about unfair competition for unskilled labor jobs among immigrants and Americans both black and white at the peak of the immigrant surge of the 1880s–1920s.[38]

How to select and who to select may immigrate into the United States under a more restricted law was and still is the basic question. In all the plans and tests and methods that were being considered in the 1920s, it is clear that there was an emerging consensus: preference should be shown to those who by reason of their personal qualities or habits would be(come) assimilated and desirable citizens. The murky idea of tying immigration to the demographic aspects of the American past began to take hold.[39]

It was Henry Curran, the Commissioner of Immigration at Ellis Island, who supposedly suggested the compromise idea for the 1924 law:

- "The most assimilable and the best kind of immigrant we could get would be that which is most nearly like the 100 million Americans who are now here." The idea was to create an annual installment that would replicate the percentage of nationalities present in the country according to the 1890 census—the "national origins of the current nation of Americans."
- "It would be a microcosm of the United States and all races would be alike on the basis of their actual proportion of the existing population," argued Senator David Reed of PA.
- The national origins base for immigration gives every national group as many immigrants to this country as that national origins group has contributed to the population of the United States, stated the senate Judiciary Committee in reviewing the proposal.[40]

The Johnson-Reed Act was adopted on May 26, 1924, after having passed the house 323–71 and the Senate 62–6. It was "a milestone, both simple and complex" according to Otis Graham. The simple version is:

> The National Origins Act limited the number of immigrants allowed entry into the United States through a national origins quota. The quota provided immigration visas to two percent of the total number of people of each nationality in

the United States as of the 1890 national census. It completely excluded immigrants from Asia even Asians not previously prevented from immigrating—the Japanese in particular—would no longer be admitted to the United States.

NOTE: The term immigration "quota" in the 1924 act can be seen to have the same connotation as immigration "permit" today, which itself is often mistermed a "visa." A visa really is a document that allows a foreign national to come to a port of entry where their particular permit—visitor student, etc.—is then confirmed. Most citizens of European countries and Canada do not need a "visa"—they are visa waiver countries; but they still need a permit and still need to be passed by the Customs and Border Protection officer at every official port of entry.

The quotas referred to the applying applicant's country of birth, except for nonwhite Asians who were required to seek entry under the quota of their country of racial ancestry regardless of their country of birth (repealed in 1968). Many in Japan were very offended by the new 1924 law, which was a violation of a turn-of-the century "gentlemen's agreement." The Japanese government protested, but the law remained, resulting in an increase in existing tensions between the two nations. But it appeared that the U.S. Congress had decided that preserving the racial composition of the country was more important than promoting good ties with the Japanese Empire.

The new quota calculations included large numbers of people of British descent whose families were long residents in the United States. As a result, the percentage of visas available to individuals from the British Isles and Western Europe increased, but newer immigration from other areas like southern and eastern Europe was limited, especially their Catholic and Jewish populations.

Quotas for all countries combined totaled 158,503 in fiscal 1965. Of these 70 percent (108,931) were for three countries:

- Great Britain and Northern (Protestant) Ireland (65,361)
- Germany (25,814)
- Republic of Ireland (Catholic 25,814).

The rest of Europe received only 40,483 quota numbers, while all other countries combined had a quota number of 9,089. Most of the Asian and African nations had quotas of only 100 persons a year.

Refugees were pretty much mixed up with the general surge of immigrants coming into the country in the decades 1880–1920. Eventually, refugee services such as the Nationalities Services of Philadelphia founded in 1921, expanded to include all immigrants without distinction:

Nationalities Service Center (NSC) was founded in 1921 under the aegis of the Young Women's Christian Association (YWCA) as the International Institute. Its mission was to assist newly arrived immigrant women with immigration and naturalization issues, and to help them learn English. Service programs evolved and expanded to respond to the changing needs of all immigrants, including men and families. The Institute's staff during these early years was composed of interpreters, immigration casework counselors, and volunteer English teachers.

The restrictionist principles of the act could have resulted in strained relations with some European countries as well, according to a State Department history of the era,[41] but these potential problems did not appear for several reasons. A variety of factors, including the global depression of the 1930s, World War II, and stricter enforcement of U.S. immigration policy served to curtail European emigration.

There were no quotas nor no limits for immigrants from Western Hemisphere countries with few exceptions, nor for spouses and minor unmarried children of U.S. citizens born abroad. Critics pointed out that many quotas would be wasted under the new quota system. Countries with the highest quotas (Britain, Ireland, and Germany) would probably fail to use them all, while immigrants from countries like Italy, Greece, Portugal, and Poland and other countries with small quotas would end up with long waiting lists.

Other older immigrant groups complained as well. "The English quota was too high; the Scandinavian and German, too low," came the angry complaints. But 33 patriotic societies voiced their support.

President Calvin Coolidge remained firmly in support of the concept of the National Origins Act. In a message to Congress on December 6, 1924, he proclaimed: "America must be kept American,"[42]

Chapter Three

Making the Law that Changed the Face of America

The Immigration and Nationality Act of 1965

On October 3, 1965, President Lyndon B. Johnson standing next to the Statue of Liberty with Massachusetts Senator Ted Kennedy—brother of the recently assassinated (November 22, 1963) President John F. Kennedy—by his side, signed unto law The Hart-Celler Immigration Act of 1965 ending quotas based on national origins.

The *New York Times* called the law "an intellectual victory." No countries, no immigrants with certain nationalities had preference or were limited.

Priorities for immigrant applicants switched from the historic labor market and skills criteria plus national/cultural heritage, to one of family reunification and kinship—a feature that came to be known as chain migration and that is still a priority today. Instead of immigration decisions being made on labor flow needs as is customary in almost every other country of the world, in U.S. immigration "today virtually all immigration decisions are made by private individuals," said Senator Gene McCarthy.[1] Administratively, the new immigration law set an annual immigration "ceiling" of 170,000 from the Eastern Hemisphere. But immediate family members and refugees were admitted outside of the cap. A ceiling of 120,000 per year was set for the Western Hemisphere—with no cap for immediate family.

Both the president and the popular Senator Ted (Edward) Kennedy assured the public that there would be no significant demographic changes to the United States brought on by the new law. At the signing of the bill on October 3, 1965, President Johnson said, "This bill that we will sign today is not a revolutionary bill. It does not affect the lives of millions. It will not reshape the structure of our daily lives, or really add importantly to either our wealth or our power."[2] While at an immigration hearing on February 10, 1965, Senator Ted Kennedy said, "The bill will not flood our cities with immigrants. It will not upset the ethnic mix of our society." Secretary of State Dean Rusk estimated the influx of only a few thousand Indian immigrants over the next five years, and other politicians. These assertions would later prove grossly inaccurate.

In fact, the law changed the face of America. The major source countries of immigration radically shifted from Europe to Latin America and Asia. The numbers of immigrants tripled by 1978. It made the country the highly diverse, multinational, multiethnic, multicultural American nation of immigrants that it is today.

Officially, the Immigration and Nationality Act of 1965 (Public Law 89–236, signed on October 3, 1965) but not officially effective until June 30, 1968, was also known as the Hart–Celler Act.[3] It abolished the National Origins formula that had been in place in the United States since the Emergency Quota Act of 1921. It was proposed by Representative Emanuel Celler of New York, cosponsored by Senator Philip Hart of Michigan, and promoted by Senator Ted Kennedy of Massachusetts.

Numerical restrictions on all visas were set at 170,000 per year, with a per-country-of-origin cap of not more than 7 percent (i.e., not more than 7 percent of all green cards could be granted to any one country) so that no country had a preference. Immediate relatives of U.S. citizens or "special immigrants" (including children born of American citizens in "independent" nations in the Western Hemisphere, former citizens, ministers, and employees of the U.S. government abroad) were not counted in the caps. Other categories such as physically and mentally deficient individuals and homosexuals no matter what their family relationship were excluded as they always had been. But any preference based on nationality were abolished (and over the next 50 decades, almost every other category as well).

How did this come about? In the 40 years between 1924 and 1965, why did the politics of immigration change from one of strict restrictions based on national origins, to a national commitment to national diversity with no limits placed on an immigrant's race, ethnic or cultural background, and religion? What conditions and personalities were the cause of this unprecedented and historic change? Could such an about-face happen again—50 years later?

It is clear that the economic, demographic, technological, and political drivers of immigration (both for immigrants to come and the country to host them) experienced great upheaval between 1924, when the restrictive national quota act was passed, and 1965 and the passage of the liberal Immigration and Nationality Act (INA). The dynamics of these drivers led very clearly to the passage of the historic change of priorities to the Immigration and Nationality Act of 1965.

THE DRIVERS OF THE 1965 IMMIGRATION REFORM ACT
1930–1965

Economics

The 40-year period between the two completely different immigration laws was an almost unbelievable time of economic change including:

- Prosperity and almost full employment in an era of restricted immigration (1924–1929).
- The Great Depression of 1929 (Black Monday was October 29) to 1939.
- After his election in 1933, FDR's series of federal social support programs and adjustments.
- World War II and a war economy between 1940–1945.
- Victory and economic renewal in America 1946–1949
- World leadership and rising economic prosperity in the 1950s and 1960s.
- Women in increasing numbers in the labor force and at universities and the GI Bill passed for returning veterans to pay for college, allowing both groups to fully participate in the new booming labor market and college-level professional jobs.
- Unemployment was less that 5 percent in 1965.

Demographics

Between 1924 and 1948 there was a great decline in immigration into the United States. Obviously that was because of the Depression, the war, and the National Origins (immigration) Act. It was a time of stabilization of the population and, as many point out, a breathing time for the masses of immigrants and their families who came in from the 1880s–1920s to settle down and assimilate to the American way of life. Many of these immigrants or their children went on to fight as Americans in the world war that was ravaging their former homelands.

But during the prewar and war period (1935–1945) the quotas also especially restricted immigration into the United States by the population that most desperately needed to find refuge: the Jews, Catholics, Romas, and other targeted populations that were facing the Nazi-perpetuated genocide that came to be known after the war as the Holocaust. They were the very populations who were specifically limited by the strict immigration quotas of the 1924 Immigration Act.

U.S. State Department policies made it very difficult for refugees to obtain entry visas. Despite the ongoing persecution of Jews in Germany, the State Department's attitude was influenced by the economic hardships of the Depression, which intensified grassroots anti-Semitism, isolationism, and xenophobia. The number of entry visas was further limited by the department's inflexible application of a restrictive immigration law passed by the U.S. Congress in 1924. Beginning in 1940, the United States further limited immigration by ordering American consuls abroad to delay visa approvals on national security grounds. Nevertheless, in 1939 and 1940, slightly more than half of all immigrants to the United States were Jewish, most of them refugees from Europe. In 1941, 45 percent of all immigrants to the United States were Jewish.

After the United States entered the war in December 1941, the trickle of immigration virtually dried up, just at the time that the Nazi regime began systematically to murder the Jews of Europe. During the second half of 1941, even as unconfirmed reports of the mass murder perpetrated by the Nazis filtered to the West, the U.S. Department of State placed even stricter limits on immigration based on national security concerns. Despite many obstacles, however, more than 200,000 Jews found refuge in the United States from 1933 to 1945, most of them before the end of 1941.

After the war and from much pressure, especially by the Jewish and Catholic communities and faith organizations, the United States slowly opened immigration to increasing numbers of the refugees amassing in refugee camps throughout Western Europe and North Africa. Along with the refugees who fled to Israel, the surge of Jewish immigrants into the United States told horrific stories of the Holocaust and confronted the world with that atrocity and with their failure to prevent or halt it.

Meanwhile, once the war was over, immigration flows from the nonquota countries of Western Europe increased exponentially. For many citizens of war-torn countries, peace was as hard as war in their nations whose infrastructure and governments were destroyed and occupied by the allies. They had to live for years under strict rationing of even such basics as meat, flour, sugar, and eggs. Thus, many Western European immigrants who did not fall under the quota system, flooded into the United States (as well as to South America), including many former Nazi party members.

It was in the decade after the end of World War II that foreign student programs were initiated; they were especially supported by President Dwight D. Eisenhower. The idea was to have a special State Department program and visa for the best and the brightest of students from war-torn countries to attend a few of America's best universities to study and train. It absolutely was expected that these top students would return to their homelands after their studies to become (American-friendly) political and intellectual leaders of their recovering countries. The foreign student and scholar program became one of the first temporary nonimmigration permits (Fs, Js, and Ms) to be established. It was very successful in its intent and the State Department even today likes to point out the hundreds of prominent and important foreign leaders who for a time, studied in the United States.

Foreign student visas were not designed to be immigration visas; they are labeled "nonimmigration visas" even today. Because of their temporary nature, the number to be given out was left to the discretion of vetted universities. Because of that temporary nonimmigrant status, then as now foreign student visas are unlimited in number. From early in the program foreign students had to show proof of acceptance for study before being allowed to enter the United States; they also had to post a bond assuring their return to their homelands—a detail retained in the 1965 INA.[4]

In the meantime, the culture and demographics of the American population were quickly changing after World War II. Marriage was up and so were birthrates. Increasing numbers of both female but particularly older male students who had been soldiers were going to college thanks to the GI Bill. The middle class was growing. Women were continuing to participate in the workforce, perhaps the first hints of the soon-to-come feminist (or perhaps better described as the woman's independence) movement, even though professional job opportunities and loans and mortgages in women's names only were generally not available.

Technology

New technologies created during the war became available to pubic consumers and America's blooming middle class quickly latched on to the growing accessibility and affordability of innovations in transportation and communication. As postwar American car production increased and became cheaper, growing numbers of families moved to the suburbs, traveled on family vacations, drove to work, and (as more and more women learned to drive) drove their children to increasing numbers of extracurricular activities. They created the American middle-class life.

Similarly, as the airline industry privatized and commercialized, easier and cheaper travel by air allowed immigrants a faster way to come to the United States. A number of major airports became official "ports of entry" for custom and border management. In the same way, advances made during the war allowed intercontinental telephone mechanisms to be improved, made more accessible and affordable, allowing especially immigrant families to communicate easier with relations in their homelands.

Hollywood movies became popular throughout the Western world. They showed the American way of life, igniting the dream of immigrating to America for millions of young people struggling with peacetime rations and struggling economics of their war-torn countries that only slowly were rebuilding and recovering.

Beginning with the Soviet launch of the first satellite, *Sputnik 1*, in 1957, the United States competed with the Soviet Union for supremacy in outer space exploration. After the Soviets placed the first man in space, Yuri Gagarin in 1961, President Kennedy pushed for ways in which NASA could catch up, famously urging action on a manned mission to the moon. The first manned flights produced by this effort came from Project Gemini (1965–1966). The space race sparked unprecedented increases in spending on education and pure research, which in turn induced many American (and foreign) students to go to college to study for these careers, which in turn accelerated scientific advancements and led to beneficial spin-off technologies and products for American consumers.

Politics

During this period, unions were still strong but changing in character. While almost decimated during the Depression, suddenly during the war years employers were facing a shortage of manpower (literally). Unions turned for the first time to women as alternatives to make labor—a movement that had been sparked in the pre-Depression, "Roaring Twenties" years.

* In 1920, the Women's Bureau was established in the Department of Labor. In 1933, President Roosevelt appointed Frances Perkins to be the U.S. Secretary of Labor; she was the first woman appointed to the U.S. Cabinet (and thus the first woman to enter the line of presidential succession) and the longest serving (12 years) Secretary of Labor.
* In 1929, Perkins was criticized by some members of Congress for refusing to deport the communist head of the West Coast International Longshore and Warehouse Union, Harry Bridges (who was ultimately vindicated by the Supreme Court). Remember that at that time, immigration matters were largely a matter of the labor committee and its agencies.

In the 1960s, social movements like the American Civil Liberties Union (the ACLU) were growing in importance. As lobbyists they were free to roam the halls of Congress in ways never permitted today. Called "gallery vultures" they developed an ecosystem of liberalism that simply doesn't exist today.[5]

Unions also remained a force in this period—especially the American Federation of Labor (AFL) founded in 1886 by craftsmen. The AFL was the largest union grouping in the United States for the first half of the twentieth century, even after the creation of the Congress of Industrial Organizations (CIO) by unions that were expelled by the AFL in 1935 over its opposition to its craft union affiliates' desire to organize on an industrial union basis. In 1955, after bitter and even violent rivalry, the AFL merged with the CIO to form the AFL-CIO a federation that remains in place to this day. The AFL-CIO was a major component of the New Deal coalition that dominated politics into the mid-1960s

The New Deal was a series of domestic programs enacted in the United States between 1933 and 1938, and a few that came later. They included both laws passed by Congress as well as presidential executive orders during the first term of President Franklin D. Roosevelt (1933–1937). The programs were in response to the Great Depression and focused on what historians call the "3 Rs": Relief, Recovery, and Reform. That is *relief* for the unemployed and poor; *recovery* of the economy to normal levels; and *reform* of the financial system to prevent a repeat depression.

The New Deal had a large impact on immigrants and the Democratic Party. Starting with the 1928 election, the Democratic Party began to win the votes of recent immigrants, in large part because candidate Al Smith rejected prohibition and displayed a sensitivity to life in urban American, where immigrants most often lived. FDR built upon Smith's gains in the 1932 general election.

It also especially energized recent immigrants and brought them into the Democratic Party. Roosevelt appointed Jews and Catholics to important positions in his administration, heartening immigrant newcomers who reveled in the appointment of their coreligionists. So great a departure was Roosevelt's attitude from that of previous presidents, whose appointments were largely restricted to white, northern European, Protestant men, that *Time* magazine featured on the cover of one of its issues in 1935 two of Roosevelt's advisers, Thomas Corcoran (an Irish Catholic) and Benjamin Cohen (a Jew).

Most important to the party's success, however, was the emotional attachment recent immigrants felt toward FDR. They believed that he was their president and saw him as a father figure who watched after their interests. It was not unusual in the 1930s for FDR's picture to hang in a prominent place in a recent immigrant's home or business. These new Americans joined the Democratic Party and they and their children would vote Democratic for the next generation.[6]

The New Deal produced a political realignment, making the Democratic Party the majority (as well as the party that held the White House for seven out of nine presidential terms from 1933 to 1969), with its base in liberal ideas, the white South, traditional Democrats, big city machines, and the newly empowered labor unions and ethnic minorities. It also was the beginning of the dominance of liberal Democrats from Northern states and the waning of the power of conservative Democrats in the South, although the latter controlled the crucial seniority positions in Congress.

Mexican and Central American immigrants had a different status during this period. The war would bring about labor shortages especially in the Southwest fields and farms. In 1942, the *bracero* program was established, Public Law 45. It was seen as a seasonal worker program for workers, not their families. The mostly Mexican *braceros* were housed and fed by the employers who could bring them in unlimited numbers. It was not meant to be an immigration visa but a temporary work visa, but *braceros* were free to come and cross the border without restrictions. They were not restricted in the National Origins Act of 1924.

IMMIGRATION INITIATIVES AND ACTIONS 1924–1964

Immigration quotas were understandably widely supported during World War II. They were seen as essential to national security and were tightened even more against Japanese when citizens were sent to detention camps after Pearl Harbor. But opposition to the quotas also was strong, especially from Italian American and Jewish organizations—and especially from Congressman Manny Celler of New York.

In 1932, President Roosevelt and the State Department essentially shut down immigration during the Great Depression as immigration went from 236,000 in 1929 to 23,000 in 1933. This was accompanied by voluntary repatriation to Europe and Mexico, and coerced repatriation and deportation of between 500,000 and two million Mexican Americans, mostly citizens, in the Mexican Repatriation. Total immigration between 1931 and 1940 was 528,000, averaging less than 53,000 a year.

In 1943, the Chinese exclusion laws were repealed.

In 1946, the Luce-Celler Act ended discrimination against Indian Americans and Filipinos, who were accorded the right to naturalization, and allowed a quota of 100 immigrants per year.

During the 1940s, the war and ,postwar years increased consciousness of Americans toward poverty and discrimination outside its shores. As America became increasingly prosperous soon after the war was over and the soldiers came home, their lives changed forever, the isolationism of America was broken. There were two significant actions undertaken by the United States under President Harry Truman that represented this new mood:

1. On June 26, 1945, the charter of the United Nations in San Francisco was signed; Eleanor Roosevelt represented the United States and most Americans this time supported the idea of helping those abroad.
2. On June 5, 1947, the Marshall Plan was initiated by U.S. Secretary of State George C. Marshall who urged that European countries decide on their economic needs so that material and financial aid from the United States could be integrated on a broad scale.

On May 14, 1948, the independent nation-state of Israel was founded by Zionist Jews and Holocaust survivors and recognized immediately by President Harry S Truman. It was the expectation that most of Europe's displaced

Jewish families would choose to immigrate first to Israel (that was billed as "the Jew's ancient homeland") before trying to get into any other country. (That expectation was not fully met.)

Between 1948 and 1964, numerous refugee laws were passed (many initiated by Representative Emanuel Celler, chairman of the Judiciary Committee) giving asylum to several hundred thousand refugees and displaced persons.

In 1950, the first "green card" appeared when the Internal Security Act of 1950 required all immigrants with Alien Registration cards, or AR-3s, to replace them with the new, green "Form I-151." Then, perhaps because Alien Registration Receipt Card was too long, everyone started calling it green card.

The 1950s also saw the rise of moderate and liberal Southern Democrats (especially LBJ), moderate Republicans (Eisenhower), wealthy Progressive Republicans (Nelson Rockefeller and Northern liberals—the Kennedys in the Democratic Party. The Progressive movement focused now on discrimination and injustice especially of the Jim Crow laws that officially separated blacks and whites in the South—"separate but equal" supposedly.

In 1952, the McCarran-Walter Immigration and Nationality Act passed in Congress over President Truman's veto retained the national origins quota but abolished the universal Asiatic exclusion as such, however, it imposed a ceiling of 2,000 "Asian" immigrants from the "Asia-Pacific Triangle"—extending from India and Pakistan east to China, Japan, and most of the Pacific Islands except Australia and New Zealand. It gave, however, preference to applicants from quota countries who had labor skills valuable to the United States or were relatives of U.S. citizens. In effect, the McCarran-Walter Act revised the quotas back to the 1920 census.

For the first time in American history, racial distinctions were omitted from the U.S. Code. As could be expected, most of the quota allocation went to immigrants from Ireland, the United Kingdom, and Germany who already had relatives in the United States.

In 1953, in his State of the Union address, President Eisenhower stated that the McCarran-Walter Act "does in fact discriminate" and he asked Congress to write an immigration law that would "at one and the same time guard our legitimate national interests and be faithful to our basic idea of freedom and fairness to all." A ten-year Refugee Relief Act was passed later that year, but basic immigration reform "failed to evolve."[7]

In his 1956 State of the Union, President Eisenhower again cited the "urgent need" for a revision of the immigration system, but Congress did not act.

In 1958 while a senator, JFK wrote and published a small book called *A Nation of Immigrants* as part of an Anti-Defamation League series entitled "One Nation Library."

In 1960, during the election campaign of Senator John Kennedy, the first Catholic ever to be elected president in the United States, the candidate saw immigration as a campaign and election opportunity (as did Nixon), but both were wary of it as divisive for their parties. Senator John Kennedy (who as a House member had upheld the Truman veto of the McCarran-Walter Act) endorsed the Eisenhower proposals for reform but did not send a comprehensive revision proposal to Congress until 1963.

On March 1, 1961, the Peace Corps was established by an executive order of President Kennedy. He created it "for talented men and women who would dedicate themselves to the progress and peace of developing countries and to involve Americans more actively in the cause of global democracy, peace development, and freedom."[8] Kennedy appointed his brother-in-law R. Sargent Shriver to be the first director of the Peace Corps.

The Peace Corps was an outgrowth of the Cold War. President Kennedy had made a strong point that the Soviet Union "had hundreds of men and women, scientists, physicists, teachers, engineers, doctors, and nurses . . . prepared to spend their lives abroad in the service of world communism." The United States had no such program, and Kennedy wanted to involve Americans more actively in the cause of global democracy, peace, development, and freedom.[9]

In 1963, the Kennedy administration omnibus immigration bill (S 1932) was only one of several presented in the Senate including comprehensive bills from Senators Philip Hart (D-Michigan), Jacob K. Javits (R-New York), and Claiborne Pell (D-Pennsylvania); in the House 55 bills identical to the administration's (HR700) were introduced and another 38 different bills were presented. Obviously, in the 88th Congress, there was a general feeling that some revision of the McCarran-Walter National Origins Act needed to be done. But while there was no significant opposition to any large increase in immigration, most congressmen did not feel sufficient pressure from their districts to push the legislation. Both the Kennedy and Johnson administrations made it clear that poverty programs and civil rights were more important.

This all changed on November 22, 1963, when President Kennedy was assassinated in Dallas, Texas. Suddenly, Kennedy's legislative goals became President Lyndon B. Johnson's passionate quest to fulfill the Kennedy legacy by passing civil rights, voting rights, and immigration reform legislation, while at the same time building a legacy for his presidency—The Great Society. On June 19, 1964, the civil rights bill passed Congress, and President Johnson signed it into law on July 2.

In 1964, during his presidential election campaign, President Johnson stated that one of his (many) priorities was passage of an immigration reform bill. In his State of the Union message he framed the issue as one of discrimination. He urged that "revisions would lift the bars of discrimination"[10] against immigrants, particularly those with much-needed skills and those joining their families. During the year, hearings were held but no action was taken. The general public did not appear to be interested in immigration as a big election-year issue.

Democratic National Committee chairman John M. Bailey credited Republican opposition to amending the immigration laws as the reason for Johnson's making a stronger showing than Kennedy had among Spanish, Italian, and Polish wards.[11] At the time, Italy had the longest waiting list of applicants, Greece was next, Poland third, and Portugal fourth.

Immigration Management — two significant changes

Two important structural changes of immigration management were made during this postwar period:

- 1933: The Immigration and Naturalization Service (INS) is created under the Department of Labor and combined the Bureau of Immigration, the Naturalization Service, and the Border Patrol under its wing. (It lasted until 2005 when it reorganized under the newly created Department of Homeland Security.)
- 1947: The reorganization of Congress placed immigration under the jurisdiction of the Judiciary Committee—out of Labor and Commerce; not coincidentally, Congressman Manny Celler was the chair and leading voice of that committee from 1923 until 1971.

This latter move was highly significant for two reasons. First, it enabled Congressman Celler to use all his powers as chairman to repeal the National Origins Quota Act, replacing it with the historically liberal Immigration and Nationality Act of 1965. But second, and perhaps even more important, it placed immigration administration in the executive branch of government under the Justice Department instead of the Labor Department. It made the focus of immigration law one of justice—family unification and antidiscrimination —instead of about work, jobs, and labor development of the country. In the zealous environment of civil rights, this change of jurisdiction carried the implication that immigration was a civil right and a matter of justice for immigrants, taking the American worker out of the picture.

THE SOCIAL MOVEMENTS THAT DROVE THE INA

Two social movements arising from society's realization of the horrendous results of discrimination were undoubtedly crucial in the passage of the Immigration and Nationality Act of 1965. This realization along with guilt and shame about America's own biases was certainly a factor that propelled the 1960 election of the first Catholic president in U.S. history, John F. Kennedy.

Painful personal experiences that all the leaders of the INA had with immigrant discrimination to one extent or another certainly propelled their sympathy toward immigrants and passage of the INA: the Kennedys grew up with stories and certainly more than a few personal brushes with bias toward Irish Catholics that made them, even as wealthy and privileged elites, become populist liberals. Similarly, his long traumatic family experience with poverty, rejection, and the struggles of Mexican-heritage workers in Texas propelled President Lyndon B. Johnson to make the passage of the INA one of the first priorities in his Great Society.

But equally, an essential driver for the passage of the INA was guilt and shame about past slavery, bias, and discrimination as the horror of the Nazi Holocaust was revealed. Americans were shocked to learn of it, of its extent, and its millions of victims as the Nazi camps were opened in the late 1940s and one by one victims and returning liberating soldiers shared their stories of the horror. It was the country's momentous lesson of the ultimate unspeakable result of bias, prejudice, and discrimination.

The Civil Rights Movement

The "modern" civil rights movement of 1948–1964 started shortly after World War II (perhaps in small part because of the successful integration of all races in the armed services). The movement became a force to make it illegal once and for all by federal law (and enforceable by federal authorities) to discriminate against anyone on the basis of race, color, religion, or *national origin*. The latter of course is what became the civil rights reason to repeal the National Origins Quota Immigration Act of 1924.

To put the evolution of civil rights and immigration legislation in the post–World War II period, here is a brief timeline of a few milestones in the modern civil rights movement:

- 1948, July 26: President Truman signs Executive Order 9981 that declares equality of treatment and opportunity for all persons in the armed services without regard to race, color, religion, or national origins.
- 1954, May 17: Supreme Court rules in *Brown v. Board of Education of Topeka, Kansas* that segregation in public schools is unconstitutional.
- 1955, December 1: Rosa Parks refuses to give up her seat in the front of a bus in segregated Montgomery, Alabama, sparking a year-long bus boycott of blacks led by Dr. Martin Luther King Jr., until buses are declared desegregated on December 1, 1956.
- 1957, January and February: MLK becomes first president of the Southern Christian Leadership Conference, which becomes a leading force in the

civil rights movement and advocates the principles of nonviolence and civil disobedience.

- 1960: The Student Non-Violent Coordinating Committee is founded and after months-long student sit-ins at segregated lunch counters at stores such as Woolworth's, swimming pools, parks, and many other public sites, leads to integration in public facilities in the South.
- 1961, May 4: Student volunteer "Freedom riders" attacked as they try to desegregate travel facilities throughout the South during the summer.
- 1962, October 1: James Meredith becomes the first enrolled black student at the University of Mississippi after riots to prevent his enrollment caused President Kennedy to send 5,000 federal troops.
- 1963: Civil rights leaders and movement participants are jailed and killed, including NAACP field secretary Medgar Evers in Mississippi on June 12. In protest, on August 28, 200,000 people march on Washington where MLK makes his famous "I Have a Dream" speech. On September 15, four young black girls are killed in a bomb at their church in Birmingham, Alabama.
- 1963, November 22: President Kennedy is assassinated in Dallas, Texas; Vice President Lyndon B. Johnson is sworn in as president of the United States. Less than one month later he passes the budget that had been stalled in a Republican Congress and enables the civil rights bill to be released out a committee lock onto the House floor through a (rarely successful) discharge petition requiring the vote of the majority of the House members.
- 1964: The 24th Amendment is passed on January 23, abolishing the poll tax in the United States, a tax used to disenfranchise poor (often illiterate) citizens. It was Ted Kennedy's major civil rights issue.
- 1964, July 2: President Johnson signs the Civil Rights Act that provides the federal government with the powers to enforce the prohibition of discrimination of any kind throughout the nation based on race, color, religion, or *national origin*.

There can be no doubt at all that the Immigration and Nationality Act of 1965 was propelled and helped greatly by—perhaps only could have been passed because of—the growing grassroots, antidiscrimination environment created by the civil rights movement. The millions of grassroots supporters and activists throughout the 1960s made discrimination against blacks and any specific, identifiable, ethnic group in any endeavor—education, housing, voting, employment—widely known and unacceptable.

The Holocaust

The joy of the end of World War II was certainly tainted by an increasing horror and even guilt and shame that American leaders, journalists, and public figures had ignored signs of the impending genocide in the 1930s and early 1940s. Some even denied knowledge of the "secret" death camps during the war even though they had been told of them as early as 1938. American leaders' reluctance to get into another world war was certainly understandable. But the cost was to ignore and even deny the unthinkable signs of genocide of Jews, Catholics, Romas, and others in the Nazi march to empire.

Millions of men, women, and children were systematically slaughtered in the genocide by the Nazis of Germany, Austria, Poland, and many other countries of Eastern Europe, or were shipped to their deaths by Nazi supporters in France, Italy, Spain, and even neutral Switzerland. (They were however welcomed in many of the nation-states of South America.) But the press and "officialdom" in Washington, D.C., ignored the signs.

> In August 1942, the State Department received a report sent by Gerhart Riegner, the Geneva-based representative of the World Jewish Congress (WJC). The report revealed that the Germans were implementing a policy to physically annihilate the Jews of Europe. Department officials declined to pass on the report to its intended recipient, American Jewish leader Stephen Wise, who was President of the World Jewish Congress. On November 24, 1942, Wise held a press conference to announce that Nazi Germany was implementing a policy to annihilate the European Jews. A few weeks later, on December 17, the United States, Great Britain, and 10 other Allied governments issued a declaration denouncing Nazi Germany's intention to murder the Jews of Europe.
>
> But the American press did not always publicize reports of Nazi atrocities in full or with prominent placement. As the magnitude of anti-Jewish violence increased in 1939–1941, many American newspapers ran descriptions of German shooting operations, first in Poland and later after the invasion of the Soviet Union. The ethnic identity of the victims was not always made clear. The news concentrated on the battles of the war, not the concentration camps. William L. Shirer, the best-selling author of *Berlin Diary*, who during the war was a European correspondent for CBS, reported that it was only at the end of 1945 that he learned "for sure" about the Holocaust; the news burst upon him "like a thunderbolt." [12]

It was during the heavily press-covered Nuremberg Trials of 1945–1946 that the true extent of the Nazi atrocities came to horrifying public light. It brought increasing pressure on the Allied powers to create a homeland for Jewish survivors of the Holocaust, would lead to a mandate for the creation of Israel in 1948. And it increased sympathy to change immigration law based on "national origin" of which being "Jewish" (or Hebrew) was considered to be a nationality and often marked in place of "nationality" on Nazi-controlled country passports.

The guilt and shame of the Holocaust had a huge impact on all of Western society that is still felt today. Perhaps it was felt particularly deeply because it had been carried out by a nationality—the Germans—who were such a part of America. Germans had helped to build America; in 1910, in almost every state of the Union, the country of birth of the majority of immigrants was Germany; by 1960, it was Mexico.[13] The German education system and classical culture was admired and emulated by elites in America and Great Britain until the Great Wars. Even the royals of England were related to Germans.

The horror of the Holocaust and the two world wars was felt in many ways. Certainly it impacted the embrace of new cultural mores, architecture, art, music, and politics—anything that was not old, classical, failed European. It certainly was behind the immediate support America and Europe gave for the founding of the new Jewish state of Israel—a development that is at the heart of many foreign relations problems between the Middle East and the West even today. For this story, it is clear to me that the Holocaust was perhaps the major reason that white America—especially young, student America—embraced the civil rights movement with such fervor and that President Johnson's Great Society goals were so quickly accomplished in two years under the banner of ending discrimination—including completely repudiating the national origins quota Immigration Act.

THE KEY PEOPLE AND INTEREST GROUPS DRIVING THE INA

While the postwar environment of the 1950s was ripe for civil rights, there were key individuals and interest groups that particularly drove that legislation. It took years for civil rights to build into the nationwide public and political movement that eventually led to the Civil Rights Act of 1964 and the many associated acts of the Great Society in 1965. But immigration reform was not really a part of that movement. Even today in all the historical events commemorating the Civil Rights Act and LBJ's great society, the INA is hardly ever mentioned.

But while immigration reform wasn't a largely visible, public movement, there were fervent advocates for it. Some key people and interest groups were crucial to its passage. Their personal stories reveal how their viewpoints were shaped and how they used their particular talents and power to direct the way the legislation was written, argued, and passed.

The Four Key Players

Congressman Emanuel (Manny) Celler

Discrimination against Jews in the National Origins Act was why the real father and namesake of the Immigration and Nationality Act of 1965 opposed the earlier act even before it was passed in 1924. Emanuel (Manny) Celler was the Jewish congressman from Manhattan since 1923 and leader of the House Judiciary Committee for some 40 years. He did more than anyone to lobby unceasingly for the repeal of the National Origins Quota Act. He is a heroic icon among the Jewish community in New York City, his lifetime home.

Emanuel Celler was born in Brooklyn in 1888. His father, Henry, owned a whiskey business; during Emanuel's childhood the Celler's basement held a 25,000-gallon whiskey tank filled with the family brand, Echo Spring. When Henry Celler's whiskey business failed, he was forced to find employment selling wine door-to-door to local residents. Soon after Emanuel graduated from public high school and entered Columbia College, his father died, and his mother, Josephine, passed away five months later. In his autobiography, *You Never Leave Brooklyn*, Emanuel Celler wrote, "I became the head of the household. . . . I took up [my father's] wine route. I went to school in the morning and sold wines all afternoon until seven o'clock in the evening."[14] Despite these burdens, Emanuel Celler was a star student at Columbia and Columbia Law School, graduating from the latter in 1912.

From the very first, Manny Celler's career reflected his lifelong interest in the plight of refugees and immigrants. Some of his earliest clients were his wine customers, most of whom were immigrants. More than one fell afoul of the immigration laws, and Celler worked hard to keep them from being deported for minor infractions. During World War I, Celler served as an appeal agent for his local draft board. After the war, Celler's law practice flourished, and the successful attorney organized two banks and served as a director of two others.

In 1922, a political acquaintance convinced Celler to run for Congress as a Tammany Hall Democrat. Celler enlisted friends, relatives, and neighbors to canvass for him door-to-door. Stressing "the evils of Prohibition and the virtues of the League of Nations," although the district had never before elected a Democrat, Celler won the election by some 3,000 votes. In March of 1923, he assumed a seat he would hold for 49 years and 10 months, the second-longest term in congressional history.

Celler made his first major speech on the House floor when he opposed the National Origins Act of 1924. The (Albert) Johnson Act passed the isolationist Congress and was signed into law. Despite this setback, Celler had found his cause, and for the next four decades he advocated eliminating national origin as a basis for immigration restriction. At no time were his efforts more critical than in the 1930s, when the United States, England, and France, among others, proved unable or unwilling to open their doors to victims of Nazi persecution and—as was later discovered—genocide.

Poignant stories about Celler's determination to fight U. S. immigration quotas are related in the Jewish Virtual Library's definitive biography of the congressman. According to historians, his drive to change the National Quota Act was particularly reinforced one Sunday during World War II when a bearded rabbi came to his home. Celler always left the door unlocked on Sundays so his constituents could enter without ringing or knocking. The rabbi in a black hat and long coat, clutching a cane, spoke forcefully to Celler. "Don't you see, can't you see?" the rabbi asked. "Won't you see that there are millions—millions—being killed. Can't we save some of them? Can't you, Mr. Congressman, do something?"[15]

Celler equivocated, asserting that President Roosevelt had told him that he sympathized with the Jewish plight but could not divert ships being used to transport war material and soldiers to bring in refugees. The rabbi's reply moved Celler to tears: "If six million cattle had been slaughtered," he observed, "there would have been greater interest."[16]

After the war, as chairman of the House Judiciary Committee, Celler resolved to liberalize the immigration laws of 1924. In 1946, Congress restricted the number of "Displaced Persons" (DPs)—a designation for refugees from the Great War—who could enter the United States that, despite the starvation in Europe, fewer than 3,000 DPs actually emigrated here. Celler's determined efforts led to the passage, in 1948, of a bill that allowed 339,000 DPs to enter the country, many of whom were Jewish.

In 1947, Celler presided over a little-noticed congressional administrative procedure that was to be key to the successful repeal of the National Origins Act. It was the "Reorganization of Congressional Committees" Act of 1947. Celler pushed that immigration be made a primary jurisdiction of the Judiciary Committee, of which he was chairman and a ranking member between 1923 and 1971. Celler now had primary jurisdiction over immigration legislation. He now had the influence and power to push through the House the historic no-national-quotas, no-national-preference, nondiscriminating, family-unification Immigration and Nationality Act of 1965 and to repeal the National Origins Act he had been opposing since its adoption.

President Lyndon Johnson signed into law an act that eliminated national origins as a consideration for immigration, culminating Celler's 41-year fight to overcome discrimination against Eastern European Jews and Catholics. Today, nearly 75 percent of American Jews descend from immigrants from Eastern Europe. Celler was defeated in the 1972 primary, becoming the most senior represenative ever at that time to lose a primary. Having served almost 50 years, he died in 1981 at the age of 93.[17]

The Kennedys: President John (Jack—JFK) and Senator Edward (Ted)

JFK   By 1952, the blue-blood, so-called WASPs (White Anglo-Saxon Protestants) who had dominated Massachusetts's elite social and political class since it had been a colony is the early 1600s. They were quickly being outnumbered by the Bay State's growing roll of voters who, like the Kennedy family, were descended from immigrants who had arrived during the great immigration wave of 1880–1920. The Kennedy's were Irish Catholics and that growing Boston demographic (controlled many police and fire stations in the city) was their political base. But Polish Americans remembered 35-year-old John Kennedy's appearances on their radio programs. A letter from the Albanian American Citizens Committee spoke of Kennedy's "deep hatred for atheistic communism." Ads in Jewish newspapers touted Kennedy's commitment to Israel. [18]

John Kennedy made immigration an issue in his 1952 Senate campaign against then Senator Henry Cabot Lodge Jr., condemning Lodge for being absent from the Senate when only three votes were needed to kill the McCarran-Walter immigration bill. "Representative Kennedy charged the act was un-American and discriminatory and said that the present limit of 154,000 immigrants is but 1-10th of 1 percent of the nation's present population." [19]

"Kennedy spotted immigration as an important thing and I suppose it was for Massachusetts politicians for a long while," said Ralph Dungan who later worked on Kennedy's Senate staff. [20]

While he was still a senator, JFK wrote a booklet, *A Nation of Immigrants*, for the Anti-Defamation League. Subsequently, after gaining the presidency, he called on Congress to undertake a full reevaluation of immigration law; and he began to revise the book for further publication. In August 1963, excerpts of the 1958 pamphlet were published in the *New York Times Magazine*. He was assassinated before completing the revision, but the book was nevertheless posthumously published in 1964 with an introduction by his brother, then Attorney General Robert F. Kennedy. In 2008, the book was reissued by the Anti-Defamation League.

The book outlines his thinking on immigration:

> "Immigrants helped give America the extraordinary social mobility which is the essence of an open society. . . . Immigration has been the foundation of American inventiveness and ingenuity. It has been the source of a multiplicity of new enterprises, and of American success in achieving the highest standard of living anywhere in the world." Kennedy's thesis was that immigration leads to dynamism and economic growth in the country. [21]

He had personal reasons for feeling so passionately about immigration. Both of John Kennedy's parents, Joseph Patrick Kennedy and Rose Fitzgerald, were born in Boston to immigrants from Ireland. The Fitzgeralds and

Kennedys lived and worked in Boston, seeking to take advantage of the economic opportunities that America offered. But they had also to overcome the harsh, widespread discrimination against Irish-Catholic immigrants at that time. The early Kennedys and Fitzgeralds worked as peddlers, coopers (barrel makers) and common laborers; later they became clerks, tavern owners and retailers.

By the end of the century, Patrick "P. J." Kennedy and John "Honey Fitz" Fitzgerald, the president's maternal grandfather, had become successful Boston politicians. Honey Fitz served in the State Senate and the U.S. House of Representatives and then as the mayor of Boston. Patrick Joseph "PJ" Kennedy was a state legislator and a ward boss, "parlaying his political power into business and real estate deals." But no matter how successful they became, the Fitzgeralds and the Kennedys, lie other "lace curtain" Iris families felt lie second-class citizens in Yankee Boston. Watching their parents advance in the world, despite having their horizons limited by social barriers, Joe and Rose were seized by a fierce desire to leave their imprint on the world through their own lives and especially through those of their children.[22]

John Fitzgerald Kennedy relished his Irish heritage. During President Kennedy's historic visit to Ireland in June 1963, he remarked to the people of New Ross, Ireland, "When my great grandfather left here to become a cooper in East Boston, he carried nothing with him except two things: a strong religious faith and a strong desire for liberty. I am glad to say that all of his great-grandchildren have valued that inheritance."[23]

Those stories were part of the Kennedy family legacy and all the children knew them. They were stories of hardship, but also of astonishing social mobility.

At the height of the civil rights movement of the 1960s, President Kennedy saw the National Origins Quota Act of 1924 as an embarrassment. He called the then-quota-system "nearly intolerable."[24] He had added the abolishment of the National Origins Act to his legislative agenda in 1963—a goal that transferred to President Johnson after Kennedy's assassination in November.[25]

Senator Edward (Ted) Kennedy Senator Kennedy also grew up with the family legacy of successful immigrants. Born in 1938, the youngest of the nine Kennedy children, from the start he was "the adored baby brother," according to biographer Peter S. Canellos.[26] Called "Biscuits and Muffins," he was chubby and cheery and became the family clown and organizer, eager to please and good natured. He was also the most considerate of the Kennedy boys.

By the time Ted was growing up, Joe had made a fortune as a banker, shipyard builder, liquor distributor, real estate investor, and movie producer, pushing his way past obstacles in Boston (where Yankee bankers had shut

out he Irish) to New York's Wall Street and Hollywood. By the time of
Teddy's birth, the two parents were away from each other more often and
their estrangement may have been visible at times to the children. But their
commitment to continuing their marriage was solid and Joe hoped that his
money would give his children the freedom that he and Rose enjoyed more
than most couples.

He set up a million-dollar trust fund for each child and told them they
should devote their lives to public service—the boys to enter public service
and burnish the Kennedy name, the girls to do some sort of social justice
work. His parents defined their parenting jobs much like partners in a fran-
chise. They worked with well-oiled efficiency to raise their children according to three guiding principles: family, faith, and country. His father's slo-
gans included, " No losers in this family," "No sour pusses," "No rich, idle
bums." The Kennedy children were expected to be cheerful, no tears, no
feeling sorry for yourself—but not to smile too much or try to charm ones
way to favor. But he punished also. "The love that gives also demands much
in return" he would say. Each child was promised $2000 if they hadn't
smoked or drank by the time they were 21.[27] Even when the boys became
members of elite Harvard clubs like the Spee Club, the Hasty Pudding Society, they never drank much except a beer. They were not allowed to touch the
hard stuff

Growing up in Bronxville, New York, a wealthy English-style village
with rolling green hills 15 miles north of Manhattan, Teddy was the victim or
beneficiary of lower expectations. "If I wanted to contribute something
worthwhile to the conversation at dinner, I would have to talk about a book I
was reading or an interesting place I had visited," he said. Jack, who was
naturally introverted and spent hours reading alone, told Ted "never be without a book in your hand." But Ted's schooling was lonely, attending lots of
boarding schools he could barely remember (10 by the time he was 11 years
old). They included Protestant boarding schools and military academies; Joe
insisted that the boys take their place with the children of Protestant power-
brokers the better to ensure their success. "He came through due to his
personality and his incredible empathy and sympathy." But Teddy had a
mediocre academic record and both parents were constantly on him about his
spelling, his marks, and his girth—weight being a family obsession.[28]

He was, however, very athletic and had the chance often to prove it. The
Kennedy children competed among themselves and against the world on
everything; anything could be turned into a contest. Touch football games
often resulted in injuries but the children were not allowed to complain. They
were even more competitive with outsiders (whom they never let into their
inner circle). At Harvard, because of his size, Ted played football—which
thrilled the family that he would play this "most manly of sports" because
Joe, John, and Bobby were too small to play. But his freshman year ended

precipitously; that spring he was in danger of flunking Spanish. He didn't like it and let a teammate take the exam. He got kicked out for two years for cheating; the family treated it as a case of bad judgment.

Ted went into the army at Fort Dix, New Jersey. Joe wrote him a letter with career advice, as help for his son's future in politics, that Teddy took to heart: "I hope you will make up your mind to get to know as many different kinds of people as you can because that kind of education is more valuable than even a college education. All kinds of people are essential for one's development."[29]

The army, in its early stages of integration, offered Teddy a lens on the wider world. Unlike his brothers who had been officers, Teddy was a grunt. He lived with black people and the working class. The experience had a profound effect on him.

Ted returned to Harvard in 1953 now "dead serious" about his studies (including earning an A- in Spanish) even though his great passion remained football. His athleticism, love of a party, and family name (John was now a senator) made him a big man on campus. He graduated in 1956 and went on to attend the University of Virginia Law School where he graduated in 1959. John was now deep in a campaign for the presidency and Ted became his youth vote outreach director. After his brother was inaugurated as the first Catholic president of the United States, Ted took a job as an assistant district attorney in Boston and his father began an unofficial campaign for Ted to win Jack's former seat in the Senate.

Presidential adviser Ted Sorenson says that "Jack was particularly sensitive about the possible charge of nepotism—that it wasn't enough [for the president] to have his brother Bobby as Attorney General but he needed his kid brother in the Senate?" Jack's advisers saw problems, but in the end they all bowed to the inevitable.[30] Ted unexpectedly beat George Lodge by a wide margin. "Even though Ted had longed to escape the smothering shadows cast by his brothers he was now headed to live and work in Washington where there were no bigger names that Jack and Bobby."[31]

Ted generally followed Jack's advice to keep a low profile during his first year in the Senate. Still, he was the brother of the attorney general and the president, so his phone calls got returned—quickly. And Jack often had him come to the White House "for cigars and laughs." As much as Bobby functioned as Jack's most trusted advisor he was often too demanding, too involved with issues. When the president wanted a break from the pressures he would call Ted. And Ted demonstrated a new maturity in his willingness to take his time and play by the rules.[32] It was Ted, on the floor of the Senate, who first got the news of Jack's assassination and told Bobby by phone.

After Vice President Lyndon Johnson (who Bobby openly detested) became president, "Ted made it clear that he didn't have to adopt his brother's personal distaste for LBJ. As much as possible he tried to keep the relationships separate. He was practical and he knew if he could remain on good terms with the Johnson White House, it would be to the benefit of his constituents and his career."[33]

In 1965, after the murders and marches in Selma advanced civil rights as the priority of the Johnson presidency, Ted sounded out prominent civil rights leaders on their legislative priorities. What Kennedy heard was "poll tax, poll tax, poll tax." It became his primary issue. "The cause showcased a new determination mixed with his usual deference."[34] He entered the debate on the floor of the Senate thoroughly prepared with his arguments, but he also remained unfailingly polite. His performance won him a new reputation in the Senate, even among the powerful Southern Democrats.[35]

Around that time, he took up another cause that was just as rife with political danger: immigration reform. Ted Kennedy led the drive in the Senate for a new immigration law that would repeal and replace the National Origins Quota Act of 1924. As a senator, Jack Kennedy had tried unsuccessfully to reform the quota system. Now Ted picked up the mantle, this time with the support of the Johnson administration.

Ted framed immigration reform as a simple matter of fairness, echoing his approach to civil rights when he had reminded people of how disadvantaged the Kennedy clan would have been had the nation never taken down the "Irish Need Not Apply" signs.[36]

"This (new immigration) bill goes to the very central ideals of our country," he said during floor debate. "Our streets may not be paved with gold, but they are paved with the promise that men and women who live here—even strangers and new newcomers—can rise as fast, as far as their skills will allow, no matter what their color is, no matter what the place of their birth."

Although the Northern Irish benefited from the National Origins Act system being one of the preferred categories, they were for the most part Protestants, while the Kennedys were Irish Catholics who were not favored. Ted staked out progressive policy that created distance between him and many of the working-class (Northern) Irish families who had always been the Kennedys' bread-and-butter supporters. Prominent Boston Irish groups lobbied strongly against the bill, but Kennedy maintained that the current system of national quotas that favored northern Europe and Northern (mainly Protestant) Ireland, violated American values.

Ted was showing he knew how to get things done in the Senate and the keys to his success were some of the same skills he had had to learn as the youngest brother of a very competitive family with so many older brothers and sisters ahead of him. He had a knack for when to jump into the fray and when to hang back.

Exhibit A was his handling of the immigration bill and in particularly handling the unapologetically racist and conservative Democrat from Mississippi and the Senate Judiciary Committee chairman, James O. Eastland. Journalist Meg Greenfield observed at one time:

> When on occasion, Eastland denounces him as a fomenter of racial violence . . . Kennedy lets it pass, knowing both the southerner's need to make is remarks for the record and their profound irrelevance to what goes on in committee. Eastland on his part, in an unprecedented bit of graciousness, permitted Kennedy to take over his own subcommittee for the period to time required, to hold friendly hearings on the immigration bill, which Eastland fervently opposed. Kennedy thus became Senate manager of the bill which he shepherded through committee and the floor with scrupulous tact, at all times willing to indulge the Southern Senators' fulminations against it—so long as they would leave is alone. As a result, the southerners conspicuously failed to try to amend it during the four days it was on the floor.

In response to critics, he also famously claimed that the change to a system to opening immigration to all nations and favoring family unification would not change the mix of the country.[37] It does not seem like Kennedy knew this statement was wrong. He might have believed it at the time, but as immigrant numbers and American demographics changed dramatically after passage of the Immigration and Nationality Act of 1965, Kennedy embraced the changes wholeheartedly. By 2007 he would say on the floor of the Senate, "Immigration is the next big civil rights issue of our time."

"That 1965 law was first big thing that he really drove himself. Ever since then, he's been making immigration policy for the country," remarked Mark Krikorian, the executive director of the Center for Immigration Studies years later. Even though in Washington tactics varied and coalition partners shifted during his 47 years in the Senate, Kennedy's core principle about immigration laws that he defended never varied.

The United States is a nation of immigrants, he said. "I look across this historic gathering and I see the future of America," he said at an immigration rally in Washington, April 10, 2006. In speeches, Kennedy often invoked the Golden Steps he could see from his Boston office, where new waves of immigrants, including his eight grandparents, came off the docks into East Boston—and a city where "No Irish Need Apply."

LBJ

"Lyndon Johnson was a genuine, true-believing revolutionary," according to the director of the LBJ Presidential Library in Austin, Texas, Mark K. Updegrove. He grew up in a small Texan town where his father was prominent and the family well off. But their fortunes changed and Johnson experienced years of hardship and even shame. He worked in manual labor to complete high school and the state Teacher's College even while being active in student government and debate. His experiences teaching poor Mexican-

American children in Cotulla, Texas, turned him into an avid FDR fan, New Deal Democrat in a state of conservative Southern Democrats. It fueled his raging ambition to one day be president of the United States.

In 1935, Johnson worked as Texas director of Roosevelt's National Youth Administration and in 1937 he ran for Congress on a New Deal platform. He served for 12 years and became a close ally of FDR even as he successfully courted and ingratiated himself with powerful Southern Democrats, particularly House Majority Leader Sam Rayburn. In 1949, he won a highly contested race for the U.S. Senate—complete with charges of voter fraud, especially in Mexican-American barrios. His extraordinary ambition, long hours, and "courting skills" of older senior senators, especially Senator Richard Russell of Georgia, the democratic leader of the Conservative coalition and arguably the most powerful man in the Senate, led to his being chosen Senate Majority Leader just two years later, in 1951. Johnson's negotiating skills earned him the title of "Master of the Senate" wonderfully recounted in Robert Caro's book by the same title[38] and, in the description of "The Johnson Treatment" by two famous columnists of the time, "Evans and Novak."

> The Treatment could last ten minutes or four hours. It came, enveloping its target, at the Johnson Ranch swimming pool, in one of Johnson's offices, in the Senate cloakroom, on the floor of the Senate itself—wherever Johnson might find a fellow Senator within his reach.
>
> Its tone could be supplication, accusation, cajolery, exuberance, scorn, tears, complaint, and the hint of threat. It was all of these together. It ran the gamut of human emotions. Its velocity was breathtaking, and it was all in one direction. Interjections from the target were rare. Johnson anticipated them before they could be spoken. He moved in close, his face a scant millimeter from his target, his eyes widening and narrowing, his eyebrows rising and falling. From his pockets poured clippings, memos, statistics. Mimicry, humor, and the genius of analogy made The Treatment an almost hypnotic experience and rendered the target stunned and helpless.[39]

"Johnson saw racial justice as a moral issue."[40] Witnessing the indignities that his black cook, Zephyr Wright, and his driver, Gene Williams, suffered during his Senate years when they drove from Washington to Texas through the segregated South—fueled his revolutionary spirit. He refused to accept pockets of poverty in the richest nation in history. He saw a nation so hellbent on industrial growth and amassing wealth that greed threatened to destroy its natural resources. He saw cities deteriorating and municipal political machines unresponsive to the early migration of Hispanics and the masses of blacks moving north.

To Johnson, government was neither a bad man to be tarred and feathered, nor a bagman to collect campaign contributions. To him, government was not a bystander, hoping wealth and opportunity might trickle down to the least among us. To LBJ, government was a mighty wrench to open opportunities for everyone, but especially the poor. He wanted his government to provide the poor with the kind of education, health, and social support that most of us get from our parents.[41]

Johnson's ambition was to be president of the United States, but he lost the nomination in 1960 to John F. Kennedy. Much to everyone's shock however (including JFK's brother Robert), the liberal Massachusetts president-to-be asked the New Deal Texan to be his vice president.

The next three years were not a happy period for Johnson, whose agony in becoming marginalized by the Kennedy administration is painful to read in Robert Caro's book *Passage of Power*. But after the assassination of President Kennedy and Johnson's immediate ascendancy to the presidency in November 1963, LBJ took on the unattained goals of JFK including immigration reform, as his own. "Like civil rights and antipoverty measures the issue flowed naturally to Johnson's agenda. He had seen the ugliness of bigotry through the eyes of his [mainly Mexican-heritage students] in Cotulla and had encouraged them to look beyond it," writes Mark Updegrove, director of the LBJ Presidential Library in his 2012 book *Indomitable Will*.[42]

Between 1937 and 1942, Johnson had helped Jewish refugees in Europe by seeing to the immigration of family members of constituents or advising them on how to obtain visas at a time when other lawmakers—and the U.S. government as a whole—were turning a blind eye to Nazi tyranny. The total number of Jews Johnson helped immigrate remains in question. None of the case files from 1937–1942 in his congressional office were saved; nor were they saved at the State Department, leaving the total extent of Johnson's involvement in the cause a mystery. There has been some speculation, found abundantly on the Internet, that Johnson was an unheralded hero to the Jews, helping hundreds to find refuge in the United States. But although Johnson's efforts were admirable, had he been involved far beyond serving his constituents' interests, it is likely he would have disclosed this in later years as a point of pride or political leverage Updegrove observes.

Johnson used his 1964 State of the Union address to condemn the National Origins Act as being out of step with American principles. "In establishing preferences," he said, "a nation that was built by immigrants of all lands can ask those who now seek admission: What can you do for our country?" We should not be asking them "In what country were you born?"[43]

Later in the year Johnson said, "Immigration reform was a matter of common sense." Two hours after his historic speech on civil rights, at 11 p.m., President Johnson asked his aide Lee White if he had called Manny Celler yet about setting up hearings for the new immigration act that he was proposing, to do away with national quotas. He even demanded that night that his aide call Ben Bradlee of the *Washington Post* to write an editorial about it.[44]

Johnson quickly tapped Congressman Manny Celler and Senator Ted Kennedy to steer his immigration bill through Congress. They were the most influential managers he could have picked on this issue—both (as we have seen) had personal family reasons to be involved in the issue. And Johnson also wasn't worried about the perceived bad blood that there was between him and Robert Kennedy ever since his nomination as Jack's vice president. Ted Kennedy had always been the friendliest of the brothers, the peacemaker. Johnson saw that giving him the management of the important immigration bill in the Senate as the way to strengthen his working relationship with the collegial Kennedy and to quash rumors about the growing strain between him and the grieving Kennedy clan (there already was a movement underway to get Robert to run for president against Johnson in 1968).

Here are bits of an intriguing conversation between LBJ and Ted Kennedy on March 8, 1965, at 9:10 p.m. (an early evening hour for Johnson):

> LBJ: This business about me being crossways with the Kennedys is just a pure lot of crap . . . and think you know something about how I feel about you. And I have no antagonisms, no antipathy, no wars to settle with anybody else. I just don't want you to let the damn press do that. . . . All I want to do is what's right.
> Ted Kennedy: We've had some good hearings on immigration. They're going—
> LBJ: Yes you have. And I heard Bobby made a helluva good statement the other days. And it looks like it might be a possibility to get it out of both houses. Do you think so?
> Kennedy: Well I think in the Senate we're in better shape than over in the House. . . .
> LBJ: Well, you've got to work on [Celler] a bit.
> Kennedy: He's a tough cookie . . . it's coming along.[45]

Overcoming predictable opposition by Southern Democrats and with much prodding by Johnson, Kennedy and Celler delivered both the upper and lower houses.

Johnson was very anxious that other issues of the Great Society *after* the civil rights act including and especially the voting rights act and education were *not framed on race* but rather on fairness, justness, equal opportunity, and equal citizenship (for all Americans, especially) *for the poor*—it was about poverty, something Johnson understood very well. *At no time did he or anyone else make it only about race or ethnic identity.* Alcohol is involved in so much of society's violence—not race.[46]

"We have to deracialize all the issues we talk about today—including violence, the culture of violence, a sickness in the culture that goes beyond race. It's domestic violence, school violence, sicknesses in society that didn't used to be," said Andrew Young[47] in April 2014 at the LBJ library during a panel discussion by Johnson administration officials who had been involved with the passage of the Civil Rights Act.

Lyndon Johnson was perpetually impatient, relentlessly restless, always in a hurry. But he also was a man of extraordinary courage and there is no doubt that throughout his life, Lyndon Johnson knew how to use power—be it the power of cajoling or threat—to get others to give him his way. His recognition of the significance of bipartisan support for controversial, but needed, domestic initiatives, and his ability to muster such support, should be studied by politicians and citizens who seek to change the world. His unique ability to make Washington work, to nourish and maintain partnerships between the executive branch and the Congress, the public and private sectors, and to focus the people on critical needs like racial justice and eliminating poverty demonstrate "Yes, we can!" to skeptical citizens who have never seen Washington get it done.[48]

> In the twentieth century, with its eighteen American presidents, Lyndon Baines Johnson was the greatest champion that black Americans and Mexican-Americans and indeed all Americans of color had in the White House, the greatest champion they had in all the halls of government. With the single exception of Lincoln, he was the greatest champion with a white skin that they had in the history of the Republic. He was . . . the lawmaker for the poor and the downtrodden and the oppressed . . . the President who wrote mercy and justice into the statute books by which America was governed.[49]

In late 2014, an epic film depicting the march on Selma on March 7, 1965, that really started the civil rights movement was released. Written and produced by an African American, Ava DuVernay, there was almost immediate criticism that in her zeal to heroize MLK, she degraded President Johnson's involvement and support of the civil rights act. "It's just a movie" she said. "I am not an historian." But nevertheless, coming during the fiftieth anniversary of the march and with an obvious eye on an Academy Award, the press quickly covered the controversy. How enthusiastic was the moderate Southern Democratic LBJ about civil rights really?

Since the film's release on December 25, critics like Mark Updegrove, director of the LBJ Presidential Library, and Joseph Califano, a senior White House aide to Lyndon Johnson, have lashed out at DuVernay for her treatment of LBJ. In the film, they point out:

> LBJ is portrayed as King's bitter antagonist—strongly opposed to compromising his sweeping domestic policy agenda by endorsing a controversial voting rights bill. Indeed, in *Selma*, LBJ's character resolutely insists that he won't touch voting rights in 1965. In real life, he informed King that he preferred to wait until that spring, by which time he expected to ram several important health, education and welfare bills through Congress. By the time this conversation occurred, his aides had been debating how and when to tackle the ballot

box for several months. As early as February 28, LBJ already had Justice
Department lawyers at work crafting policy options on voting rights. The
distance between LBJ and MLK was a matter of weeks, not years.

DuVernay called the criticism "jaw dropping" and "offensive to SNCC,
SCLC and black citizens who made it [Selma] so." "Bottom line," she continued, "is folks should interrogate history. Don't take my word for it or LBJ
rep's word for it. Let it come alive for yourself."

DuVernay is entirely correct that Lyndon Johnson did not originate the
Selma campaign. King decided on and launched the initiative well before his
January 15 phone call with the president. But Updegrove and Califano only
scratch the surface when they insist, correctly, that LBJ was committed to
passing a voting rights bill in 1965 and that he relied on King to help build
consensus for such legislation. More problematic than what the film ignores is
what it invents out of whole cloth. [50]

In July in a message to Congress, Senator Kennedy asked for a repeal of the
National Origins Act that "discriminates among applicants for admission into
the United States on the accident of birth." He argued that the national quotas
system should be ended in five years and replaced by a selection system
based on individual skills and family reunification, "first come first served."
There would be a minimal increase in total numbers from 157,000 quota
immigrants to 165,000, he noted several times as an argument for passage.

But in truth, there was no great demand for immigration reform in 1965.
"It is a very minor issue," said American Jewish Committee lobbyists Myer
Feldman, Norbert Schlei, and Abba Schwarz, all Kennedy advisers inherited
by the Johnson administration. [51] That was true among the general public and
in political circles. There were no real demonstrations, broad-based, national
grassroots, public demand to change immigration policy as there was for
civil rights. There was obviously no widespread demand or even political
support to increase the number of new immigrants into the country.

There were however significant interest groups who wanted to do away
with nationality preferences.

Interest Groups for and against New Immigration Legislation

In favor

Ethnic groups, religious groups (especially Jewish and Italian Catholic), and
labor organizations lobbied heavily in favor of the administration's new Immigration and Nationality Act that ended the national origins quotas and
favored family unification over work skills. Jewish and Catholic organizations had labored since 1924 to unweave national origins quotas by admitting
family members on nonquota visas.

- Jewish organizations, including The B'nai B'rith Women and the American Council for Judaism's philanthropic fund, among other Jewish organizations, supported this reform legislation while it was yet in subcommittee in the winter of 1965.
- Roman Catholics had the twin motivations of still-evolving social justice doctrine and the potential windfall of a mass influx of coreligionists from Latin America.

Liberal political organizations included:

- Americans for Democratic Action.
- The ACLU: David Carliner testified before Congress on March 12 that "provisions of the bill should be rewritten to permit admission on a continuing basis of persons from any area who were 'oppressed or persecuted, or threatened with oppression or persecution because of their race, color, religion, national origin, adherence to democratic beliefs, or their opposition to totalitarianism or dictatorship . . . uprooted by natural calamity or military operations who were unable to return to their usual place of abode.'" The ACLU also recommended "a ten year statute of limitations on deportable offenses; any alien admitted to the United States as a permanent residence prior to his 14th birthday be immune from deportation; and anyone on nonimmigrant visas (students, seamen, visitors) could transfer to permanent residence status."[52]
- The National Lawyers Guild.
- The Communist Party USA, which supported higher immigration on the grounds that it destabilizes working Americans.[53]

Some groups linked the passage to reaction to the horror of the Holocaust. The director of the Lutheran Immigration Service of the National Lutheran Council endorsed the bill during testimony in Congress on March 22 by saying, "The view of man underlying the national origins quota theory is not too dissimilar from that which ended in tragedy and death for millions in Europe within our lifetime."[54]

A broad lobby pushed for the greater emphasis on families. It included churches, ethnic groups whose members still had family in the Old Country, and the AFL-CIO. The union was worried about competition from too many high-skilled newcomers, so they preferred to see the new law put a priority on family members rather than skilled workers.

> This was not only Italian Catholics with their large families. The family focus made absolute sense to Asian Americans as well. "If you think about families and you know, if you think about the roles that say your parents play when you have children and how they help you, you know, take care of the newborns and

provide support for you or how your brothers and sisters in the Asian community, what often happens is brothers and sisters get together and they buy a home together. They pool their money and they buy a business together. And so it, you know, family is very important not just to the social, emotional well-being, but also the economic well-being of these communities," said Karen Narasaki Director of the Asian American Justice Center in Washington, D.C., in an NPR All things considered radio interview in 2006.[55]

Mike Masaoka of the Japanese-American Citizens League pointed out that under the McCarran-Walter Act, Japan's waiting list was "backlogged through 1990." But he also expressed "grave reservations regarding the first-come first-serve basis as a provision since Europeans had an "eight-year head start" on registration over Asian countries.[56]

Jack Wong Sing of the National Chinese Welfare Council supported the increase in the number of Chinese scholars, scientists, engineers, and others with skills to add to the descendants of the first immigrants.

The president of the International Union of Electrical, Radio and Machine Workers of America (IUE) James B. Carey, also secretary of the AFL-CIO, testified in "wholehearted support" of the Senate Bill. "It will do little or nothing to add to unemployment," he said. By 1970, "only about 24,000 quota immigrants will have joined the labor force each year and at that time we will have a labor force . . . of 86 million. The newcomers will constitute three-thousandths of one percent of that group of workers and we can expect that a good number . . . will bring badly needed skills to this country."[57]

The American Veterans Committee representative Frank E. G. Weil endorsed the new law for many of the same reasons the ACLU cited. In addition he said his organization "opposed a provision which would revoke the citizenship of immigrants who evaded military service by leaving the United States, or who were court marshaled."

These groups did not exert much influence especially because many "showed little knowledge of the legislation and seemed mostly concerned with the threat of communist subversives slipping across national borders."

African American leaders in the 1960s also could not be counted on to take the restrictionist positions staked out by Frederick Douglass, Booker T. Washington, and A. Philip Randolph. They were beginning a move toward political solidarity with all the world's "people of color" and against discrimination of all kinds based on race, creed, and religion, and including national origins.[58]

Opponents to the LBJ Bill, and Favoring Keeping the National Origins Act

"Many Europeans natives who had benefited from the current system and whose family immigration journeys were fresher and less complete than the Kennedys saw danger in the reform."[59] This comment when talking about

Ted Kennedy's split with many of his Massachusetts constituents was referring mainly to Northern Protestant Irish and English immigrant heritage families for whom there was no "quota" (i.e., permit) limit for their extended families as they were considered high preference immigrants to the United States. Ending the National Origin Quota Act would have ended that preference for northern European heritage families.

In February 1965, Representative Feighan held public hearings in Cleveland, Ohio, on immigration and asked various groups including the press, organized labor, immigration committees of bar associations, women's organizations, and leaders of nationality groups to answer a questionnaire. His survey showed that respondents thought that there should be

- an annual ceiling on immigration
- a limit set by Congress
- a repeal of the national origins system
- in congressional law, safeguards for U.S. laborers
- limits placed on the number of new refugees each year
- retention of 300,000—the number currently allowed—for new immigrants

Two organizations that were particularly against the new proposed law were the American Legion and the American Coalition of Patriotic Societies. The Baltimore District Director of the ACLU testified that "the rich sounding words do not cover up the fact that American workers will be hurt."[60]

There were other groups in opposition as well who appeared to testify in Congress, as reported in CQ's Almanac 1965.

Mark M. Jones of the National Economic Council said, "There is no need for immigration within two or three years at least in the national interest." The New Jersey Coalition's Myra C. Hacker supported the Feighan bill that "does away cleanly with the allegedly offensive national origins quotas and sets a definite and realistic maximum limit on annual immigration."

The president of the Republican Committee of One Hundred, Inc. and author of *Invasion Alert*, Mrs. Ray L. Erb, testified on June 24 that the proposed immigration legislation would "enormously increase the number of immigrants permitted to enter the United States annually for permanent residence." "Are we willing to permit the American population makeup to be based rather on the makeup of foreign lands whose natives can get in line fastest in the greatest number under a first-come first-served scheme of entry?"

Representatives of other groups who testified in opposition to the bill included the following:

- National Council of Agricultural Employers

- Association of American Physicians and Surgeons
- Baltimore Anti-Communist League
- Doorstep Savanna
- League of Christian Women

A Harris Poll released in May 1965 showed the public "'strongly opposed to easing of immigration laws by a 2 to 1 margin: (58 percent to 24 percent)."[61]

But while representatives of these groups testified in Congress, in fact they did not organize a "bone and muscle" opposition to the 1965 bill, as they had in other attempts to repeal the National Origins Quota Act in the past. Part of the reason was that the Johnson administration agreed to make substantial revisions in its initial proposals, responding to initiatives proposed by subcommittee chairman Feighan—especially on a quota for Latin Americans. The end cap of 300,000 was far below what opponents had objected to in the administration's initial bill of 350,000 with no limits on Latin Americans; it was enough along with the environment of the times to effectively neutralize the major opposition forces

PASSING THE INA

Timing is everything. LBJ, the consummate politician, knew that the civil rights movement needed an explosive focal point to bring public demand around to the cause. "In the 1960s, social movements like the ACLU were huge. Still, Johnson was scared that the civil rights and voting rights bills could not pass with all his legislative skills and knowledge of parliamentary tricks if they couldn't find a big cause, a big (well-organized) confrontation. Selma was it."[62]

In the 1960s, reforming immigration policy and writing a new immigration law was not a highly visible, public process (as it has been since 2006). As can be seen from above, there were only a few legislators and lobbyists really interested. The process in the 1960s went slowly through the legislative committee and subcommittee process. It wasn't without political controversy, although the tide of the times favored it.

But it might not have even been considered by a major committee if it weren't for the largely ignored administrative process that took place in 1947: the reorganization of congressional committees and their jurisdiction under the Legislative Reorganization Act of 1946–1947. In the reorganization of 33 standing congressional committees down to 13, the jurisdiction for immigration law was changed from basically the Commerce and Labor Committee and a series of temporary select joint committees on immigration, to the official jurisdiction of the Judiciary Committees in the House and the Senate.

To the point, the long-time chairman and ranking member of the House Standing Committee on the Judiciary from 1923 to 1971 was New York Congressman Manny Celler. He also was majority leader of the Joint Committee on Immigration and Nationality Policy between 1955 and 1969. There can be no doubt that Representative Celler's passion to overturn the 1924 National Origins Act and his position on the Judiciary Committee were key to having that committee take on the official jurisdiction over immigration law.

Senator Kennedy served as a member of the Judiciary Committee and chair of the Senate Immigration Subcommittee through much of his 56 years in the Senate. These positions gave him power over the agenda and witnesses for immigration bills. Of course as brother to the assassinated President Kennedy and to Attorney General Robert Kennedy, his influence also was almost mythical. While LBJ in his nine short years in the Senate became its "Master," Ted Kennedy in over 50 years became its "Lion." The reform bill could not have had better legislative advocates and shepherds.

The actual legislative process from the time the bill was reported out of the House Judiciary Committee, through passage in the House, passage in the Senate legislative committees, passage in the Senate, passage in a conference committee, and signed into law took slightly less than two months!

- Reported and amended by the House Judiciary Committee (H Rept 745) on August 6, 1965 as HR2580
- Passed and amended by the House on a 318–95 roll call vote on August 25, 1965
- Reported and amended by the Senate Judiciary Committee (S Rept 748) on September 15,1965
- Passed by the Senate on a 76–18 roll call vote on September 22, 1965
- Conference report (H rept 1101) agreed to on September 30, 1965 by a 320–69 roll call vote of the House and by voice vote of the Senate
- Signed into law (PL 89-236) by President Johnson at the Statue of Liberty on October 3, 1965.
- Became effective in mid-1968 after a three-year transition period

As seen above, both the Kennedys and LBJ mentioned the need for immigration reform in their political campaigns in the 1950s and 1960s. But the real legislative process for reform began in 1962 with a series of hearings leading to some 17 reports in assessing global population (migration) with special attention to anticipated immigration pressures from Mexico, Central America, and the Caribbean. The intention was to link U.S. immigration policy to global and national demography—which in the 1960s meant maintaining strict limits on incoming numbers. But "policymakers and the press ignored the early reports and demographic trends were little mentioned in subsequent debates. It was understood that real action waited on the president's agenda," writes Otis Graham.[63]

By 1963, when Kennedy was moving on civil rights legislation, it seemed natural among liberals to link the two causes, with the joint target being *discrimination.* The net effect was to eliminate race and national origin as the basis of preference for admission to the United States from non–Western Hemisphere nations, and by eliminating all country-by-country quotas as well as the Asian ancestry provisions. One immediate result was expected to be sharply increased, immigration from Italy, Greece, Poland, and Portugal while some countries that previously had had no quotas (such as Northern Ireland) might experience waiting lists.

The Controversy Over Latin Americans

But organized labor organizations objected. They insisted in hearings and lobbying, efforts that notable provisions be made to protect American workers against job competition from immigrants—particularly from the Western Hemisphere; particularly from Mexico and Central, and South America. They demanded that a specific 120,000 annual limit on immigration by imposed on natives of the Western Hemisphere "closing off the possibility of a very substantial increase in future immigration from the one area on which there previously had been no numerical restrictions."[64]

This controversy developed into a heated jurisdictional dispute and a personal feud between two of the opposing legislators. In July 1965, Celler was the chairman of the full Judiciary Committee that determined whether or not legislation would reach the floor. Representative Michael A. Feighan (D-Ohio) was chairman of the House Judiciary's Subcommittee on Immigration having replaced in 1963, the long-time opponent of any repeal of the National Origins Act, Representative Francis E. Walter (D-Pennsylvania). Feighan, however, was also chairman of the all-but-defunct Joint Committee on Immigration; as such, he tried to obtain funds to reactivate the committee that had not been active for almost 14 years in order to take over the immigration reform efforts. He accused Celler of trying to "strangle the purposes of the Joint Committee and prevent the Congress from establishing control over immigration policy."[65] Celler aggressively opposed the move and the dispute became personal, but he was able to keep funds from going to the Joint Committee. Celler claimed that the Joint Committee lacked legislative authority.

While it was never stated publicly, some lobbyists said Celler (and several pressure groups supporting the administration bill) were afraid Feighan might use the Joint Committee's studies as an excuse to delay action until

1966 or beyond. Even more, he and others feared that Feighan might plan to use the Joint Committee to engage in a "witch-hunt" on immigration security risks.

As it was, the main point of controversy during consideration of the bill (HR2580) in the House and in the Senate remained the contentious issue over the ceiling on immigration from the independent countries of the Western Hemisphere, mainly Mexico, Central America, and South America.

The Johnson administration opposed setting a ceiling of 120,000 annual immigration from the Western Hemisphere, arguing that the existing-maximum policy was justified by mutuality of interests between the United States and other hemisphere nations, by good neighbor attitudes, and by the "special relationship" between the United States and other Western Hemisphere countries, Previously there had been no numerical limits for Western Hemisphere countries except for Jamaica, Trinidad, and Tobago. It is particularly understandable that President Johnson, having grown up with Mexican and Central American immigrants in Texas, would feel strongly about maintaining unlimited immigration from Latin America. His experience teaching their children gave him a lifelong sympathy toward them and the discrimination he saw they suffered (very much as President George W. Bush had some 40 years later).

The limitation was strongly supported by Representative Feighan, the Irish Catholic Democrat from Ohio, and Clark MacGregor, a moderate Republican from Minnesota; they barely lost an amendment setting a 115,000 annual limit on Western Hemisphere immigration after strong administration pressure succeeded in defeating it.

Feighan agreed not to insist on the limitation during the House vote (even though he favored it) in order to get it past House Democrats (and probably because he knew that the stronger, more influential, Senate Democrats would take up the fight). And indeed, two powerful members of the Senate Judiciary Committee prevailed: San J. Ervin Jr. (D-North Carolina) and Evert Dirksen (R-Illinois); they led Attorney General Nicholas Katzenbach to a reluctant agreement to drop the administration fight against the limitation, that was then set at 120,000. Ted Kennedy, the bill's manager, agreed, although he was opposed to it personally. A detailed accounting of the struggle between Celler and Feighan can be found in the CQ Almanac 1965.

The administration was also overruled on other Feighan proposals that it initially opposed. The original administration bill gave first preference for immigration from non–Western Hemisphere areas to applicants with special talents and needed skills; and second preference to family. This was switched in the end. Some observers said that the administration's agreement to accept a number of Feighan's proposals helped neutralize opposition to an immigration bill overall and led to its passage.

At the end of April, Representative Celler published in the *Congressional Record* an outline that was "designed to correct mistaken notions" about bill HR2580. He pointed out that instead of admitting an excessive number of immigrants, the effect of the bill would be "quite insignificant" on the U.S. population. The bill would not let in "great numbers of immigrants from anywhere," including Africa and Asia, and that there was "no real evidence to back the charge that the bill would increase unemployment even though it did not (as under current law) require an immigrant to prove he had a job waiting for him upon application for immigration."

The House debated bill HR2580 beginning June 17 and reported it out of committee on August 6 after adding substantial amendments drawn from Feighan's bill. The House passed it after two days of debate on August 25, with the majority of Republicans and northern Democrats supporting it and the majority of southern Democrats opposing it. CQ Almanac 1965 reports the reactions of various key parties to the debate.

Celler, who was the Dean of the House and the only then-current member who was in Congress when the quota system was enacted said, "I am glad I have lived to see my theories vindicated."

Congressman Durward G. Hall (R-Missouri) stated that "the present law is 'more liberal' than that of any other nation."

The Senate held hearings between February 10 and August 3 on the administration's bill. Attorney General Nicholas Katzenbach, Secretary of State Dean Rusk, Labor Secretary W. Willard Wirtz, and the Secretary of Health, Education, and Welfare Anthony J. Celebrezze were among cabinet secretaries testifying in favor of it. Senator Robert Kennedy (D-New York) said that the new immigration act would not have any significant effect on the ethnic composition of the United States.

The Senate Judiciary Committee reported the bill on September 15, with committee chairman James O Eastland (D-Mississippi) and John L. McClellan (D-Arkansas) voting against it. In a joint remark they stated, "Why is it that of all the nations of the world, the United States is the only one that must answer to the rest of the world and be apologetic about its immigration policy?"

Senators Ted Kennedy, Philip Hart, and Jacob Javits criticized the imposition of a ceiling on Western Hemisphere immigration, suggesting that "at no other time in the history of our immigration policy have we disturbed or altered the unique relationship that exists among the nations of the New World."

The Senate passed the bill on September 22 by a 76–18 roll call vote after four days of debate. On the floor Edward Kennedy said, "This bill is not concerned with increasing immigration to this country nor will it lower any of the high standards we apply in selection of immigrants." His brother Robert said, "A system which allows an American citizen to bring to this country a maid or a gardener overnight—but forces him to wait eight years for his sister—makes no sense."

Senator Allen Ellender (D-Louisiana) said, "It makes little sense to me to continue accepting large numbers of immigrants when we have almost four million unemployed in the United States at the present time."

Spessard L. Holland (D-Florida) asked, "Why for the first time are the emerging nations of Africa to be placed on the same basis as are our mother countries, Britain, Germany, the Scandinavian nations, France, and other nations from which most Americans have come?" (ignoring the some 20 million African American citizens living in the country at the time, almost 11 percent of the total population).

The conference bill (H Rept. 1101) was reported out of the committee on September 29 and adopted by the Senate on September 30 on a voice vote and by the House the same day by a 320–69 roll call vote. It was signed on October 3 by President Johnson next to the Statue of Liberty (whose Liberty Park he had just declared a national monument on May 11, 1965).

The final bill contained many concessions from the original house bill:

- It reversed the priorities to first preference for applicants based on family unification and second to those with special talents and needed skills.
- It imposed a 120,000 limit for the Western Hemisphere.
- It refused to grant the administration an Immigration Board and to provide the president with discretion to reallocate certain quotas.

The new bill did however contain the major presidential request: repeal of the national origins quota system.

It also contained some provisions offering discretion by the attorney general on deportation and adjustment of status to that of lawful admission of individuals heretofore deemed ineligible for immigration. They included:

- Alien crewmen who requested residency who entered before June 20, 1964
- Persons who had been free of mental illness for a period of time sufficient to indicate recovery
- Aliens who had entered the United States illegally prior to June 30, 1948. (Existing law provided for adjustment of status if the entry was before June 28, 1940; the Senate bill to set the date at June 28, 1958, was defeated in the conference bill.)

Proposals for special residency quotas for Cubans were referred to the Western Hemisphere Commission for further study. Homosexuals were still banned.

The *Congressional Quarterly* listed five reasons for the passage of this historic bill despite the acknowledgement of everyone in the know that "the public at large was not greatly interested in immigration reform nor especially concerned about the national origins quota system."

Many of the immigration bill's most ardent supporters told the *Congressional Quarterly* that they attributed the success of the 1965 legislation to the following factors:

1. The 2–1 Democratic majorities in each chamber that were generally responsive to President Johnson's wishes—an unusual parliamentary situation.
2. Relatively strong support from the Johnson administration for this particular bill because of various significant considerations: (a) general conviction that the national origins quota system was invidiously discriminatory (especially against Jews from Eastern Europe); (b) desire to ease U.S. relations with nations receiving unfavorable treatment under the national origins quota system—particularly Italy; (c) desire to win or retain political support of minority groups who might benefit from the repeal of the national origins quota system—particularly Italian American, Catholic American, and Jewish American groups.
3. The chairman of the House Judiciary Subcommittee on Immigration Representative Feighan was more in favor of repeal of the national origins quota system than the previous subcommittee chairman Francis E. Walter (D-Pennsylvania, 1933–1963) had been (in fact he had blocked all previous efforts at revision).
4. The willingness of the administration and many of the ethnic, labor, and religious groups supporting the bill to compromise on the overall numbers of new immigrants (particularly from Mexico, Central and South America) and on family unification to neutralize past opponents.
5. Changing attitudes in the United States toward race and national origins. The "fear of an invasion by undesirable immigrant ethnic and racial groups simply was not as great as in the past" *Congressional Quarterly* was told by lobbyists.

To these five reasons and particularly as a corollary to the fifth must be added the sincere but usually unspoken horror and shame of the Holocaust: shame especially among liberals over America's denial, failure to do anything, and rejection of millions of Jewish and southern European Catholic refugees who tried to enter the United States before, during, and after the war. "The shame of the Holocaust created a temporary anomaly wherein anti-Semitism became socially unacceptable," wrote Charles Krauthammer on Jan 29, 2015.[66]

In the case of the passage of the historic Immigration and Nationality Act of 1965, it was not a result of massive, grassroots organization and demonstrations that caused it to pass, unlike the Civil Rights Act. For that legislative moment, President Johnson cautiously waited for just the right time and just the right situation to launch the legislation; he purposely chose the march on Selma as the launch. "At this time, on this issue there must be no delay, no hesitation, no compromise with our purpose" he said of the march and of civil rights in general.

The Voting Rights Act was an even easier case to make before the public. "The command of the Constitution is plain. There is no moral issue. It is just wrong—deadly wrong—to deny any of your fellow Americans the right to vote in this country," Johnson said before Congress in 1965. "There is no issue of States rights vs. national rights. There is only the struggle for human rights . . . it is not just about Negroes but really it is about all of us who must overcome the crippling legacy of bigotry and injustice," he said, adding the sentence that was to become the rallying cry of the civil rights movement: "And we shall overcome."

At those words, "seventy-seven year old Manny Celler—a lifetime of vigorous often futile fights for freedom behind him—"leaped to his feet cheering as wildly as a school boy at his first high school football game," Princeton history professor Julian Zelizer noted in his recent book on the civil rights movement.[67] But Professor Zelizer did not mention that for Celler the battle of his life was to repeal the National Origins Quota Act; it well could be that what brought Celler to his feet was the recognition that the time had suddenly come for the realization of that quest. He certainly aggressively pushed for the abolition of the poll tax—the civil rights issue on which Ted Kennedy was most focused—through the House Judiciary Committee, even though the proposal had been rejected in the Senate for fear it would jeopardize passage of the civil rights act. Celler adamantly disagreed and the abolition of the poll tax was included in the House bill. Although Johnson's demand prevailed in the final conference bill, Celler's willingness to fight for its removal was very possibly when he and Ted (who had been a senator for less than two years) became allies for the battle that Celler was really focused on—repeal of the National Origins Act.

As it was, victory in the Civil Rights Act in 1964 and the Voting Rights Act in August 1965 opened the gates for other Great Society successes. "If Johnson had made his mark in 1964, the Eighty-Ninth Congress would be virtually pliant to his vision for America, making 1965 among the most transformational years in American history."[68]

The election of 1964 produced the most liberal Congress since the Democratic landslide of 1936. "There were so many Democrats," noted the young

Illinois representative Donald Rumsfeld, "that they had to sit on the Republican side of the aisle."[69]

"Liberal and moderate Democrats now so outnumbered conservatives that for the first time in decades, the conservative Southern Democrats were seriously worried about retaining their power," writes Professor Zelizer in the first sentence of his new book's chapter entitled "The Fabulous Eighty-Ninth Congress"[70] It was also the subhead of a chapter about JFK's "Indomitable Will" by Mark Updegrove, director of the LBJ Library; he also called it "The Fabulous Eighty-Ninth Congress."[71]

President Johnson being the legislative "Master of the Senate" that he was, took full advantage of his skills to pass as many of his Great Society initiatives as he could. He knew it was a unique time for big government initiatives. And he knew it wouldn't last. "The short period in which Congress enacted most of the Great Society programs was more an aberration than the norm," Zelizer comments. "This period of liberalism was much more fragile, contested and transitory than we have usually remembered"[72]

The passage of the Immigration and Nationality Act occurred not because of any great social movement for or against it outside of a few obvious interest groups. It was more because of the political environment of the times, repulsed by horrible instances of discrimination in America and in Europe, wanted to repudiate any instances of discrimination in postwar society. It was a time of liberals and a great trust in the idea that government—good, responsible, liberal government—could fix the ills of society.

It didn't last for long. There may never be a time like that again. The 1965 Immigration and Nationality Act may be the most liberal immigration law that will ever pass in the United States. On its enthusiastic passage, maybe the savvy politicians like Johnson knew it might be as good as it would ever get. Ted Kennedy went on to fight to get it better for the next 50 years, even with a new "comprehensive immigration reform bill." During his lifetime, he could not repeat the success of his second year in the Senate in the Fabulous 89th.

"In 1965, huge unmet needs festered across America and the notion of addressing them via Big Government still retained both a certain novelty and wide public acceptance. It made sense to assume that social progress could result from the sheer application of federal resources," writes Charles Lane, a *Washington Post* editor and columnist.[73] But, the *Post* editor concludes, "Even in those optimistic early years, though, skeptics worried about unrealistic goals and unintended consequences."

Chapter Four

Impact and Unintended Consequences

It can be said that "no one who supported the passage of the INA so eagerly in 1965, openly recommended what it would turn out to be," wrote history Professor Otis Graham in his 2004 book *Unguarded Gates*. "The law's two chief results were unintended."[1]

1. Increasing the volume of immigrants back to over one million legal permanent residents a year, as it had been in the 1920s when the restrictive National Origins Act was passed; in addition, over two million immigrants come in each year on temporary visas and over 500,000 illegal immigrants a year either sneak across the border (about 60 percent) or overstay their temporary visas—totaling close to four million new immigrants each year who stay in the country.
2. Altering the United States ethno-racial-national population to "resemble the world" rather than the nation that had grown out of thirteen British colonies (and thousands of African slaves).

In the fiftieth year of the Immigration and Nationality Act, its impact is both highly visible and at the same time, unnoticed because it has become so taken for granted. The INA created the multiethnic, multicultural, multinational, multilingual, multifaith mix of people who are American citizens today. Every aspect of our culture has been affected. That includes from the food Americans eat, to the point where in almost every American city one can find grocery stores and restaurants offering once such exotic fare as Asian noodles, Thai rice, sushi, tacos and enchiladas, falafel wraps, and shish kabobs; to the clothes and shoes we wear from the sweat shops of Africa and Asia; to the multitude of languages spoken in the streets and taught in schools (Chinese- and Spanish-immersion elementary schools are increasing popular throughout the country).

All of this is due to the millions of immigrants who came pouring into the United States from every nation in the world after 1965 with no restrictions as to race, creed, religion, or national origin, bringing their cultures with them. Of course none of these cultural changes are "pure" from the foreign national's point of view; they have all been Americanized. Irrefutably they have enriched and diversified the American culture. Today, 50 years later, most Americans from the now not-so-young boomer generation that so enthusiastically embraced civil rights and the INA in the 1960s, to the millennials and their younger sisters and brothers today, generally see our cultural diversity as perfectly natural, perfectly American.

Yet today, almost every political leader from every political stripe claims that our immigration system, the INA, is broken. "Reforming" the INA is the subject of increasingly heated political debate, disputes, and disagreements. Some say that immigration reform will be the make-or-break legacy issue of President Barrack Obama.

How did the INA become so controversial? What happened in the past 50 years to cause this law that changed the face of America into such a diverse culture to become the target of outrage by almost every political activist?

The numerous impacts and results of 50 years under the INA can be grouped together under three categories:

1. Increasing numbers of legal immigrants;
2. Increasing numbers of illegal immigrants;
3. Increasing confusion about immigration principles: that is, is it a civil right or enforceable law? Should some nationalities be preferred after all (like Mexican and Salvadorian agriculture and construction workers, or Indian and Chinese engineers)? What is it to be a Nation of Immigrants as we enter the twenty-first "globalized" century?

INCREASING NUMBERS OF LEGAL IMMIGRANTS: PERMANENT, TEMPORARY, AND REFUGEES

The facts are easy to find. The total number of foreign-born residents in the United States almost tripled after implementation of the Immigration and Nationality Act of 1965.

- In 1960, 9.7 million foreign-born immigrants were living in the United States, 5.4 percent of the total population.
- In 1980, 14.1 million, 6.2 percent of the total population.
- In 2000, 31.1 million, 11.1 percent of the total population.

- In 2010, 40 million, 12.9 percent of the total population. Of these 5.6 percent were naturalized and 7.3 percent—some 22.5 million were noncitizens (a little over half or 12 million were estimated to be residing illegally in the country, 8 million illegally employed, about 55 percent came in over the southern border, and about 40 percent overstayed legal visas).

Note: The percentage of foreign born today is still not as great as during the period of 1880–1920—when the foreign-born population doubled from 7 million to 14 million and made up 13.3 percent of the population. Those 40 years saw the biggest wave of immigrants into the United States in our history, and as noted in chapter 2, that drove the passage of the highly restrictive National Origins Quota Act of 1924. It is estimated that by 2020 the foreign-born population in the United States may also rise to nearly 14 percent, with a faster growing percentage from Asia than from Latin America.

The percentage of immigrants granted legal permanent residency status (i.e., green cards) from South America, the Caribbean, Asia, Africa, and Eastern Europe, rose every decade from 1961 to 2000, while at the same time the percentage of immigrants from Europe and Canada decreased exponentially. The major source of immigration to the United States rapidly changed from Europe before 1965, to Latin America and Asia after implementation of the INA.

Europe and Canada: 45.9 percent to 17.1 percent
Latin America and the Caribbean: 39 percent to 47.2 percent
Asia: 13.4 percent to 30.7 percent
Africa and other: 1.8 percent to 5 percent[2]

This significant change in the number of immigrants, much less the demographics and culture of America, was not the intention of the framers of the 1965 INA, President Johnson, the Kennedys, House Judiciary Committee chair Emanuel Celler—or at least, not their stated intention. "Expert after expert testified before Congress that little would change. Secretary of State Dean Rusk repeatedly stressed that the issue was not the numbers. "No more people were likely to come. It was simply the principle."[3]

The central purpose of the new immigration law was to reunite families, according to Rice University sociology professor Stephen Klineberg. "The government's newfound sense of egalitarianism (in the Civil Rights movement) only went so far. Congress said nothing is going to change demographically because we're going to give preference to the (extended) families, to people related to those already here."[4] The idea was that those demographics would just expand slightly for their relations.

But it didn't happen that way. "The new selection system they were advocating based on family unification, would build streams of family flows from a base in the newly arrived—who mainly were Mexicans—and from huge refugee flows, mainly Jewish. Family preference was the leverage for especially Asian and Latin American newcomers to increase their numbers as immigrants, leaving long-term immigrant residents (mainly from Northern Europe) who had few immediate family abroad, with diminished influence over immigration streams shaping the nation's future," UCSB Professor Otis Graham wrote and said on NPR.[5]

Why did framers of the INA miscalculate the numbers of immigrants who would come in as a result and its impact in completely changing the face of America? Were they deliberately deceptive? How much did they know and not want to share for fear of the bill's not being passed?

"When I first started studying this, I thought, 'They're lying because they want this thing (the INA) to pass,'" Graham said on NPR in May 2006. "But I changed my mind. In my research I found so many lobbyists that followed this issue, so many labor union executives, church people, and others involved all said the same thing. Maybe ignorance is the answer . . . ignorance three feet deep."

Historians of the era decline to call this outright deception, believing instead that the reformers had not given much thought to the system they were putting in place for they were looking forwards. . . . Their main impetus . . . was not practical but ideological. They were expunging what they took to be a legislative blot on America's internationally scrutinized record on human rights, more intent on dismantling an inherited system than in the careful design of a substitute.

A formidable coalition had mobilized behind repeal of the old law and for a vaguely defined "liberalization." The coalition included the numerous members of religious and ethnic organizations associated with the "new immigration," strategically in northeastern and midwestern urban states—homes of the growing, powerful, liberal and progressive Democrats. The "oddly enfeebled opposition was unable to take aim against the assurances of the new law's proponents that the numbers and demographics wouldn't change, because that was not only being denied at every turn but was never proposed nor anticipated."[6]

In retrospect it is hard to see why it was not obvious to the proponents of the new immigration law that it would almost immediately begin to change the demographics of the United States. The reasons for it now seem obvious.

Reasons for the Increase of Legal Immigrants

Several causes for the unexpected increase in *legal* immigrants, permanent and temporary, include:

- Basing immigration priority first on extended family unification—which led to what has become known as "chain migration" (that one naturalized immigrant can bring in numerous, close, adult relatives who, once naturalized, can continue the chain).
- The expectation and relative ease to naturalize—become an American citizen.
- The continual creation of an ever-growing alphabet soup of temporary visas (the Hs for workers, the Fs and Js for students, etc.).
- The rising number of temporary relief visas for asylees seeking refuge from natural and manmade disasters, especially from Latin America and Cuba.
- The growing number of miscellaneous ways to get legal status, including the diversity lottery, birthright citizenship, and legally buying a green card.

Priority on Family Unification

In the United States, *immigrant* is the term usually applied to a foreign national—also referred to in legal parlance as an *alien*—who has a legal and official U.S. permit to live and work permanently in the United States. This permit is known popularly as a "green card." In recent years, the U.S. Citizenship and Immigration Services grants over one million new permanent immigrant legal status—more than any other country.

A Legal Permanent Resident (LPR) immigrant can stay their lifetime in the United States with almost no restrictions on working (except perhaps in positions requiring top secret clearances), traveling, owning property, doing business, receiving public benefits, and other privileges of permanent residency. The main thing s/he is not allowed to do is to vote. The right to vote remains the exclusive privilege of a U.S. citizen, particularly in federal elections—it is a felony crime for a noncitizen to cast a ballot. However, a few communities around the country are granting voting privileges in local elections to LPRs. The green card can be revoked if the LPR commits certain crimes or is found to have "abandoned" their green card by living abroad for more than six months without notifying the citizenship and immigration services.

Under the INA, only about 20 percent of green cards every year were to be granted on the basis of work skills of the primary head of household. The rest—some 80 percent at first, now less but still the majority—are granted each year on the basis of family kinship to the primary worker. The primary green card holder normally can obtain green cards without restrictions for a spouse and minor children, who are not counted in the LPR overall cap.

In addition, since the Immigration Reform and Control Act of 1965, the primary permanent immigrant also can apply for green cards for his/her adult children and their spouses and children, adult brothers and sisters and their family members, grandparents, and other dependent relatives including cousins—in other words, extended family members (this is often referred to as "chain migration"). These "preference visas" are limited in number (minimums) by prioritized criteria including relationship, age, and status of the family sponsor. First tier, family sponsored preferences for a green card include:

- unmarried sons and daughters of citizens—about 23,400 visas given out annually
- spouses, children, unmarried sons and daughters of permanent immigrants—114,200
- married sons and daughters of citizens—23,400
- brothers and sisters of adult citizens—65,000

A minimum of 140,000 employment-based preferences for green cards also are allotted by law as follows:

- Priority workers—28.6 percent
- Advanced degree holders or exceptional ability—28.6 percent
- Skilled worker—28.6 percent
- Certain special immigrants—7.1 percent
- "Employment creators" such as investors in low-populated, rural areas—7.1 percent

Outside of these restrictions, of course, the United States does not discriminate in granting green cards on the basis of age, disabilities, gender, and/or cultural differences. A little known fact about new permanent immigrants is that senior citizens and disabled family members who are granted green cards are immediately eligible for social security insurance benefits, regardless of whether they or any family member ever paid into the system.

The Immigration Act of 1990 modified and expanded the 1965 act; it significantly increased the total immigration limit to 700,000 and increased visas by 40 percent. Family reunification was retained as the main immigration criteria, with significant increases in employment-related immigration. Other modifications include expanding the number of green cards given to certain investors and their families under certain conditions, and for foreign students graduating from American universities with advanced degrees (MS and PhDs) in the STEM (Science, Technology, Engineering, and Math) fields. (To date the foreign student visa is only a temporary nonimmigration permit.)

The green card is the only status from which a foreign national can apply for citizenship. It is not a requirement! No permanent resident is ever required to become a U.S. citizen and they can (and most do) live their entire lives in the United States without ever becoming a citizen.[7]

Ease of Naturalization—Becoming a U.S. Citizen

It is rarely acknowledged that the United States is relatively friendly and welcoming to the idea that immigrants become citizens, that they "naturalize." The public expectation that they do so is certainly far more than in many European countries. Americans often expect immigrants to become citizens as soon as they can; most Americans believe that immigrants come to the United States because it is their dream to become a citizen. Americans welcome new citizens, with ceremonies and parties put on by community organizations after the naturalization ceremony. The process is a fairly easy one relatively, but of course there are requirements.

In general, in order to apply for U.S. citizenship, a foreign national must have been in the United States on a permanent residency green card for at lest five years (spouses of American citizens, three years) with a clean criminal record. The application processing time can take up to a year and includes a test on U.S. history and constitutional principles, and an English exam (usually oral). Both tests were upgraded in 2006 and 2007. The application fee was also raised in 2007 from $330 for adult applicants and $255 for minors plus a $70 fingerprinting fee, to $595 for adults and $460 for minors plus a $80 fee for biometric identifiers. Additional increases and charges are to be expected. There is no fee for applicants serving or who have served in the U.S. military.

To get some perspective on how relatively easy the U.S. process of naturalization is, compare it to that of another country—Switzerland. (Note: The author lived in the Swiss canton [state] of Vaud for five years.) There, a foreign national who wants to become a Swiss citizen must reside in one community—one canton—for 10 years with a valid Swiss working visa, not an easy thing to get (the visa that thousands of foreigners get to work for the United Nations or the many NGOs around the Geneva area do not count, no matter for how many decades they and their families live there). After 10 years of residency, the process of forms and interviews for Swiss citizenship starts at the local level, then proceeds to the canton level if one passes local scrutiny, including perhaps paying the arbitrary fees (sometimes substantial) that any Swiss town may impose independently; and finally to the national level for Swiss citizenship.

The whole citizenship process in Switzerland can easily take two or more years. It certainly includes proving one's fluency in the language and culture of the canton (Switzerland's 26 or so cantons are language pure in three different languages—1 Italian, 4 French, and the others German, including dialects thereof). Standards differ for each canton and locality; Switzerland is a confederacy after all, not a federation. In some cantons, foreign-born children who attend local schools for 10 years can apply for an expedited citizenship.

For young people, citizenship comes with a 30-year plus commitment to serve in the local unit of the cantonal Swiss national guard, to train yearly, to practice shooting skills monthly at the local shooting range, and to always possess in their homes, functioning fire arms and ammunition. In turn, the locale of which one is a citizen is ultimately responsible for its citizens' welfare and support should they become indigent. Switzerland is not part of the EU so the benefits of that association (jobs, education, visa-free passage, and so on) could vary according to changing times and diplomatic agreements. In general, the Swiss people are not personally very encouraging nor enthusiastic about immigrants taking on Swiss citizenship; relatively few immigrants go through the rather arduous (in comparison to the United States) process.

The relatively easy process for a green card holder to become an American citizen has increasingly become a focus of immigrant advocate groups hoping to expand the number of voters who are personally invested in the passage of comprehensive immigration reform. The naturalization campaigns by Latino political activists has especially been helped by the fact that some countries such as Mexico, enable their citizens to take on American citizenship while still being able to keep their Mexican passports—to be dual-nationals, to have two passports, two nationalities, two citizenships. This was not always the case. Before 1998, any Mexican citizen who became a naturalized U.S. citizen lost their Mexican citizenship. But in March of that year, Mexico joined Colombia and El Salvador—large immigrant source countries to the United States—and changed its policy to allow dual-nationality.[8]

It is really up to each sovereign nation-state to decide if they will allow their citizens to be dual-nationals or not. As "modern nationality law evolved at the beginning of the 20th century, as nation-states were created out of empires, the prevailing theory was that each person should have only one nationality so as to avoid conflicting loyalties in times of war. Many countries followed the policy that citizens who voluntarily naturalized in a foreign country automatically lost their original nationality."[9] But after World War II, the overwhelming majority of governments in the world began to distinguish between nationality and citizenship and have come to tolerate or embrace dual nationality. Most do not encourage it, however, because of the legal and practical complications it can cause.

According to the U.S. State Department, "U.S. law does not mention dual nationality or require a person to choose one citizenship or another." A U.S. citizen who automatically becomes a citizen of another country (through birth or marriage or, in the case of Israel, falls under the requirement of their

"Law of Return" or is "half Jewish") does not lose their American citizenship. But, a person who acquires foreign citizenship by applying for it may in fact lose U.S. citizenship. Under a 1964 Council of Europe convention, dual nationals are the responsibility of the nation-state in which they usually reside.[10]

But in reality, to date the majority of green card holders in the United States do not naturalize, although the proportion is slowly increasing. The number of green card holders who naturalized each year increased from an average of about 150,000 a year in the 1970s to over 600,000 in the 1990s. Then in 1996–2008, the naturalization numbers peaked to just over 1,000,000 per year. The annual numbers add up to more than the number of visas issued in those years because around 1.4 million of those who were granted amnesty by IRCA in 1986 (now numbering over three million) actually became citizens (less than half it should be noted).[11] Many immigrants do not immediately apply as soon as they are eligible, or do not pass the test on the first attempt. This means that the counts for visas and the counts for naturalization will always remain out of step—from 1960–2000, under half.[12]

Green card holders from Latin America, Mexico especially, are the particular target of advocates who want to increase the number of immigrant naturalization and voter registration. Their numbers increased exponentially because of the family unification priority of the INA. But in fact, that population in particular is slow to naturalize.

"Most Latino immigrants just don't bother. The high costs for naturalization may be one factor that discourages low-income immigrants from naturalizing at the same rates as higher-income immigrants," stated an "Immigration Facts" report of the Migration Policy Institute in February of 2007.[13] Mexican green card holders "have a comparatively lower tendency to become U.S. citizens than other nationalities" according to the Pew Hispanic Center report in 2014. Certainly proximity of their homelands have much to do with this.[14]

"Latinos aren't that interested in becoming citizens," said Congressman Luis Gutierrez (D-Illinois) to a group of Latin American journalists at the National Press Club on April 18, 2007. "Most of them just want to be able to go back and forth from their homelands to work in the U.S. with ease."[15] Panelists included Congressmen Luis Gutierrez (D-Illinois) and James Sensenbrenner (R-Wisconsin); former INS Secretary Doris Meissner, Director of the Migration Policy Institute; Pamela Constable, Deputy Editor, *The Washington Post*; and Jose Carreno of El Universal. No transcripts were made or are available at the time of printing but I have heard Gutierrez make the quoted statements on various occasions both in English and in Spanish. The seminar was part of an International Center for Journalists program for 21 community journalists from Latin America to meet U.S. leaders.[16]

A major factor causing some immigrants' reluctance to naturalize is that green card holders can do almost anything a citizen can do except vote and hold high security jobs. Some green card holders have told me they don't want to have to serve on an American jury because they don't believe in the death penalty and they don't want to be put in a situation to have to decide that. One advantage of citizenship may be that a naturalized citizen is generally not liable to be deported unless perhaps convicted of an act of terror or of being a traitor. Even then the deportation process would be highly unusual.

Most legal permanent residents who have been here for decades don't see the need for citizenship. They may not speak, read, or write English easily; they may live in comfortable neighborhoods surrounded by immigrants from their same homeland, possibly even their same village. Their children are citizens and can help them with all the official necessities of life.

There is another factor, too. It is easy to dismiss the reluctance of legal, permanent immigrants to naturalize as just being lazy or because the benefits of permanent legal residency are too generous. But traditional Americans tend not to realize that to change citizenship is a highly emotional decision for many first-generation immigrants, especially older adults with long relationships with their homelands, whose ties and pulls of culture, language, and family history in their homelands are fresh and strong. Many take seriously the pledge of loyalty and do not want to give up primary loyalty to their homeland even if they could, as American citizens, retire in their homelands if they choose. Some don't want to return to their homelands as foreign citizens.

Refugees

The United States's refugee program is an immigration program that lies outside the regular green card system and has its own highly restricted, numerical limitations that often have been set by the president. Refugees are desperate men, women, and children from specific geographic areas who are facing mortal danger in their homeland and must leave to survive. The U.S. refugee program is managed by the Departments of State, Health and Human Services, and Homeland Security, but is codified in immigration law.

Basically, the program identifies, interviews, and accepts refugees who meet stringent refugee qualifications, including that they can prove (or at least convince a judge) that they face likely persecution if they returned to their homelands. Once passed, refugees (and often their families) are transported to a specific town where they are met by town sponsors (usually from local churches or nonprofit organizations) and given a place to live and help for children to get into public schools, aged members to get onto applicable public benefits, enrollment in English classes, and getting a job or into job training or higher education programs. After a year, the refugees are allowed to apply for a green card.

The U.S. refugee program was a major source of legal immigrants between 1950 and 2000 and after World War II and the Korean, Vietnamese, Cambodian wars, and others in which U.S. forces were involved. But the programs changed character in the twenty-first century, and the United States as a whole now takes in far fewer refugees from Middle East conflagrations, even from Iraq and Afghanistan where we were intensely involved, than do small towns in Sweden.

In 2007, the number of refugees allowed to come to the United States under the refugee program was 70,000 a year. However, only about 50,000 actually were accepted. "This is partly because many refugees coming out of war countries are found to have committed disqualifying violations, mainly in terms of accepting material support from an organization that the United States considers to be a terrorist support group," according to Kelly Ryan of the Bureau of Population, Refugees and Migration.[17] The "material support" limitation was part of the REAL ID Act that was passed by Congress in 2005. "It paralyzes America's traditionally generous refugee admission program," *Washington Post* editorial writers charged in April of that year.[18]

Legislation was introduced in 2007 to resettle into the United States 15,000 "special immigrant status" Iraqis and their families for each of the next four years. But priority for Iraqi resettlement has faded since with increasing new waves of refugee seekers and refugees from Haiti, Central America, Somalia, Ukraine, and certainly from the ruins of Syria, putting the lives of those Iraqis who worked for Americans during the war in grave danger and with little hope.

Diversity Lottery

There is another unique way that hundreds of thousands of foreign nationals have gotten green cards since passage of the INA. It's the Diversity Immigrant Visa program (DV immigrants), a congressionally mandated annual lottery program also known as the Green Card Lottery. The lottery is administered by the Department of State, as codified by Immigration Act additions in 1990. It makes available 55,000 permanent resident visas annually to (supposedly) randomly selected natives of countries deemed to have low rates of immigration to the United States. Candidates are supposed to apply from their homelands. Country eligibility varies. Some countries (like Russia) are eligible some years and other years not. Somehow, a surprising number foreign students at U.S. universities and at research institutes like the National Institutes of Health in Washington, D.C., get lucky and "win" the green card lottery. Complaints of fraud have increased over the years.

During the Senate hearings for a comprehensive immigration bill in 2013, there was much discussion about doing away with the diversity lottery and converting its 50,000 PLR permits into green cards for foreign students who had graduated from American universities with advanced degrees (MS and PhDs mainly) in the STEM fields. Both Democrats and Republicans and especially President Obama, favored the idea of green cards for foreign students, but not at the expense of the "diversity" visa. Perhaps that was because of the label "diversity" or perhaps that was because, although not said, it was recognized that most of the green cards going to STEM graduates would go to lucky recipients from mainly two nationalities: China and India. In other words, not diverse.

Birthright Citizenship

The United States also grants a truly unique right to citizenship to just about every child born in the United States to noncitizens, no matter what their immigration status. It has been and continues to be a primary source of direct citizenship for millions of foreign nationals in the United States. It's called "birthright citizenship."

The number of U.S. births to nonresident mothers rose 53 percent between 2000 and 2006, according to the most recent data from the National Center for Health Statistics. Total births rose 5 percent in the same period. All were considered to be U.S. citizens. [19]

The basis for this right is the first half of the first sentence of the 120-year-old 14th Amendment of the U.S. Constitution that states, "All persons born or naturalized in the United States and subject to the jurisdiction thereof, are citizens of the United States."

This has been interpreted simply to mean that any child born in the United States is automatically a citizen. Millions of babies born to foreign nationals in the United States have been granted full U.S. citizenship because of this clause. No other country in the world gives out citizenship in this way.

But birthright citizenship has become controversial. First, there is concern that it abuses the very core meaning and intent of citizenship. Second, practice has ignored the second condition of the clause, the one that begins with "and" that grammatically indicates that there is an additional condition to be fulfilled in order to get birthright citizenship: (1) to be born (documented) in the United States (or of U.S. citizens abroad), and (2) to be subject to the jurisdiction thereof—meaning the parents and thus their newborns must be officially subject to all the laws of the country. Some legislators question and would like to see these two alleged abuses adjudicated.

Birthright citizenship has become the vehicle for a growing international business of "birth tourism"—where tens of thousands of pregnant mothers, especially from Asia, have come to the United States for a few weeks as tourists with the express purpose of giving birth and thereby having their newborns be granted U.S. citizenship. Many of the birth tourists sign up for a package deal that includes a three-month visitors visa; and comprehensive maternity, birth, and newborn pediatric medical services in special birth-tourist hostels and clinics sensitive to the language and customs of the tourists. The "tours" conclude of course with the return of the mother and child to their homeland with the baby's U.S. passport in hand. The typical cost of one of these tour packages was estimated to be $45,000 per mother. In 2006, it was estimated that almost 8,000 babies were born to birth tourists; the number could well be over 10,000 a year by now.

Birthright citizenship also has been a significant factor in the growth of the Hispanic populations in the United States. Until 2009, Latinos were the fastest growing demographic in the United States, although since 2009, the Asian growth rate has surpassed that of Latinos. The primary source of both Hispanic and Asian population growth until 2000 had been from immigration, including millions of illegal immigrants. Latinos comprise almost 60 percent of the illegal immigrant population; Asians comprise 30 percent of young adult "DREAMers" (so called for the Development, Relief, and Education for Alien Minors [DREAM] Act) who are illegally in the country.[20]

But since 2000, the growth of both these populations, especially Latinos, has swung from immigration to native births. Between 2000 and 2010, there were 9.6 million Hispanic births in the United States, while the number of newly arrived immigrants was 6.5 million. Overall, U.S. births alone accounted for 60 percent of Hispanic population growth.[21] The government does not track what proportion of the births to noncitizens are to mothers who are illegally in the country. Births to indigents are covered by the hospitals, which are forbidden by law to turn anyone away.

There have been discussions in Congress the past decade about whether or not citizenship for the children born of short-term tourists and of parents who are living and working illegally in the country is a misinterpretation of the 14th constitutional Amendment. It was ratified on July 9, 1868, before immigration law became federalized; it was one of three amendments to assure that African Americans were considered full citizens. At the time there were no national immigration laws, no tourist visas or immigration statuses like "temporary" and "illegal."

Many media pundits claim that the amendment can only be changed through an arduous national constitutional-change process requiring the approval of two-thirds of states legislatures. But in fact, the interpretation and practice of the phrase "subject to the jurisdiction thereof" can be changed—by legislation or a by an order of the Supreme Court. It's been done twice before.

According to the Congressional Research Office of the U.S. Senate, in 1868 there were actually four groups of people that were not subject to the jurisdiction of the U.S. laws and therefore whose children would not have the right to U.S. citizenship at birth. Of the four, one is still in force (though not necessarily enforced): the children born of recognized diplomats with full immunity from U.S. laws; they are not subject to the full jurisdiction of U.S. laws and therefore their children are not eligible for U.S. citizenship under the 14th Amendment. Of the other three, one was changed by legislation in 1921 (Native Americans born and residing in their own nations were neither considered citizens nor eligible to vote until the Indian Citizenship Act of June 24, 1924). One is by a Supreme Court ruling in 1898 (*U.S. v. Wong Kim Ark*, see chapter 2) established that children born to Chinese who were *legal* immigrants but not eligible to be naturalized, would themselves be citizens under the 14th Amendment). And one is universal and only occasionally used abroad—the children born of "invading warriors"—according to the Senate Congressional Research Office.

Does citizenship really include short-term tourists, who are legally in the country but whose permit is for a short-term visitor with no intention for their birthright-citizen children to stay or form any kind of attachment or loyalty to the country of their birth? Does "being subject to the jurisdiction thereof" really include foreign nationals who knowingly and continually break numerous laws and yet increasingly are being excused and deferred from the jurisdiction of those laws by advocates and presidential executive orders? Whether these groups of foreign nationals should qualify for birthright citizenship will undoubtedly be a subject of discussion at future immigration hearings. Until then, the amendment is a source for millions of babies of immigrants to get citizenship, as well as a basis for demands that their multimillions of parents be given a pathway to citizenship—green cards and amnesty.

Buying a Green Card

Since 1965, there have been a number of amendments and additions to the INA that have enabled hundreds of thousands of foreign nationals to obtain green cards outside of the normal immigration regulations. These opportunities are all legal. Several have bipartisan support to be extended in the future. There are many details and qualifications that limit who can take advantage of obtaining these special visas, but they have one thing in common: they cost money to varying degrees.

Described in brief below, and somewhat with tongue-in-cheek, are some ways to "buy a green card," starting with the most expensive to the least:

• Investor visas: For $1 million of unborrowed funds, a foreign national investor willing to put their money in a new, qualifying, commercial project can get a green card for him/herself and his immediate family if, within two years, the investment creates at least 10 full-time jobs for U.S.

citizens or legal immigrants with work permits (not including the investor's spouse or children). For $500,000 the investor can get the same deal if the money goes to a government-targeted project in a high-unemployment or rural area "that benefits the U.S. economy through job creation and capital investment." About 10,000 investors visas can be granted a year.

- Foreign students graduating with an advanced degree in STEM fields may be granted a green card if new legislation supported not only by both Democrats and Republicans, but also most especially by President Obama passes. Since foreign students often pay not only full price at private universities, but also a special non-waived, "out-of-state" fee at public universities, it can be estimated that most foreign students pay around $40,000 a year for tuition alone and easily another $40,000 for annual living expenses for themselves and often their families. As most foreign students take two-to-four years to complete an MA/MS degree, and 7–10 years for a PhD, that green card along with their degrees could cost them between $200,000 and $800,000.

- High-skilled visa conversion: Many if not a majority of the millions of immigrants who come into the United States to study or work often look into converting their temporary visa (usually good for three years, with the possibility to extend it another three years) to a permanent green card. This is literally the bread and-butter business of most immigration lawyers who can charge what they want. Just from anecdotal information from immigrants who have gone through the process, the costs can range from $5,000 to $25,000 or more for the temporary visa holder and their families.

- Amnesty: Arguably the cheapest way to obtain a green card—the proverbial pathway to citizenship—for immigrants who have been living and working in the country illegally is to wait for Congress to pass an amnesty. In 1986, over three million immigrants paid as much as $300 in fees and fines to get a green card after the amnesty law was signed by President Reagan. New proposals for amnesty or legalization or a pathway to citizenship for illegal immigrants include higher fines, fees, and up to 11 years of probation with initial costs being proposed at $600–$900.

Temporary Visas

Temporary nonimmigration visas are by far the biggest source of rising numbers of *legal* immigrants into the country. By 2010, over two million were being given out every year to foreign visitors, students, workers, professionals, performers, scholars, teachers, religious leaders, conference goers, journalists, and fiancées. Every year, more categories seem to be added to the alphabet soup of temporary visas.

This may not have been a completely unexpected consequence to the fathers of the Immigration and Nationality Act of 1965. As seen earlier, many legislators in 1965 wanted the new immigration law that repealed the Nationality Origins Act to first prioritize needed skilled workers over family unification. When that didn't happen, the temporary work visa outside the number of permanent immigration visas was a natural alternative.

Officially, a "temporary permit holder" is a foreign national who enters the country legally on one of dozens of different kinds of temporary permits. Nearly two million foreign nationals enter the United States legally every year on such temporary permits. Many of the temporary permit categories (such as tourists and foreign students) are unlimited in number. Others (such as H-1B and agricultural workers) are limited in number. But all temporary permits have the same kinds of conditions.

Most temporary permits

- are time limited albeit for varying periods of time—for instance, a tourist or visitor permit is good for three to six months; professional or skilled workers are usually on a three-year permit with a possible extension for another three years; a foreign student permit is good for the duration of studies plus a year or two of practical training; a seasonal agricultural worker (H-2 permits) good for a "season";
- are for work restricted to a specific employer;
- do not allow dependent spouses or children to work;
- carry the proviso that the holder has promised to leave the country once the temporary period is over or be considered illegally in the country if they "overstay"; and
- are not encouraged by the United States to be "adjusted" to another permit while in the country, such as from a tourist visa to a student, or a scholar to permanent green card, unless the holder returns home and applies from there—a proviso from which thousands of immigration lawyers through-out the country make it their often-lucrative businesses to find exception. The only permit that does not have this restriction is the H-1B, which allows "dual intent" (see below).

The kinds and numbers of temporary permits have grown exponentially since 1965 in part because of the elimination of the work skills that for 200 years had been the basis of granting immigrant status in the United States. Because most of the available green cards today are granted on the basis of family ties, not work skills, the need for foreign labor in certain job catego-ries has increasingly been met by these temporary work permits.

Many advocates for comprehensive immigration reform, including the CEOs of large dot-com companies such as Facebook and the heads of U.S. chambers of commerce, seem to love them. They demand more temporary visas and fewer regulations for skilled workers of every category. Universities recruit ever-growing numbers of foreign students each year (in 2015 close to 900,000) to help fill their classrooms, coffers, and research labs. The temporary nonimmigration visa allows them to recruit foreign students to their campuses in unlimited numbers—something they depend on.

But temporary visas are also criticized by advocates of comprehensive immigration reform. "This guest worker program is the closest thing I've ever seen to slavery," Congressman Charles Rangel (D-New York), chairman of the House Way and Means Committee has been quoted as saying.[22] "The temporary visas create a permanent, second-class tier of laborers in America," Latino activists pushing for citizenship for illegal and temporary workers often proclaim. And "The Congressional Hispanic Congressional will not support any immigration reform bill that includes temporary visas that do not lead to a pathway to citizenship," Illinois Congressman Luis Guticrrcz, and immigration spokesperson for the Congressional Hispanic Caucus often warns on record to reporters.

But perhaps the biggest unintended consequence of temporary visas is their role as the fastest rising source of illegal immigrants. It is often cited that some 40 percent of the unauthorized immigrant population today (about 4 million of the estimated 12 million) came in legally on temporary visas and then ignore the time limits, "overstaying" their visas and becoming "illegal aliens."

The following is a brief description of some of the most popular temporary visas that both enrich the United States and have added to the unintended increase of millions of immigrants residing and working in the United States.

The H-1B Permit

The H-1B visa category was established in the late 1980s under the INA as a way for specific employers to bring in professionals with college degrees. It became known as the high-skilled, tech workers visa. But it has been used increasingly for lower-level tech workers in research labs and computer production companies, as well as for skilled medical techs, teachers, semiprofessional trainers, and even stablemen and party valets.

Mainly it is specific to the employer who is awarded the visas and offers them to his/her prospective international employees. As the visa is employer specific, it is not mobile for the employee; if their employment situation changes, they can't take their visa with them. Each H-1B is applied to and awarded through the employer. The duration of the visa is three years with a possible three-year extension.

In 2000, The American Competitiveness Act (AC2000) eased some of the restrictions on mobility of the H-1B employee after accusations that it was being used as a system of indentured servitude. But there is a rather involved process of approval to get the mobility. The subject of mobility comes up often in discussions about comprehensive immigration reform.

During the early 1990s, the INA cap of 100,000 H-1B visas was rarely reached. But by the mid-1990s it was filled increasingly by the first-come, first-serve system. In 1998, the cap was increased to 115,000 with some 20,000 reserved for advanced-degree applicants. As more and more high-tech companies developed and learned of the visas, the cap filled faster, and by 2010 the new cap of over 212,000 H-1Bs was being oversubscribed days before it opened. But always a certain number—around 20,000—were reserved outside the cap for graduating foreign students. Universities and corporate employed have kept up a constant pressure to increase the number of H-1B visas and to expedite their processing.

The six-year limit for an H-1B has remained en force, however, but visa holders have been allowed a unique proviso for a nonimmigration visa. The H-1B visa is one of the few that is "dual intent"—that is, unlike other nonimmigration visas such as the foreign student and scholar permits, where an applicant could be denied the visa or have it removed if an intent to immigrate was proved while on the visa, the H-1B allows the holder to have the intent to apply for a green card while applying for or working in the United States under the H-1B. The idea was to enable particularly valuable genius employees to stay on permanently in the United States, even to become citizens.

Meanwhile, the spouses, children, and other dependents of H-1B visa holders are given H-4 visas that allow them to reside in the United States as long as the primary visa holder, and to attend school, get a driver's license, and open a bank account. But they are not permitted to work or to get a social security number. Under the 1986 amnesty act, if an employer hires an H-4 visa holder, they are committing a felony. It is safe to say, however, that the ruling is ignored and not enforced.

In 2006–2007, a campaign was conducted by various universities and CEOs of dot-com companies to include in immigration reform bills significant expansion of the H-1B visas for graduating students. They argued in congressional hearings and in the press that the United States surely would lose competitiveness, prosperity, and future generations if the number of H-1Bs were not increased by hundreds of thousands immediately. In a unique single-witness hearing before the Senate Education Committee in the spring of 2007, Bill Gates made a case to attach a green card to the diploma of every foreign student graduating with an advanced degree from a U.S. university in a science or engineering field. (Increasingly, foreign graduate students dominate these fields of study and research at many U.S. colleges and universities.)

Over the years other categories of H visas have developed to enable foreign nationals to work temporarily in the United States. Thousands of summer employees, mainly from Eastern Europe, are often hired as hotel and shop workers and especially lifeguards in summer resort cities, at most U.S. national parks, and often at large condominium swimming pools throughout the country. School teachers (especially in math), medical technicians, and nurses increasingly come to the United States from countries like the Philippines and work for low wages, but making multiple times more money than they could in their homelands. Summer help for festivals and parties come increasingly from South America.

In most cases, employers claim it is impossible to find American teenagers to do this work and they are forced to hire foreign workers from May through September. Often the eager young foreign workers take on two or three jobs during a summer to make money to live on during the rest of the year and live with up to a dozen other summer workers from their homelands, sleeping in shifts in small apartments.

Foreign Student Permits

Of all the temporary permits, the foreign student visa is perhaps the earliest and certainly the most generous and venerated of all. Since the late 1940s when it was established to allow bright young people from war-torn countries to have a chance to pursue their studies, it was always regarded as a temporary nonimmigrant visa. The numbers were few; most were elite students going to elite universities. But over the decades that changed.

By 2014, the number of foreign nationals studying in the United States on foreign student visas had grown to close to 886,052—an 8 percent increase from 2013 and a historic high. It can be expected that the numbers will grow to over one million in the next few years. "International education is considered to be America's fifth largest export, bigger than medical services," according to the International Institute of Education's (IIE) annual "Open Doors Report" of 2013.

There are two main kinds of foreign student permits:

1. F: mainly for college degree programs (associate degree to PhD) and English-language programs offered by colleges. Since 2004, more F1 college students are graduate students than undergraduates. Fs can also be used for exchange students in elementary and secondary schools.
2. J: for research scholars and visiting professors at universities, think tanks, and research labs. Usually these carry a three-year, nonrenewable limit.

These international student and scholar visas are unlimited in number and given out by colleges, universities, and some research institutions like the National Institutes of Health that have been vetted by the U.S. State Department. Some 3,000 institutions of higher education throughout the United States are approved to host foreign students and scholars.

Recently bipartisan initiatives were proposed to give green cards to foreign students graduating from American universities with advanced degrees (MSs and PhDs) in science, technology, engineering, and math. President Obama has supported the idea in every State of the Union Speech since 2009. It is not clear if advocates understand that hundreds of thousands of students would qualify, the majority citizens of mainly two countries: China and India.

Some university and State Department officials have mixed feelings about the idea of giving Permanent Legal Residency immigration status to foreign students. While the prospect of an automatic pathway to citizenship might help the recruitment of what is often referred to as the "best and the brightest students in the world," the initiative could also threaten the "unlimited" aspect of the current foreign student visa. If hundreds of thousands of graduating foreign students are to be given automatic green cards, that could impact the principle of caps on the number of permanent immigration visas given out every year and of the nationality diversity of new permanent immigrants. Currently, universities thrive on the fact there is no national limit to the number of foreign student visas that can be given out since they are temporary. Increasingly, postsecondary education institutions depend on the growth of foreign student, full-tuition revenue as state support for American students decreases. Many officials don't want the foreign student visa to be limited in number.

The State Department also supports the temporary nature of foreign student visas that requires the potential America-friendly leaders of countries throughout the world to return home as advocates for America. Diplomatically they don't want to be seen as draining the brains from other countries and they count on the good will that foreign student gain toward America during their studies. "We do not favor foreign student visas becoming part of the permanent immigration system," Evan M. Ryan, Assistant Secretary of State for Educational and Cultural Affairs said at the November 2014 launch of the International Institute of Education's annual report on foreign students, "Open Doors," at the National Press Club in Washington, D.C.

Temporary Protected Status Asylees

Asylees under Temporary Protected Status (TPS) are another large source of temporary permits that can be extended for decades. TPS asylees come from countries that are designated (since 2003) by the Secretary of Homeland

Security as too dangerous for the applicant to safely return due to ongoing armed conflict, environmental disaster, or other extraordinary and temporary conditions. Citizens of designated countries also can be granted TPS if it is deemed that the country is unable to handle the return of its nationals adequately.

But the status is different from that of a refugee. It is temporary. It does not come with a permanent immigration visa after a year, although beneficiaries can apply for a green card and perhaps get it if they qualify.

TPS beneficiaries can apply for the temporary asylum status either outside or inside the country after initial review of their cases (prima facie eligible). They cannot be removed (i.e., deported) from the United States and are given employment authorization documents (EAD)—a working permit by the Citizenship and Immigration Services bureau of the Department of Homeland Security. Their period of asylum is limited to a specified amount of time (often two years), which also can be extended as a class, multiple times. But this causes confusion. The TPS can be in a state of limbo for years.

El Salvadorian TPS recipients are a good example. In 2008, 229,000 El Salvadorian nationals were eligible to register for TPS, adding to the some 340,000 LPRs in the country at the time. By 2011, the U.S. Census found more than two million U.S. residents were of El Salvadorian heritage. By 2014 their "temporary" protective status and "temporary" work permits had been extended so many times that now the immigrants are demanding they be given permanent residency status and the rights of citizenship. El Salvadorian consulate offices have recently sprung up all over Washington, D.C., where El Salvadorians are the largest Latino immigrant nationality.

It is unclear if the tens of thousands of Unaccompanied Alien Minors (UAMs) from El Salvador who surged over the border in the summer of 2014 would be granted a new long-term TPS status. Most of their advocates are seeking refugee status for the children (the vast majority of whom are teenagers: 15–18-year-old males seeking work and females with toddlers and babies). After entering the United States, most sought protection from the border patrol and were either united with family members living in the United States (often illegally) or were placed under the care of the Department of Health and Human Services child services in cities and states throughout the country.

Unlike Mexican UAMs, the children fleeing Central American countries could not be returned immediately. Many came expecting amnesty and advocates urge that they be granted refugee status with automatic green cards within a year. It is expected, however, that most will not qualify for refugee status, but that few if any will be deported.

INCREASING NUMBERS OF ILLEGAL IMMIGRANTS

Decades after the Immigration and Nationality Act of 1965 was implemented, Senator Kennedy was asked about the unexpected increase in the number of immigrants from what he, President Johnson, and just about everyone else who had supported the bill predicted. Senator Kennedy often blamed it on "illegal immigration."

He was partly correct. No one had predicted in 1965 that by the new century, some 12 million foreign nationals would be living and working in the United States illegally. In 1986, President Reagan passed an amnesty act, which legalized over three million illegal immigrants in the country at the time (three times more than the one million that had been estimated by the bill's sponsors). Kennedy had promised that this was a one-time deal, that it would not be needed to be done again. The major goal of the act had been to end illegal immigration forever, but the enforcement measures that had been put in to stop it were not enforced.

In the 1990s the numbers of unauthorized immigrants in the country began to surge, hitting a peak of 12.2 million in 2007, up from 3.5 million in 1990. In 2008–2009 the number dropped to 11.5 million, before rising again in the past few years according to the *New York Times* in 2013.[23] (Note: Pew Hispanic Center researchers derive their estimates with a complex formula that calculates the number of legal immigrants in the country and subtracts that from the overall foreign-born population, which was 41.7 million last year. About 28 percent of that total was immigrants here illegally, according to the Pew Research Center Hispanic Trends Project published September 23, 2013.)

Experts seem to agree that approximately 55–60 percent of illegal immigrants in the country today (about 7 million of the 12) sneak into the country mainly over the Mexican border. While the numbers vary every year, an average of about 500,000 are estimated to come over every year. Not all are Mexican nationals. Every year, close to 20 percent of the people who come over the Mexican border illegally are what the border patrol refers to as OTMs—"Other than Mexicans." Most are from Central America, a growing percentage from Latin America and Brazil, and the rest from Asia and the Caribbean. In 2010, 1 percent was estimated to be from the Middle East.

Not all make it either. The U.S. border patrol has been increasingly successful in turning back a number of immigrants sneaking over the border thanks to the Bush and Obama administrations' emphasis on detention and removal at the border rather than the "catch and release" process of the 1990s. There has been some controversy that the Obama administration counts the rising numbers of immigrants caught and turned back at the border as "deportations"; technically deportations are an action taken against mainly illegal immigrants living and working inside the United States.

Since 2005, the number of forced deportations has also increased, however. Before the Department of Homeland Security (DHS) was established after 9/11, there was no agency in the United States responsible for internal enforcement of immigration laws. The creation of the Immigration and Customs Enforcement (ICE) bureau in the new DHS gave that agency that unique charge. The second secretary of the DHS, Michael Chertoff (2007–2008), announced in 2007 at a speech at the American Enterprise Institute that he would emphasize immigration enforcement at the workplace. After a public relations disaster, when ICE agents were seen on TV arresting and handcuffing hundreds of illegal immigrant workers at a Swift meatpacking plant in Iowa, the department turned its enforcement focus on the employer, not employees.

Because of increased enforcement in the mid-2000s, together with the U.S. recession that particularly impacted the construction industry where a large proportion of illegal immigrants from Mexico and El Salvador work, the numbers of unauthorized immigrants decreased noticeably in 2006–2008. From 2007 to 2009, a Pew Hispanic report stated that more unauthorized Mexicans left the United States than came here illegally. It has risen again since then.[24]

While the number of illegal immigrants who sneak over the border fluctuates, the percentage of immigrants who came into the country legally and then overstayed their visas making them unauthorized, has grown to an estimated 40 percent of the total. This includes many of the some 100,000 Irish nationals who are in the country illegally today. Some are vocal indeed for a "comprehensive" immigration reform that includes legalization of all illegal aliens. Often, groups of young Irish adults who are in the country illegally attend the various immigration hearings in Congress and lobby especially the Irish-heritage members of Congress to demand that they "Legalize the Irish"—the name of their organization that appears prominently on the backs of their green T-shirts. The Irish youths often pass out bright green brochures proclaiming, "We need *Your* help to keep the Irish in America." The brochure includes quotes and photos of smiling Senators John McCain (R-Arizona), Hillary Clinton (D-New York), Ted Kennedy (D-Massachusetts), Sam Brownback (R-Kansas), and Charles Schumer (D-New York). "You are really here on behalf of what American means," Hillary is quoted to say (let's hope she is not referring to their illegal status!).

By law, being in the country illegally is a misdemeanor, not a felony. Every "illegal alien"—the official term that is used by Supreme Court Justice Sonia Sotomayor for one—in the United States is committing at least a civil offense just by being in the country without a permit. While a "minor crime," the offense is still punishable with removal or sometimes up to a year in prison and a fine of up to several thousand dollars.

But the criminal status of an illegal alien can easily escalate to a felony if a crime is committed, if false documents are used, or if the foreign national reenters the country after having been forcibly deported—all punishable by deportation and a permanent criminal record, making them ineligible to enter the country in the future.

The level of criminal offenses for illegal presence in the country varies. For instance if an illegal alien

- overstays a legal visa, it is a civil offense
- enters the country illegally it is a misdemeanor
- obtains false documents and uses them for any purpose such as getting a job, buying a home, getting insurance, s/he has committed a felony
- purports in writing to be in the country or the state legally (such as on a voting registration form or a public college application to avoid out-of-state tuition); such written statements often are not or cannot by law be questioned at the time of signing
- defies an order for deportation, then their residency becomes a felony. Reentry after deportation is a felony; failure to depart is a civil offense penalized with a formal order of removal and 10-year bar.

Since 1986, knowingly employing any immigrant without a work permit is also a crime punishable by a fine and even incarceration. This was embedded in the Amnesty Act and was supposed to be the way to stop illegal immigration—by "halting the driver" for it: the ability to get a job, to be hired. But there are many loopholes and legal paradoxes in the laws that regulate the employment of immigrants. For instance:

- While all employee applicants in the United States are legally required to present documents showing that they are in the country legally and have a work permit, employers do not have to verify that the documents presented are valid.
- While it is illegal for an employer *to hire* an illegal immigrant, it is not illegal for that immigrant to *seek* work—an effort that Arizona tried to criminalize but was rejected by the U.S. Supreme Court.
- While it is illegal to be in the country without authorization, it is only a misdemeanor and a far lesser "crime" than knowingly buying and using false identification to get benefits like a job, which is a felony. Hence, it is a far more serious "crime" for an illegal immigrant to use false documents while being called "undocumented" than it is to be in the country illegally and be labeled an illegal immigrant.

To get around some of these difficulties in an effort to stop illegal immigration, in 2005 or so the DHS together with the Social Security Administration started developing an electronic verification system that would make it as simple for an employer to check an employee's immigration status as swiping a credit card. It's called E-Verify and it's nationally accessible. But usage of the system is voluntary, not required. Arizona is one of the few states to make it mandatory for an employer to use E-Verify in order to qualify for a state business license (a regulation that the U.S. Supreme Court upheld in 2011), but congressional efforts to make it a national requirement have so far failed.

Whatever the violations, however, the continued presence and employment of an illegal alien puts both immigrant and employer at risk of sanctions. All immigration misdemeanors and felonies are punishable by deportation. The immigrant with a deportation notice faces two choices:

1. "Voluntarily withdraw" (the legal term, although presidential candidate George Romney made its nomenclature "self deport" famous and pejorative). Leaving voluntarily will not affect future legal entry into the United States. Future illegal entry, however, is a felony that not even deferred action has excused to date.
2. Wait to be caught, detained, and involuntarily and forcibly removed. This action will be on an immigrant's record and can result in being banned from entering the United States legally at least for a period of time.

Both of these options are common immigration enforcement measures used worldwide and do not constitute crimes against humanity.

There are many reasons for the increase of illegal immigrants into the United States over the past 50 years as there were for the unexpected increase in legal immigrants. With hindsight, most of the reasons are very predictable and understandable. One was the passage of the INA itself. The passage of the1965 Immigration and Nationality Act coincided with the greatest global population growth in world history, populations that were eager for paid work. The INA opened up the possibility for families from every country in the world to immigrate to the United States.

With green card priority on nationality diversity and family unification, new immigrants did not need to prove they had needed work skills. Many were unskilled and willing to work at any job. They in turn encouraged extended family members—especially young cousins—to come in (often on very loosely regulated visitor visas) with the expectations that they would get eventual green cards under family unification, amnesty, or deferment from deportation together with an open job permit; in the meantime, they stayed on and worked "under the table" with impunity.

Waiting Lists

The waiting list of eligible, completed applications is years long for countries where visa demand exceeds the per-country limit (aka the "oversubscribed list"). Countries at present that are on the so-called visa prorated list are Mexico, mainland China, India, and the Philippines. For other countries like Iceland, for instance, there is rarely a waiting list based on that nationality. But once the total number of limited preference categories (some 400,000) have been accepted for any year, all other applications received are put on the waiting list by country and date of receipt. "It is impossible for us to accept all the eligible applications we receive from family members alone every year."[25]

There is an agreed upon total number of applicants for Permanent Legal Residency permits (aka: green cards) of around one million—the most generous total in the world. Anyone who is denied or who has been on a waiting list or who has a family member on a waiting list for years complains that this is unfair, but do you have a better idea? We can't have "open borders." This explains the often-heard complaint of a legal resident that they have been waiting for years to bring in their adult child or parent, aunt or uncle, grandparents, and so forth, all of whom are eligible for eventual family unification green cards, but have to wait their turn. They are frustrated of course. They are doing things legally and feel they have the right to bring in their numerous relatives when they want.

From the immigrant's point of view, waiting years for a legally eligible family member to get a green card is heartbreakingly unfair. They know also that staying in the country without a permit and "living in the shadows" is not only illegal, but also stressful and dangerous. They can be detained and deported at any time. For millions of illegal immigrants, their families, and their advocates in the United States, the only fair thing ro do, the right thing to do, the humane "American" thing to do is to legalize them. They cannot understand how anyone could be against that. But they never talk about stopping illegal immigration itself.

By the mid-1970s, illegal immigration had become what journalist Roberto Suro (a founding Director of the Pew Hispanic Center) called "a hot second-tier issue." It centered mainly in the Southwest.

Seasonal Agricultural and Low-Skilled Workers

The end of the *bracero* program in 1965 and the beginning of the INA with its nationality diversity that limited, for the first time, immigration from Mexico and Central America changed the dynamics of labor for the Southwest's ranches and mega-farms. Waves of Mexican and Central American farm workers streamed into the Southwest—California and Texas particularly—seeking work for any wage they could get and inevitably displacing some Americans, including Hispanic and African Americans at the bottom of the wage scale. California labor leader Cesar Chavez and his United Farm Workers tried in vein to stem the tide of the now mostly illegal workers employed by farmers who "held down food prices by holding down farm workers' wages. They undercut the economic and social gains of Americans of Hispanic descent."[26]

According to the Department of Labor, the only legal mechanism through which to contract people from outside the United States to work on farms here is the H-2A work visa program. A key prerequisite for issuance of H-2A visas is certification by the Department of Labor that the specific jobs for which foreign workers are sought could not be filled from the U.S. resident labor supply. Agricultural employers have to demonstrate a labor shortage to import foreign workers on a temporary basis under terms and conditions that will result in no adverse effect to U.S. workers.

There are many bureaucratic hurdles to meet before the permits can be granted. Beyond the certification that the foreign farm workers are not taking jobs away from native and naturalized citizens and LPRs, employers must also meet several required terms of employment of H-2A workers, including provision of transportation from and back to their home country, housing while here, and a state-specific "adverse effect" pay rate generally higher than minimum wage. It is not surprising then, that most foreign agriculture workers do not come in under the H-2A program. According to Marcos Camacho, General Counsel for the United Farm Workers at a congressional hearing:

> Today, we have reached a situation in agriculture that demands urgent action. There are about 2.5 million farmworkers in this country, not including their family members. More than 80% percent of them are foreign-born, mostly but not all from Mexico. Virtually all of the newest entrants to the farm labor force lack authorized immigration status. The helpful reports from the National Agricultural Workers Survey by the U.S. Department of Labor state that about 53% of farm workers are undocumented. But most observers believe the figure is 60% or 70%, and much higher in specific locations. Many employers now hire farm labor contractors in the hope that they can shield themselves from liability for hiring undocumented workers in violation of our immigration law and from liability for labor law violations. The labor contractors compete against one another by offering to do a job for less money, and the cut-throat competition means that the workers must take lower wages. When one labor contractor is prosecuted for violating labor laws, he is easily replaced. Our current immigration system is causing employers to attempt to evade responsibility for their employees, while undocumented workers are too fearful of being deported to demand changes. In many cases, due to inadequate enforcement of labor laws, employers take advantage of undocumented workers by subjecting them to illegal wages and working conditions.

Many proposals have been included in various immigration reform bills and in stand-alone bills, especially by Senator Diane Feinstein (D-California), to make it easier for employers to hire foreign farm workers for particularly the bend-over agricultural labor on American farms. All of these bills have failed to date, due largely to the fact they are usually included as part of a gigantic omnibus or comprehensive immigration package containing controversial elements such as legalization and a "pathway to citizenship" for farm workers presently in the country illegally. After the first bill failed to pass cloture in early June of 2007, Senator Feinstein remarked on the floor and on the record to an empty Senate chamber that the bill was "probably too massive and it might be best to break up some of the pieces and try to have them pass on their own." I attended the Senate debate and vote, and noted the senator's remarks that were also cited in the *Congressional Record* for June 7, 2007.[27] She meant of course the agriculture jobs bill piece.

But Feinstein tried that in December of 2006 and her separate bill also failed. The bill included a "pathway to citizenship" for illegal immigrants working in agriculture (60–80 percent of field workers according to experts). But the legalization of illegal workers poisoned the bill. On October 31, 2007, I asked Agriculture Committee Chairman Senator Tom Harkins (D-Iowa) if he was expecting Senator Feinstein to add the AgJOBs amendment to the farm bill to be voted on the next week. He answered firmly: "She told me she would propose it and I told her I would not support it. Even though I supported it in the immigration bill, I don't want to drag down the farm bill with a filibuster or anything like that. It is an immigration matter. It is part of comprehensive immigration reform and we won't get to that until 2009 or after." To date, it still hasn't been legislated.

Migration to the United States proved critical to the economic strategies of many Latin Americans and many Latin American policymakers after World War II. Wages earned in the United States and sent back to the homelands of immigrants became one of the leading sources of foreign revenue (read, dollars) in many parts of South and Central America.[28]

The situation of course is the same for the vast majority of illegal immigrant workers who do not work in agriculture or bend-over labor but increasingly work in construction or in the hospitality industry (hotels, restaurants, resorts, and the like). The need for these workers may imply opening up additional work permits for these occupations, or it may better show the need for enforcement of labor regulations regarding wages, benefits, and immigration status. It should not be assumed that immigrants—illegal and legal—are doing jobs that Americans can't or won't do. This is particularly true of workers who come in on temporary visas of all categories.

Overstaying Temporary Visas

As has been noted, the number of foreign nationals who came into the United States legally on one of the multitude of temporary visas described above but overstayed and became unauthorized, make up some 40 percent of the total number of illegal immigrants in the country today and growing. They are people of every nationality, profession, and stage of life. Many are invisible to the system, especially if they don't work. They live next door; their children go to school with your children and grandchildren; they are active in community organizations. Many are valued colleagues and workers. Often close family members don't know of their illegal immigration status. They are millions of people who are living in the shadows.

There are several visas that are particularly vulnerable to overstaying. Tourist visas for one, especially of young people who find they can stay on for years as college students—especially at state and community colleges that in most states practice a "don't ask don't tell" policy regarding immigration status. Students increasingly work at part-time jobs that are not known for a strict adherence to checking immigration status.

Similarly, it is estimated that over 50 percent of the some 900,000 foreign students presently studying in the United States five or more years, will stay after their studies are completed, even though their F visas require them to return home after their studies and a temporary "work training" period. Eventually, many find legal ways to stay: They will be able to earn enough to pay a lawyer to "adjust" their temporary permits to a green card or to obtain another temporary permits, usually the H-1B. Some will marry U.S. citizens, some will win the lottery, and some will stay on as university and research scholars.

In most cases, the staying-on of foreign students is considered a positive thing. Increasingly, American politicians ask, "Why are we kicking out the best and the brightest of the world's students in whom we have invested years of education and research facilities and who can add to the job creation and prosperity of our country."

But it is also true that many of the 9/11 terrorists had come in on foreign student visas. One of the first regulations that passed Congress after the terrorist attack of 2001 was SEVIS—the Student and Exchange Visitors Information System. It required universities and colleges to input basic information about their foreign students, including field of study and intended date of graduation, into the national electronic database. It is maintained by the DHS and accessible to the FBI. But it only includes information about students as long as they are registered at an institution. It does not track them after they leave or never registered even though they were granted a student visa from that institution.

The illegal staying-on of foreign students is not the part of the foreign student visa for which university officials feel responsible. Although they are vetted by the State Department to issue the foreign student visa and thereby receive the lucrative benefits of hosting foreign students, officials of the National Association of Foreign Student Advisors (NAFSA)—now renamed the more politically correct Association of International Educators—continually make it clear that it is not the duty of their advisors to enforce the "return home" part of the visa, nor indeed to even know where their foreign student is after they leave the campus.

Free Public Education and Medical Care for Minor Illegal Aliens, *Plyler v. Doe.*

Certainly, illegal immigration could be said to have been encouraged since 1965 by a number of very liberal rulings by the Supreme Court giving educational, medical, and other public benefits to illegal aliens and their children. One such case is *Plyler v. Doe.*[29]

In 1982, the Supreme Court held, in a 5–4 vote, that children living illegally in the United States have the same right to a free public education as American citizens. The case had originated in Texas five years earlier. Lawyers for a group of children illegally in the state filed a class-action lawsuit seeking a free public education. Lawyers for Texas school districts argued that an influx of illegal students would ruin the public schools. A district court ruled in the plaintiffs' favor. The ruling was upheld on appeal, first to the 5th circuit and then to the Supreme Court in 1982. Under the Act, "schools have to be careful of any unintentional attempts to document students' legal status which could lead to the possible 'chilling' of their Plyler rights" warned John Willshire-Carrera, Esq. of the National Coalition of Advocates for Students, Boston, Massachusetts.[30]

In-State College Tuition

In some states, illegal alien, young adult children who graduate from a state's public high school, are allowed to attend the public colleges of that state at the in-state tuition rate, not the much higher tuition that out-of-state American students, legal foreign students, and the children of temporary permit holders (such as H-1B holders) must pay.

In-state tuition is a huge subsidy paid by state taxpayers amounting to tens of thousands of dollars per student depending on the state. But as a state benefit, it is up to state voters and legislators to decide whether to give it to illegal immigrants or not and what are the qualifications—usually graduation from a high school in the state and at least two years residency in the state. It can be highly controversial. By 2014, some 15 states allowed illegal immigrants to get in-state tuition if they had graduated from a state high school. But international students—youths coming from countries throughout the world on foreign student F and scholar J visas, do not get in-state tuition nor are they waived from it during their studies.

The permission to get in-state tuition does not alter the student's illegal immigration status nor allow them to get a work permit. Many advocates believe that amnesty will eventually come for these students that will give them permanent residency status and open job opportunities. It happened in 1896 and 1996. But this is just for students who are illegally in the country. No foreign student nor college student on a legal temporary visa can "dream" of getting automatic permanent status and jobs. Lucky for them, most employers don't know that or ignore it.

Amnesty

The concept, even the very word *amnesty* has become a highly charged buzz word in the immigration debate—a bristling connection for an entire idea: to grant open job permits and permanent immigration status to millions of foreign nationals who have broken U.S. immigration and labor laws by living and working in the United States without a permit, visa, or authorization. The strange thing is that those who want to do so (often Democrats), refuse to call it amnesty and those who oppose the action, do call it that. *Amnesty* has become a contentious word and concept.

But what is amnesty exactly in legal terms? *West's Encyclopedia of American Law* defines *amnesty* as a governmental act that grants a group of persons who have broken the law immunity from prosecution. And amnesty can (and almost always does) have stringent conditions ("seriously qualified" in legal terms).

The action of a government by which all persons or certain groups of persons who have committed a criminal offense—usually of a political nature that threatens the sovereignty of the government (such as sedition or treason)—are granted immunity from prosecution.

Though amnesty can be broad or narrow, covering one person or many, and can be seriously qualified (as long as the conditions are not unconstitutional) it cannot grant a license to commit future crimes nor forgive crimes not yet committed.

Amnesty allows the government of a nation or state to "forget" and forgive criminal acts, usually before prosecution has occurred. Amnesty has traditionally been used as a political tool of compromise and reunion following a war. An act of amnesty is generally granted to a group of people who have committed crimes against the state, such as treason, rebellion, or desertion from the military.

But amnesty is not a pardon. Both derive their legal justification from Article 2, Section 2 of the Constitution, which gives the president the power to grant *reprieves* and *pardons* for offenses against the United States. The main difference between the two actions however is as follows:

- Amnesty is usually given to a group of people who have committed a crime against the United States but have not been convicted of the crime in a court of law; it is given *before* prosecution.
- A pardon is given by the president to a specific individual *following* a conviction for a crime.

"Forgiving" and "granting" permanent visas to millions of people *as a group* is what is so politically contentious about the idea of amnesty for illegal immigrants. It has become the line in the sand over which strong proponents and opponents will not compromise. It is the basis of "comprehensive" immigration reform over which Democrats, especially the highly vocal proponents of comprehensive immigration reform such as the Congressional Hispanic Caucus, will not compromise to date.

Amnesty has become the standard by which one's immigration stance is judged to be "pro-immigrant" or "anti-immigrant." It has been the poison pill that has killed legislation that otherwise seemed deemed to pass. So why do proponents refuse to call it *amnesty*? Because opponents insist that massive group amnesty (conditional or not) only will only encourage millions and millions more of illegal immigrants to come, stay, and work illegally, form mixed-status American families with U.S.-born children, work their way into our hearts, and wait for the inevitable next amnesty. Amnesty is seen as another gateway for illegal immigrants.

Why do opponents of amnesty say this?

Because it has happened before.

In 1986, thanks to Ted Kennedy, working with President Ronald Reagan (another Westerner like President Johnson who was very sympathetic particularly to Hispanic and Asian immigrants in California), the amnesty of 1986 was argued as emotionally and passionately by advocates for illegal immigrants as "comprehensive" immigration reform is today. One of its major focuses was that it would be a one-time deal only; that it would stop future massive illegal immigration while humanely dealing with the estimated one million illegal immigrants "living in the shadows" in 1986.

It was called the 1986 Immigration Reform and Control Act (IRCA).[31] By 2015 some three million illegal aliens in the country have been given what at the time was openly called "amnesty under the act." Nearly everyone admits that the 1986 amnesty was a humane act that was supposed to be a "one-time legislation." In 1982, in a letter to his colleagues on the Senate Judiciary Committee, Senator Edward Kennedy addressed the issue of legal status for illegal aliens in the pending bill. "A critical feature of [the bill] is the proposed legalization program. . . . It is both humane and sensible to *undertake a one-time legalization program*, as was unanimously recommended by the Select Commission."[32]

But Kennedy was wrong (as he was in 1965). By the turn of the century there were 12–20 million immigrants living and working in the United States illegally.

IRCA is considered by many to be a failure. Illegal immigration grew by multiples since amnesty was instituted. While the reasons for the failure are many, because few if any of the enforcement sanctions embedded in the bill were enforced. That includes fining and even arresting employers who knowingly hired immigrants without work permits. It is common sense to understand that amnesty without enforcement encourages more illegal immigration.

Because of the failure of IRCA to stop illegal immigration, present day proponents for legalization and citizenship for illegal aliens make every effort to deflect their actions from being called "amnesty." They employ other language (e.g., earned citizenship; legalization; bringing "them" out of the shadows; following the American dream; pathway to citizenship; extension of temporary working visas). They insist that what they are proposing is not amnesty because their legislation imposes harsh conditions and requirements for an illegal alien to meet before getting legalization and citizenship.

Conditions include registering the migrant and documenting work history, job skills, length of stay, family status, and arrest record. Some of the proposed legislation imposes complicated requirements such as: "touch backs" (returning to their homelands for a certain period of time and applying from there), going to a port of entry to be issued a temporary visa, or maneuvering a "pathway to citizenship" that takes years, before being granted a permanent green card. Various fines have been proposed that have to be paid by the illegal alien before getting legalized; fees range from $500 to over $10,000. By imposing these conditions and requirements and punishment in the form of fines and fees, proponents say it is not giving amnesty.

But amnesty is a *blanket forgiveness by Congress* for breaking federal law given to a specific "class" or group of people who have not been convicted of the crime. Conditioned or not, mass forgiveness is amnesty.

There is one other way, however, for a large group of people who have broken federal immigration law to defer, delay, and perhaps even just waive arrest, detention, and deportation. It happens when the president offers "prosecutorial discretion" through an executive order or executive action to people who meet specific qualifications. It can't be done as a single action for a whole group of people however; discretion can only be granted on a case-by-case basis.

Executive Orders, Executive Actions

Ever since the legalization of illegal immigrants became a contentious issue
and blocked in Congress, advocates have urged that the president use another
process to affect the change: an executive order and executive actions. The
idea is that with a single order, the president could expedite the legalization
of millions of immigrants who are facing at least potential, if not actual,
deportation.

The terms executive *order* and *action* are often used interchangeably, but
they should not be. They actually refer to two different processes.

1. "A presidential executive order 'is a directive issued to federal agencies, department heads, or other federal employees by the President of
   the United States under his statutory or constitutional powers,'" according to Robert Langley writing at usgovinfo.about.com, and reported on "The Two Way" on NPR on November 20, 2014, by Scott
   Neuman. "In many ways, presidential executive orders are similar to
   written orders, or instructions issued by the president of a corporation
   to its department heads or directors." They are legally binding. An
   executive order is just that—a mandate that the executive (president)
   gives to one or more of his agencies about how to implement laws that
   Congress handed to him. In the case of prosecutorial discretion, the
   president can only dictate that discretion can be used—persecution
   deferred or temporarily waived—for individuals who the agency must
   ascertain have met certain requirements on a case-by-case basis. It is
   not a class-action law; the president can't legislate.
2. "By contrast, a presidential executive action is kind of a catch-all
   term. An NBC newscast quoted an unnamed administration official in
   2011 as saying: 'It just means something the executive branch does.
   The use of any of a number of tools in the executive branch's tool-
   box.'[33] Political writer Tom Murse says, '[Most] executive actions
   carry no legal weight. Those that do actually set policy can be invali-
   dated by the courts or undone by legislation passed by Congress. . . . A
   good way to think of executive actions is a wish list of policies the
   president would like to see enacted.'"[34]

"The terms executive action and executive order are not interchangeable.
Executive orders are legally binding and published in the Federal Register."
They have been around since the first days of the republic. George Washington issued eight of them. Perhaps the most famous example was Abraham
Lincoln's Emancipation Proclamation. House minority leader Nancy Pelosi
recited a list of dozens of presidential executive orders in one of her first
speeches on the floor to the new 114th Congress that was considering a bill

to defund that part of the DHS that was to implement President Obama's executive order of November 2014 to legalize millions of illegal immigrants. "Critics say there's no specific constitutional authority for them, but precedent has outweighed the critics."[35]

Executive actions have been used on immigration matters in the past, most famously after Congress passed and the president signed the amnesty bill of 1986. Soon after, advocates realized that the children of adults getting amnesty were not included, so President Reagan made an executive order to have that happen. Soon after, Congress passed a law legislating it. It affected thousands of illegal immigrants.

In 2012 and again in 2014 President Obama made an executive order to defer prosecution and deportation for DREAMers. Some two million individuals were said to be potentially eligible; by 2014 when the order was extended another two years, some 600,000 had been granted the waiver. In 2014 the president again ordered a temporary deferment of illegal immigrants who were the parents of DREAMers and the parents of U.S.-born citizens—again on a case-by-case basis. Some five million are generally said to be qualified but again it is doubtful that more than a million will apply and be accepted.

While deferring certain illegal immigrants from immediate deportation in order that the department can run more efficiently is within the president's prerogatives, it is less clear that he has the right to give full work permits to millions of immigrants without such permits. In addition, thousands of new government employees will be needed to implement the program out of the CIS—a cost that eventually may be covered by the fees collected from the applicants, if the numbers pan out.

The big question is this: Do such amnesties and executive orders and actions actually encourage more immigrants to disobey immigration laws, come in illegally, be hired illegally for usually below-standard wages, and enjoy protections and benefits that even most legal immigrants, especially temporary, get—especially the expectation of an eventual amnesty? There is much proof that the surge of hundreds of thousands of unaccompanied minors from Central America who traveled thousands of miles, crossing the Mexican border into the United States without permits, were encouraged to do so because of DACA and other executive actions and amnesties that led eventually to a pathway to citizenship, a green card, permanent residency, and full access to U.S. jobs for millions of illegal immigrants.

Clearly, Ted Kennedy was conflicted about illegal immigration. He blamed it as the reason for the great unexpected increase in immigration than ever had been imagined when he pushed for the Immigration and Nationality Act of 1965. But over the years as he became the voice of civil rights in the Senate, it seems that his only solution to end illegal immigration was to legalize everyone who was illegally in the country at the time and pass laws that would discourage future such migration.

Didn't happen. Those laws were not enforced, and deportation didn't happen because Kennedy and other leaders could not bring themselves to endorse deportation.

Unenforced Laws and Sanctuary Cities

Another significant reason for the continued rise in illegal immigration obviously, is the highly visible reluctance by the public and by U.S. officials to enforce immigration laws in the interior of the country. The Obama administration particularly has experienced increasing pressures by advocates for illegal immigrants to end President Bush's policies to punish employers who illegally hire immigrants without work permits, or even to deport illegal immigrants who commit multiple misdemeanors and felonies. While it is true that since 2008 the Obama DHS has deported some two million immigrants—"more than ever in history"—that is less than 350,000 a year, less than the number of new illegal immigrants who come in or overstay their visas in a year.

The vast majority of those deported have either been convicted of a violent felony or have defied previous deportation orders and actions—an unforgivable felony even for prosecutorial discretion at the time of this writing. However, the president has promised that only convicted criminals of serious felonies (implied to be violent assault and murder) are to be deported in general. Adversaries on both sides continually find exceptions to this ruling.

But it is difficult to argue against the growing perception that almost all of the 12 million or so illegal immigrants in the country are increasingly protected from sanctions and certainly from deportation. Most Americans are very sympathetic to illegal immigrants and can't seem to stomach punishing them, especially young immigrants—certainly not by deportation. Several court and administrative rulings have watered down, if not eviscerated, any but the most stringent federal actions to sanction illegal immigration. They include:

- In 1982, the Supreme Court ruling in *Plyler v. Doe* made it illegal for anyone seeking admission in a school or hospital to be asked their immigration status.
- Starting in 2009, the Obama administration effectively dismantled two Bush administration programs that facilitated cooperation between DHS and state and local law enforcement agencies. They were referred to as ICE Access programs—most especially Secure Communities. The Secure Communities (S-Comm) program involved the identification of aliens wanted for deportation through checking electronically collected finger-

prints at the local level and matching them with fingerprints on file at DHS for persons sought for deportation.

- The 287(g) provision was enacted into the INA in 1996 under the Clinton administration and in reaction to the 1992 terrorist attack on Wall Street. In this program, state and local law enforcement officers were to be trained by the federal government in immigration law enforcement and then deputized to act as immigration agents. As originally designed, the persons locally identified as illegal and deportable aliens were taken into custody by the federal authorities and put into deportation proceedings.

Some states and counties who used to require their law enforcement personnel to ask about the legal status of those stopped even for minor infractions, have now mostly withdrawn the ruling for fear of legal cases brought on by civil rights groups. Other jurisdictions have forbidden it for years.

Even the few entities that are required by law (state and federal) to ascertain the legal status of an individual, such as employers (including individuals hiring people to work in their private homes and gardens), U.S. immigration service and enforcement bureaus, state departments of motor vehicles, public colleges or universities, and social security offices, rarely follow up on the order. Usually the requested status is supposed to be designated in writing (usually by checking a box marked "citizen" or not) on a written application. If the box is marked "citizen" or if a status document (like a social security card or a state driver's license) that the holder ascertains is legal is presented (even if it is fraudulent), most institutions like colleges and small employers are not allowed to query further. Usually most never will ask for the holder to prove if a presented document is valid or not.

In a number of American cities, local legislators have been pushed by constituents (particularly the Catholic Church and immigrant advocacy organizations) to become sanctuary cities for illegal immigrants. Cities like Anchorage; Los Angeles; Chicago; Cambridge, Massachusetts; Portland, Maine; Tacoma Park, Maryland; Detroit; Minneapolis; New York City; Houston; Seattle; Madison, Wisconsin; and New Haven, Connecticut, openly give illegal workers identity cards, offer them benefits such as free job training and searching, health services, language education for adults, and legal advocacy and protection (mainly noncooperation) and especially sanctuary against U.S. Homeland Security Immigration Enforcement inquiries. They forbid their local law enforcement officers to ascertain the legal status of anyone, including criminal detainees, and to not participate or help federal law enforcement officials in enforcing federal laws regarding labor law and employer sanctions.

This doesn't just happen in liberal cities. Recently, a panel of three mayors, all Republican, from Aurora, Colorado; Salt Lake City, Utah; and Anaheim, California, admitted that they treat everyone who resides in their cities equally—equal benefits, rights, and protections.

"We have so many problems that we cannot take the time to distinguish what someone's immigration status is. We will not take the time to call in immigration officials to report on any illegal action to detain or certainly not have them deport any of our immigrant families. We are all a community and equal. It's the only sensible way to govern. It's the only humane thing to do."

"Cities are the bottom of the totem pole and we have no choice about who is coming to live in our municipalities. We just have to deal with them and the impact on our (locally funded) schools, hospitals, roads, services, housing and jobs," said Ralph Becker, the two-term mayor of Salt Lake City, Utah, at a panel of mayors sponsored January 20 by the *National Journal* in Washington, D.C., on "The Next America: Population 2043 Town Hall."

"I just don't have time to deal with it [details of immigration status and enforcement]," said Aurora Colorado mayor Steve Hogan forcefully. "I will do what I have to do for my city at the moment and deal with the niceties of political philosophy later (if ever)."

"Our main purpose is to keep people in our community safe," all the mayors agreed. "We just do what we can. We don't have time to argue. We don't have the power or the resources to enforce immigration laws. We just deal with everyone in the community the best we can to keep everyone safe."

"We rely heavily on nonprofits to help—especially (religious) faith groups," agreed the mayor of Anaheim, California, Tom Tait, who described his city's demographic as majority Latino and most of the rest as Asian and Arab. "We can't get caught up in the past histories of these populations—we all have blood on our hands; we have all been victims; now we just have to deal with the present. We're all in it together now equally."

When asked what the impact of 50,000–60,000 unaccompanied minors from Central America who had been brought into the city the past year, Becker replied, "We've had many refugees come to stay in our city. I wish we had more resources, but we find a way to help them. If we can help, then that's good. I can't identify any bad from it."

Enforcing national immigration law is obviously a distant concern for these mayors (who by the way were all Republicans).

Americans also are generally very reluctant to support the enforcement of the "limited time" aspect of every temporary, nonimmigration, time-limited visa. The idea of "internal" enforcement by ICE somehow sounds *Nazi*. Even those congressmen (most often Republicans) who want more internal enforcement rarely call it that—it is almost always referred to as "border security"—even though that is not what ICE does. Really, the only somewhat bipartisan agreement is for sanctioning large employers who knowingly hire large numbers of illegal immigrants at abusive wages, and for a national requirement for E-Verify—eventually, maybe. But for many liberal Democrats, the very idea of "temporary" visa smacks of second-class status, indentured servitude, and even slavery. They'd like to have all temporary visas have the possibility of leading to a "pathway to citizenship"—a green card. Obviously, increased enforcement of temporary visa limits and the deportation of visa overstayers, seems unlikely to ever be popular. Without enforcement however, the temporary visa may very well become the biggest source of illegal immigrants.

It is little wonder that illegal immigrants believe the advocates who tell them that they have a "right" to come in, live, work, and stay for a lifetime in the United States without any legal status at all. It's no wonder that confusion is rising over just what immigration is all about.

INCREASING CONFUSION ABOUT IMMIGRATION

A Civil Right?

Several times in 2007 and 2008, congressional journalists (including me) watched Ted Kennedy pound his Senate desk in passion, declaring that "immigration is the next big civil right."

He was wrong, of course, immigration is not a civil right, and certainly it is not a civil right for a foreign national to enter, stay, and work in any country illegally. But over the past 10 years, increasingly the vocabulary of many advocates for comprehensive immigration reform has taken on the rhetoric of civil rights.

There was a civil rights implication almost from the beginning of the INA in 1965. The repeal of the 1924 comprehensive bill was clear in an era of civil rights when that law was based on clear discrimination and preferences based on national origin. But there was more, as Otis Graham describes it. Immigration became a "safe" issue in civil rights:

> As supporters and lobbyists from religious and ethnic organizations from Northern and Midwestern urban states coalesced around the Johnson Ted Kennedy INA, they were joined by business leaders and organizations including Western "big agriculture"—especially the mega farms of California's central valley. Sympathetic to these lobbying groups with a reasonably direct stake were mostly liberals, for whom immigration reform had surfaced as a smaller theater of the Civil Rights Movement and one that did not involve the dangers of marching in Mississippi. The INA was supported enthusiastically by all those who had also supported civil rights legislation and saw immigration based on national origin as discriminatory and hence against civil rights. "No Congressman wanted to risk being seen as 'racist' by opposing the Kennedy-managed legislation."[36]

Boston Globe biographers of Senator Ted Kennedy went further. "Kennedy regarded illegal immigrant workers as an exploited minority, reforming the nation's immigration laws was akin to protecting people's civil rights. He said that the INA reflected the nation's changes in attitude toward ethnic minorities.[37]

As the decades pass and the numbers of illegal immigrants continue to rise and the demands for more immigration visas that lead to citizenship become more heated, it is beginning to sound like even the idea of selection of immigrants is discrimination, racist, and against civil rights. Even to designate the status of an immigrant as temporary or illegal is considered to be offensive by advocates and to be avoided. "There is no such thing as an illegal person," is the argument often heard. The rhetoric of many liberal and libertarian advocates demands "rights" for immigrants without distinction.

The problem for liberals about immigration, however, is that it is not only not a civil right, but also that all immigrants are not equal. Civil rights are rights belonging to an individual by virtue of citizenship.

Immigrants by definition are not citizens. The basic right of citizenship—to vote—is not allowed for immigrants (with a few controversial exceptions where a local jurisdiction allows permanent legal residents to cast ballots in local elections). But throughout the United States, federal law makes it a felony for a noncitizen to vote in a national election.

The true cold fact is that ardent liberals in particular have an almost unsolvable ideological problem with immigration, according to Boston University Professor Alan Wolfe in his book *The Future of Liberalism*.[38] Their inherent dilemma is that they not only believe in liberty, but even more importantly, they believe in equality, the equality of all people no matter who. The problem with immigration is that while immigrants are people, they do not all have equal rights—not even equal civil rights in a sovereign nation-state in which they are not a citizen. Immigrants have different rights from citizens under immigration law, and from other immigrants, depending on their immigration status or category:

- Permanent immigrants have almost all the rights of citizens including the open right to work almost anywhere except where there are stringent restrictions for national security clearances; permanent immigrants are subject to deportation for violent felonies mainly.
- Temporary immigrants have many rights, but not all have the right to work or have mobility in their working visas
- Illegal immigrants have very few rights under the law; especially they do not have an inherent right not to be sanctioned for breaking U.S. laws and not to be deported.

But of course these are the laws; and then there is the humanity of immigration. Most illegal immigrants are hard-working, good, family people whom almost everyone knows, meets, associates with in their schools, stores, and restaurants and especially at construction sites and hospitality businesses. They contribute much to our economy, as there are no restrictions for illegal immigrants to run a business, seek work, use and contribute to public facilities and nonprofit organizations. But because they do not have a legal permit to work, it is not unusual for illegal immigrant workers to be paid less than legal immigrants and citizens, and sometimes not at all. Like many American workers, their injuries are not covered by the employers (even though it is a fineable misdemeanor for those employers to knowingly employ an immigrant without a permit).

This is the territory that civil rights activists have stepped into so eagerly. In their enthusiasm to find ever-new areas of discrimination and racism, civil rights advocates have made illegal immigrants a new category of abused American.

Nationality Diversity

Another element of growing political confusion and dispute comes from the very intention of the INA itself—the idea of ending preferences and discrimination on national origins. It is the very essence of the law, to obtain what in modern parlance can be called "nationality diversity."

Throughout the decades, the INA has been lauded for ending discrimination in immigration. Using the parlance of the civil rights movement, one can say that with the INA, Ted Kennedy and the U.S. Congress committed the United States to immigration diversity by nationality when they repealed the National Origins quota act. (In the context of the times it should be remembered that in most European countries of the 1930s and 1940s and beyond, to be Jewish was considered a "nationality." For instance Latvian citizens who were Jewish carried Latvian passports with the nationality stated as "Jewish").

But others point out that while it ended discrimination for some nationalities that had heretofore been limited by quotas (particularly Asians and Africans), it actually increased discrimination for other major nationalities that had not been limited before, including Northern Europeans (English, Northern Irish, Germans, Dutch, Scandinavians, etc.) and Mexicans and Central and South Americans.

President Johnson famously said, "We ought never to ask 'in what country were you born?'" in the new immigration and nationality act.[39] But still, nationality preference is a tricky thing.

For one thing it has always been the case that many more immigrants from certain countries (Mexico, India, the Philippines come immediately to mind) want to come into the United States more than others (e.g., from Denmark). How could the criteria be "no preferences" and "first-come, first-serve" and yet not allow immigration to be dominated by immigrants from a few nation-states, especially Mexico, from where so many immigrants could cross illegally into the United States with impunity?

There had to be established a system of equality between nationalities; it was officially established around 1975 and is referred to as the "7 percent rule" by the few immigration specialists who know of it. Most immigrant advocates and congressmen do not know of it and call the waiting list proof that there is a quota.

The 7 Percent Rule

The number of green cards given out to any one specific country has always been restricted and fought over. In 1965, it was around 170,000; by the 2000s, more than one million green cards are given out annually.

But in trying to be inclusive and fair and true to the spirit of the 1965 Immigration and Nationality Act that made every nationality equal and gave a preference to family unification, a percentage system was developed. No more than 7 percent of the total number of green cards given out every year were to go to one nationality. The formula gets complicated from there. According to Michael Hoefer, DHS Director of the Office of Immigration Statistics, here was the breakdown as he found it in 2007:

- 226,000 minimum number of employment-based green cards given out;
- no more than 25,620 green cards granted to family members of employ-ment-based immigrants from *any* one country;
- dependents limited to 7,320 or about 2 percent of the total;
- completed applications are counted in the order received on a first come, first serve basis;
- once a country's numerical limit has been reached, any further completed applicants received from citizens of that country will be put on a wait list in order of receipt.

This is not a well-known fact among congressmen. Most advocates spin the fact that there are waiting lists as proof that there are quotas, even at a House hearing on June 6, 2007, that confirmed the above numbers.[40]

The problem is of course that some countries (like Ireland and Mexico) feel they have been placed under a quota, a numerical limitation that they did not have before. Mexicans particularly feel they should be an exception since they are a neighbor and have a historical precedent of coming and going over the border without restriction for centuries.

And then there is Cuba.

The Cuba Exception

In 1966, Congress had to face the issue of migration of Cuban citizens from the nearby Communist regime. The question had been laid aside in order to pass the 1965 INA. But there were strong demands that Cuban refugees should have a special exception in the new immigration system of no nationality preference.

Since 1966, "Cubans have been the most privileged immigrants in the United States all compliments of the Cuban Adjustment Act (CAA), passed just one year after Congress repealed the national origins preference quotas act of 1964 in favor of the INA," a *New York Times* op-ed, "Why Are Cubans So Special?," proclaimed on January 31, 2015.[41] It's a fast track to permanent residency—a green card—for any Cuban national who can make it physically into the United States, no matter how.

Under the CAA, Cubans receive unique and highly favorable treatment, including granting of permanent residency a year after arrival, as well as being eligible for government benefits, such as Medicaid, supplemental social security income, child care, and disability. It was passed in 1966 to adjust the status of some 300,000 Cubans who found themselves in legal limbo after fleeing Cuba's socialist revolution of 1959. "No other foreign nationals enjoy these benefits except for the few who are granted political asylum," according to a Reuters article by David Adams and Tom Brown, "Cuban Perks under Scrutiny."[42]

In 1995, the CAA was revised to specify that the physical presence had to be on dry land—just one toe, one "dry foot"—not in or on water or "wet foot."

These days an average of about 36,000–40,000 Cubans arrive each year. Many are selected by a visa lottery, others come under a family reunification program, and there are a handful of political asylum cases. Roughly 10,000 arrive without visas each year, smuggled by boat or via the border with Mexico.

Cuba has protested the policy for years, claiming that it causes brain drain in the country. Civil rights advocates in the United States claim the policy was initiated due to a class and race preference. During the first two decades of the policy in the 1960s and 1970s it was mainly Cuban businessmen and entrepreneurs who left; "they were large white, educated and middle or upper class," write Bardach in the *New York Times*.[43] But consequent waves of Cuban immigrants were poor—including the elderly and supposedly convicted felons released from Cuban prisons and forced to emigrate. That is when the dry-foot/wet-foot policy was initiated.

The CAA raises a perennial question about the INA and a ban on immigration policy based on preferred national origins. If Cubans get special preference, then why not other nationalities—especially Mexican, a poor neighbor whose workers, particularly agriculture workers, have been valued in the United States and whose national heritage makes up a large percentage of the population in the Southwest.

The only answer is that such preferences need to be fully debated and legislated in Congress.

Nationality Clustering

It is unquestionably natural for first generation immigrants to cluster in nationality groups when they first come, raising their babies and toddlers in the homeland culture and language. This eases the adjustment for new immigrants of that nationality to settle. It's also encourages other immigrants to come from that nationality—legally and illegally.

Often nationality groups will cluster around common jobs where they will help each other get the job, speak the language on the job, sometimes end up dominating that profession, making it uncomfortable for immigrants from other nationalities and even Americans to work there. Throughout the nation and in individual cities, one sees this clearly. Examples abound in Washington, D.C., where

- Today almost every construction trade like carpentry, painting, dry wall, roofing, brick, and tile laying that in the 1990s were almost all done by African Americans and provided a ladder to the middle class for them and their families, are now nominated by Latin Americans. (In D.C., especially those from El Salvador, hard-working crews of skilled compatriots talk, laugh, and even sing in Spanish as they work.)
- It's hard to find a taxi not driven by an Ethiopian man or a fine hotel (Four Seasons, for instance) without cheerful, polite, friendly, and seemingly always smiling Ethiopian and Eritrean and other African women in the service areas.
- Nail salons are almost always owned and staffed with young non-English-speaking Asian men and women—from Vietnam, Thailand, Korea in particular. Even the high-end hair salon next to the Four Seasons is owned, and staffed mainly with hair stylist professionals from Turkey.
- Chinese students dominate university graduate programs in STEM fields (science, technology, engineering, and math) as well as many of the research labs, classes, and postdoc fellowships at NIH (where purportedly some 80 percent of the researchers are foreign scholars on temporary, six-year maximum J visas).
- Former students from India and their children run IT departments in universities and the government, including for the first term, the brilliant Aneesh Chopa, the "first Chief Technology Office of the U.S. government

instituted" by the Obama White House (and author of *Innovative State: How New Technologies Can Transform Government*).[44]

Throughout the United States there are famous immigrant neighborhoods where anyone from that nationality could be at home: Chinese in San Francisco; Italians in New Orleans and Baltimore; Norwegians in Minnesota, and now Somalians. Every community has its proud immigrant "old towns" that are still referred to the original nationality even though that nationality is long gone (Chinatown in Washington, D.C., comes to mind). But there is no question that it is perfectly natural for the first generation of any immigrant population to cluster.

All of these examples of productive clusters of immigrant nationalities bring into question the whole idea of doing away with national preferences. Doesn't our splendid history of assimilation (or if you will, the more politically correct term: *integration*) make clustering only a first-generation immigrant problem? Should there be any concern about nationality diversity when it comes to some occupations? Will it matter in the end that a high proportion of computer technicians are Indian; or scientists, Chinese; or construction workers, Latino? The apex of this confusion is the situation with Mexican nationals in the United States.

Mexicans are the largest nationality comprising Hispanic-heritage residents in the United States; they make up the majority in more than a dozen states and this number is increasing every year. They stand apart in most Latino communities, especially in the Southwest, by their number and closeness of their neighborhoods often made up of multiple generations from the same village. It is understandable that they dominate given the proximity of Mexico geographically and historically. The question becomes, should they be given special immigration status as a close and economically struggling neighbor with a population that is increasingly intermingled in the American identity? Should nationality diversity be put aside especially for Mexican nationals?

SEGUE TO THE TWENTY-FIRST CENTURY

It is obvious by seeing the many impacts of the "Immigration and Nationality Act of 1965 and its many additions and addendums, that this law in effect would become the nation's most sweeping immigration law, forever changing America's cultural fabric and broadening its promise," concludes Mark Updegrove of the LBJ Library in Austin. It was a result of Johnson's success with the 89th Congress—which he "affectionately referred to as 'the fabulous Eighty-Ninth.'" Of the 115 bills Johnson sent to the Hill in 1965 and 1966, 89 became law. It was a "prodigious record for its sheer volume and success ratio [over 77 percent] but more for the magnitude of change the laws delivered."[45]

Republicans who were shaken by LBJ's crushing defeat of conservative Barry Goldwater in 1964 participated in passing most of his Great Society bills. There was in the land a feeling among the public and legislators, that the American people had given Johnson a mandate to pass legislation "dedicated to the liberal idea that government had an obligation to ensure a decent life and equal opportunity for all its citizens . . . especially including African Americans," wrote a *Washington Post* Book World editor Wendy Smith in a book review of Zelizer's book *The Fierce Urgency*.[46]

That sentiment held despite the significant losses Democrats experienced in the midterm election of 1966 and their losing the White House to Republicans in 1968. "You could argue that liberalism has been on the defensive ever since," writes Smith.[47]

Even so, 50 years later, many if not of all the safety networks and programs of the Great Society endure. "So embedded are Great Society's policies and politics in the nation's fabric that many citizens cannot conceive of life without them,"[48]

Certainly that is true of the broad principles of diversity and ever-expanding beneficiaries of the INA—the law that changed the face of America. But over time, a political environment can change due to dramatic and far-reaching events. Fifty years later, the future of the Immigration and Nationality Act and its precepts are very much in contention in twenty-first century America.

Chapter Five

Reforming the INA in the Twenty-First Century

An essay appearing in the *Washington Post* in mid-January 2015 during the convening of the new 114th Republican-dominated Congress describes well the broad context in which the issue of immigration reform falls today in the twenty-first century:

> There may be some cosmic historical cyclicality revealed this year in the fact that, half a century ago, no event was more consequential than the convening of the 89th Congress in which one party (in 1965 the Democrats, in 2015 the Republicans) enjoyed huge majorities in both houses. The "fabulous (Democratic-dominated) 89th" went on to pass a legacy of transformative and beneficial policies that ironically defines today's Republican leaders' agenda—and problems.
>
> Evidence mounts that the great acts of 1965 now yield diminishing returns or, in some cases, have actually turned counterproductive. . . . Most Americans do not want a radical change of their 1965 benefits, but do feel "a thoroughgoing reform of our 1965 vintage government is both necessary and desirable. The goal should be a modern efficient sustainable government . . . that works through bipartisan compromise. That means overcoming not only demands that have made the Republican mainstream hostage to their right wing, but also demands that have silenced mainstream Democrats, demands made by their left wing who tend to demonize even modest tweaks to the Great Society.
>
> "The dilemma of 2015 legislators," according to Charles Lane, a *Washington Post* editor and columnist, is that "too much government is confined by 1965 ambitions."[1]

That describes the INA and immigration reform today. It seems they have become confined by 1965 zeal. In 2015, 50 years after the passage of the law that changed the face of America, immigration reform has suddenly become one of the hottest political issues of the times in the media and the political arena. But the rhetoric is that of 1965 civil rights: "a fight for justice," "the right thing to do," "pro and anti" forces of good and evil. By February 2015, after the Democrats lost the Senate to the Republicans in the midterm election, the immigration "debate" had morphed into a gotcha-politics battle, driven by advocates from both parties using bullying, moralistic, and scare oratory that is repeated, distributed, fanned, and hyped without question and only too eagerly by a growing, voracious, commercialized, 24-hour, increasingly online, unedited, unvetted news media.

Yet no "fierce urgency" underlies comprehensive immigration reform as did the civil rights movement in 1965. There are no massive, broad-based, public marches of citizens demanding that immigration laws be changed immediately to bring in tens of thousands more IT workers and engineers, and to legalize all illegal immigrants. As will be seen in this chapter, the idea that there exists a monolithic, perennially liberal, Democratic, Latino voting bloc whose trigger is blanket amnesty is only the expected exaggerations of political activists. The "Latino voting bloc" is the product of never-ending political election-season hyperbole that is repeated constantly without question or balance even by many senior, well-known, media anchors, panelists, and newspaper editorial writers, who seem to be stuck in the twentieth century when it comes to immigration.

The need to update the INA of 1965 is clear and necessary. Times have changed. The many drivers of immigration reform today are vibrant, complicated, and multilayered. But two things are certain:

1. The vast majority of Americans like and want immigrants. They relate to them as they do to their own family immigration histories.
2. But they also want immigration policy to reflect the needs of America today and the laws governing it. They know immigration laws can and will change, and that that process takes (and should take) a lot of time, discussion, and compromises. Most certainly the majority of American citizens want that debate to be civil, even if passionate. They want the decisions to be made in a bipartisan manner. And until the laws are changed, the laws that exist have to be honored and enforced. Americans want their government to work within the rule of law.

THE DRIVERS FOR REFORM OF THE INA

Key Social Movements

In November of 2014, an epic movie *Selma* was previewed at the White House and hit the movie theaters. Fifty years after the march that propelled the civil rights movement, the movie made the story come alive again. It became the media buzz of the month. "Selma showed that . . . Martin Luther King Jr. and the civil rights movement must be seen not as 'dreamers' but as the motor force for change that transformed America. To make America better, look to movements, not presidents, people in motion, not legislators in session," wrote the liberal Democratic editor and publisher of *The Nation* magazine.[2]

In 1965, public officials were galvanized to support the most liberal legislation of our time because of public demand for civil rights. It started as a movement for justice for African Americans who faced harsh discrimination in the South because of the Jim Crow laws. But the movement quickly came to include other groups facing discrimination—including children, the poor, and immigrants—who were being discriminated against by the 1924 National Origins Law.

The success of the civil rights movement created historic victories for President Johnson's Great Society agenda including the passage of the Immigration and Nationality Act. Even more, the verve and expansion of the movements for justice created a political environment of can-do optimism among Americans for the next four decades. Most young people growing up in that half of the twentieth century, came to believe fervently that outrageous injustices could be challenged and won, and that progressive government could fix nearly everything.

From the beginning of the twenty-first century, however, the mood has increasingly become one of doubt, fear, and anxiety. The century started out on the very first minute in an atmosphere of almost hysterical anxiousness. Remember Y2K? No one was sure that computers across the world could handle the change of dates from 1999 to 2000, and hence the entire operational systems of the world might crash at the moment of the new millennium. IT managers across the globe spent midnight of New Years Eve in their offices anxiously watching the computer networks of their employers, not sure what they would do if there was a meltdown. The fear of the moment passed without a hitch, but the anxious feeling of vulnerability and fear of change remained. The theme of the century had begun.

The presidential elections of 2000 reflected that doubt and unease. The furious disputes and controversies of the election battle between Al Gore and George W. Bush culminated in November with hanging chads and double-voter recounts. It ended suddenly, dramatically, breathtakingly with the historic ruling by the Supreme Court *Gore v. United States* that George W. Bush had won the election. Four years later Bush shocked Democrats again by handily winning reelection despite the furious liberal public outrage over the Iraq war and the fruitless search for WMDs, and without the help of hanging chads or SCOTUS. Also (maybe even more shocking to progressive Democrats) the younger President Bush accomplished what his father couldn't; he won a second term with the support of a high percentage of Hispanic voters.

Perhaps the one good outcome that advocates for comprehensive immigration reform hoped for from the 2000 and 2004 elections was that President Bush—a strong supporter of comprehensive immigration reform—would pass a bill. He not only promised it would be his top priority the first year of his presidency, but he began immediately to lay the groundwork for it. Mexican President Fox was the first foreign government leader he invited for an official visit to the United States (in the past, that honor usually went to the British or Canadian leader). On May 5, 2000, he even hosted the first-ever Cinco de Mayo celebration to be held at the White House. Some people were calling him our "first Latino president" and comprehensive immigration reform seemed a sure thing.

But then 9/11 happened. Republican congressional leaders turned against immigration reform in 2006 and 2007. Advocates could only wait until 2008 and presumably the next Democratic president to get it done.

That election turned out to be historic as well. Americans voted for the first African American heritage president of the United States, Barack Obama, the son of a foreign student from Kenya and the adopted son of an Indonesian stepfather—surely someone who knew immigration issues personally.

So it was that two dramatic events, rather than movements, took place in the first decade of the twenty-first century that changed the way immigration and immigration reform are perceived and argued today.

1. On September 11, 2001, foreign terrorists attacked the World Trade Center in New York City and the Pentagon in Washington, D.C., killing over 3,000 people. It immediately changed the focus of immigration into a national security issue and resulted in the establishment of an entirely new bureaucracy to enforce immigration laws on the borders and in the interior of the country: the Department of Homeland Security (DHS).
2. In November 2008, Americans by a large margin, elected the first black president of the United States, just months before Ted Kennedy the last liberal lion of the Senate, passed away. For many Americans it was a culminating point, one could say the peak, of a civil rights era focused on ending centuries-long discrimination against African Americans. It also was the visible turning point for the civil rights movement, converting it to a broader focus where emerging identity groups such as illegal immigrants suddenly were framing their issues of discrimination under the ever-broadening umbrella of civil rights.

The other drivers of immigration were changing significantly as well from the earliest days of the twenty-first century.

Economic

Briefly, in the 50 years since the passage of the Immigration and Nationality Act of 1965, the United States experienced waves of prosperity and economic crisis and then a long recession starting in 2007. By 2012, the country had begun a gradual financial recovery, albeit with very slow job growth—a so-called "jobless recovery." Stagnant middle-class wages and devastating, bursting, financial asset bubbles, have kept the majority of Americans in a low-consumer mood. Continual commercial globalization has brought about stunning income growth in the top sector of society (the so-called 1 percent).

At the same time, there is a rising awareness and unwillingness to accept passively that "globalization does have some losers." Anger is rising about income inequality that is growing to levels of the 1920s Gilded Age. The top economic worries of most adult Americans are whether or not good middle-class jobs and an American Dream, middle-class lifestyle will be available in the future for their children and grandchildren. Many worry about losing their own jobs or being able to find a new one or a better one. In 2014, the unemployment rate was decreasing but still worrisome, especially for African Americans

> While jobs have been created in droves since the recession has ended, many of those positions were low-wage or part-time positions. Most affected by the dearth of full-time, higher paying positions have been Blacks and Latinos.
> However, it appears that even Latinos are doing better than Blacks in this current economic upswing. According to the [National Urban League's 38th annual "State Of Black America"] report's numbers, 13.1 percent of African Americans are unemployed compared alongside 6.5 percent of whites and 9.1 percent of Latinos.[3]

The majority of Hispanic voters, like most middle-class whites, are worried about getting better jobs and about access to a good quality education for their children, health care for their families, and eventually enough retirement income to not be dependent on their children. Immigration reform is not the top issue of any of these American voters.

It is clear that decades-long, uncertain job and wage growth inevitably will affect the general public's attitudes about immigration. Most Americans want to believe that immigrants do not displace Americans in their jobs, but instead get jobs based on their hard work and entrepreneurship. Most Americans believe and hope that innovative immigrants will open up new working opportunities for everyone. Americans want that all employees be paid fairly based on their work no matter what their gender, race, or immigration status. They want everyone in America to not only work to make a better life for themselves and their own families, but also to enrich the nation's culture and economy.

But as the numbers of immigrants competing for jobs rise exponentially and the number of jobs decrease; as immigration laws are increasingly not enforced and millions of illegal immigrants willing to work for less than Americans are legalized and given job permits to take better jobs; and as advocates for illegal immigrants increasingly demand that they be given the full benefits that citizens enjoy based on emotional appeal alone, that belief in the unquestioned benefit of immigration is beginning to change. In 2015, it can be seen that public concern is growing about the potential negative impact of unregulated immigration on job opportunities for Americans and on community resources, both short term and long term. They worry about the credibility of the rule of law.

Demographics

In general, population growth has been slowing in the United States in the new century. Census data shows that in 2013, an aging baby population and slower immigration rates, combined for a nearly stagnant U.S. population growth that year. Also in 2013, the total number of residents increased at the slowest pace since the Great Depression. Growth for the 12 months ending July 1, 2013, was 0.71 percent, or just under 2.3 million people—the slowest since 1937, according to Brookings Institution demographer William Frey, who called this year's growth "underwhelming." In 2011–2012, the U.S. population grew at a slightly higher 0.75 percent rate. [4]

Hispanic and Asian heritage populations grew in the first 15 years of the twenty-first century to become the dominant "minority"—especially in once-traditional black communities and cities. Latino growth derived increasingly from the native born, however, not from immigration. In 2009, the growth rate of the Asian population in the United States overtook Latinos as the fastest-growing demographic in the country. PEW Research Center studies show that both demographics are intermarrying especially with each other and whites. [5]

Boomers (approximately 50–68 years old) are reaching retirement age and make up 16 percent of the population. They are retiring "kind-of sort-of," although AARP statistics show that over 20 percent of an American retiree's income is earned. Boomers are staying on the job longer or are retraining and moving into "second chance" jobs, often doing things like teaching, which they may have always wanted to do before but couldn't afford to, but also opening up businesses to make money. Many are "moving down" when they become "empty nesters"—increasingly choosing to move to smaller residences in active cities and university towns rather than gated golf communities. That is, if their adult children haven't moved back before they sell the family home.

The boomers' kids—mostly "millennials" approximately 18 to 33 years old—are proving to be a unique demographic. They are in many ways extremely different from today's older generations and very different from how their parents were when they were the millennials' age. In some ways, they are the kind of kids the generation of the 1960s had hoped they would have: extremely diverse, tolerant, family oriented, and not highly consumer oriented (in the McMansion sense). Maybe they're an example of "be careful what you wish for"!

The Millennial Generation

This new generation is forging a distinctive path into adulthood. While demographers may disagree slightly on the age range, millennials are generally young adults who graduated from high school and entered adulthood around the turn of the century—hence "millennials." In general, they are relatively unattached to organized politics and religion, linked by social media, burdened by college debt even without degrees, distrustful of large organizations including government and big educational institutions, in no rush to marry—and are surprisingly happy and rather optimistic about the future. They are also America's most racially diverse-everything generation.

The Pew Research Center surveys show that half of millennials (50 percent) now describe themselves as political independents and about three in ten (29 percent) say they are not affiliated with any religion. These are at or near the highest levels of political and religious disaffiliation recorded for any generation in the quarter century that the Pew Research Center has been polling on these topics.[6]

Other studies of millennials agree. One by pollster John Zogby in his book *First Globals: Understanding, Managing, & Unleashing the Potential of Our Millennial Generation*[7] shows that they have low expectations for their futures and especially of any help from any large organizations including federal and state governments, large universities, mega churches, and nationalized NGOs (Non-Governmental Organizations or charity groups) with mega staffs making mega bucks.

In general, millennials put family relationships above professional ones. They love their families including their social-media friend-families. It is truly amazing for boomers and the silent generation before them to hear millennials say sincerely how much they like their parents, like to hang out with them (not just on their couches), and consider them to be among their best friends. Many live at home after college or the military, and while most intend someday, in their mid-to-late-30s or so, to have their own families and homes, they are not anxious about marrying or purchasing their own home or condo on a mortgage. According to Zogby, many millennial professional couples will live separately in different cities, even different countries (often exotic ones) at some time during their relationships, even when they have children.

Millennials don't tend to be obsessed about possessions—at least not of the McMansion variety. They don't expect to have long-term jobs or to get social security or retirement after decades of working at a wide variety of jobs and professions. They don't seem to be worried about what used to be called "insecurity" (or still is in insurance and stock broker ads); they just accept that that is the way it is going to be. They do want to work, like to work hard and be useful. But they want jobs that "do good" rather than "are good" (aka high paying). They'll work 24/7/365 at something they love but will quit if it isn't good any more—and go back and live with mom and dad. Many would rather work for themselves or with a few friends in a "start-up" enterprise using money collected through crowdsourcing or the like. Some boomers call that lazy . . . (such was the accusation on the cover of a *Time* magazine) but some old hippies-turned-yuppies might be envious.[8]

This new 20-something generation is amazingly (though one shouldn't be surprised) tolerant of everything. They and their friends and families are increasingly multicultural, multinational, multiracial, multilingual, multireligious, multisexual, multi-everything. They are therefore generally very flexible. They shrug their shoulders a lot. Maybe a good alternative name for them is the "whatever" generation. But one thing is for sure: millennials not only "*get*" diversity, *they are* diversity in all its living forms. Perhaps that is why they are essentially apolitical and secular and earth conscious. They are so twenty-first century!

Millennials take population mobility and immigration for granted (although according to UN statistics only 3.2 percent of the world population lived outside of their home country in 2013. Some 232 million people out of a total world population of over seven billion people live abroad according to an article in the *Daily Mail* in April 2014.[9] In the United States, close to 20 percent of millennials now are of Hispanic heritage and that number is growing. It is interesting to note that many of the characteristics of millennials are actually those of Latinos—close to their families, multinational, not wildly ambitious for Wall Street jobs, and so forth. I expand on this idea in my 2014 feature article in *The Hispanic Outlook*, "Are Hispanic Millennials Leading Their Generation?"[10]

The diversifying of America's demographics, is largely driven by immigration. But it's not just the first generation of immigrants from the twentieth century that did it, but also the second and third who, like President Obama, are products of intermarriages between immigrants from every nation, race, faith, and creed in the world. The demographics of today reflect the principles imbedded in the Immigration and Nationality Act of 1965 as they play out in the twenty-first century. The monocultural immigrant "old town" enclaves of multigenerational immigrant families, are now so twentieth century. Today's twenty-first-century immigrants and their children are mobile, diverse, and tied in to the new technology.

Technology

The past 50 years has seen technological changes that have touched and changed the lives of people in all but the most remote villages of the world. All of these changes have affected immigrants and immigration to some extent, but some have had a special impact on immigration. In the centuries that immigrants came to the United States, the expectation was that they were leaving their homelands probably forever, that they would probably have little communication with their families in the homelands and be able to see them just rarely if ever again. But the technology of the past 50 years, especially of the twenty-first century, has truly changed that expectation, that consequence of centuries of immigration.

Space

Technology has impacted especially air transportation through the once-active space program NASA. The National Aeronautics and Space Administration was created on October 1, 1958, this is such general information available through various resources on the web that provide for research into the problems of *Sputnik 1* and to address a technology gap crisis that had become part of the Cold War. In the next 50 years it certainly accomplished its mission with the following :

- The first manned flights produced Project Gemini (1965–1966).
- The Apollo program, despite the tragic loss of the *Apollo 1* crew, achieved Kennedy's goal by landing the first astronauts on the moon with the Apollo 11 mission in 1969.
- With détente, a time of relatively improved Cold War relations between the United States and the Soviets, the two superpowers developed a cooperative space mission: the Apollo–Soyuz Test Project.[11] This 1975 joint mission was the last manned space flight for the United States.
- The Space Shuttle flights that have been described as the symbolic end of the "space race" occurred in 1981.[12]

The NASA budget peaked in 1966 at $43,554 million. It has been going down ever since. In 2014, the NASA budget was $17,646 million; the requested budget for 2015 is $17,460 million, with commercial flight, cooperative partnerships budgeted to take $848 million of that.

"The commercial flight budget for 2015 includes buying launches from commercial companies like SpaceX, and I'm all for that," writes Slate's Phil Plait. "These types of capabilities may be better handled by private companies that can do so more cheaply, motivated by NASA funding."[13]

The Space Race sparked unprecedented increases in spending on education and pure research. That accelerated scientific advancements and led to beneficial spin-off technologies in every field, but most especially air transport and communication systems, both of which hugely facilitated the mobility of immigrants. It also cemented international cooperation between scientists and engineers throughout the world.

Social Media

In the 1950s, a telephone call abroad was an expensive and often hectic process. Like many Americans, I recall my mother-in-law in Germany spending precious minutes of the occasional international call with her son in California first having to be assured that everyone was OK "since why would you be calling if it wasn't an emergency?" and then urging her son to hang up quickly because it was "costing too much." The Internet has completely changed that dynamic, particularly for immigrants with extended families overseas. A brief history of the Internet puts this significant change of the past 50 years into perspective.

The earliest forms of the Internet, such as CompuServe, were developed in the 1960s but were not widely known or used. It can be said that a particular world elite became aware en masse of the wondrous reality of instant and personal long distance and wireless communication that is e-mail at a rather unexpected place: during the 1984 Los Angeles Olympic Games. Every one of the over 10,000-person badged staff, athletes, and officials were given an e-mail address that they could use on the thousands of computers dispersed throughout the three Olympic villages (at USC, UCLA, and UCSB) and numerous Olympic sports venues and hospitality centers. Long lines at each station proved that the computer e-mail stations were vastly more popular with Olympic athletes and their coaches than the video games and TVs placed about. I was a director of the UCSB Olympic Village in charge of the National Olympic Committee relations department; I saw how e-mail and the ease of communicating by Internet was introduced to usually broad and influential, popular, world elites—the best athletes and coaches of every nation in the world. (Note: while all the nations of the Soviet Union except Romania boycotted the Olympic Games in the summer of 1984, all of their delegations and many of their athletes had made several visits to the Los Angeles Olympic Organizing Commitee in the years preceding the games, including to practice games in the summer of 1983; many told me that their most exciting training experience was learning how to use their e-mail.)

Public Internet relay chats, or IRCs, were first used in 1988 and continued to be popular well into the 1990s.

In 1999, the first blogging sites became popular, creating a social media sensation that's still popular today. After the invention of blogging, social media began to explode in popularity. Sites like MySpace and LinkedIn gained prominence in the early 2000s, and sites like Photobucket and Flickr facilitated online photo sharing. YouTube came out in 2005, creating an entirely new way for people to communicate and share with each other across great distances.

By 2006, Facebook and Twitter both became available to users throughout the world. These sites remain some of the most popular social networks on the Internet. Other sites like Tumblr, Spotify, Foursquare, and Pinterest began popping up to fill specific social networking niches . . . [creating] an environment where users can reach the maximum number of people without sacrificing the intimacy of person-to-person communication. [14]

By the time of this publication, several of the above named sites could well be obsolete and new ones taken their place.

SKYPE

But by far the most significant technology for most immigrants and their families in the United States and abroad, besides the Internet, is SKYPE, a computer (and now mobile devises) international telecommunications system that was first released in August 2003. It was developed initially by six young European techies (a Dane, a Swede, and four Estonians) who literally started it and ran it for years out of home offices mainly in Tallinn, Estonia. It went through many derivations and for years the founders had trouble finding start-up and operational funds. There were serious issues about privacy: at first too much (so there were concerns that criminals could use it easily without a trace); and eventually, too little (so that individual calls could be traced and hacked too easily). The fantastic can't-make-this-stuff-up true story of the development of Skype is dramatically told in the article: "How Can They Be So Good?: The Strange Story of Skype," by Toivo Taenavsuu. [15]

Eventually, Microsoft bought SKYPE for $8.5 billion, and by 2014, 40 percent of international calls were made on SKYPE— that's over 214 billion minutes! On January 21, 2013, it was recorded that more than 50 million SKYPE users were online at one time, many if not most of them using the visual capability that allows them to see each other as they talk. Grandparents read bedtime stories to their grandchildren on SKYPE, saw their first steps, a wedding or a funeral or a baptism or a bris or a *quincinera*. Immigrants can be involved with their families' daily and ceremonial lives from long distance without being there physically.

The growing ease of international transportation thanks to space research and the ever-increasingly widespread use of Internet and SKYPE technology bring immigrant families together without having to travel or to immigrate. It challenges the need for an immigration policy with a priority for green cards on unification of the extended family, as is imbedded in the 50-year-old INA .

Politics

The environment of partisan politics, the big issues and who the main interest groups for those issues are, also of course changed greatly in the 50 years since the "fabulous 89th" liberal Congress and the passage of the 1965 immigration act that changed the face of America. Just as the changing demographics of America were driven by the new economics of transportation and communication, so were the politics of immigration. Old alliances and evolving interest groups combined into new political partners and adversaries, a new political dynamics of immigration.

As noted above, the new century began with the historic dispute over the presidency that ended up in the Supreme Court. But it is also a tribute to the American polity that once the decision had been rendered, the country settled into it peacefully. After 9/11 the country was unified as only a war caused by an attack can do—until President Bush decided to invade Iraq in a fruitless search for WMDs (weapons of mass destruction). The partisan divide remained fierce through the 2004 election, but then a strange thing happened. The liberal icon of the Democratic Party, the Lion of the Senate, the Northeast's scion Ted Kennedy, came together with President Bush and former POW and senior Senator John McCain of Arizona, the Southwest, to develop a comprehensive immigration bill. There was sympathy on both sides of the aisle in the House and in the Senate.

In truth, the political parties are split over immigration reform, despite how the press tries to depict them as "two sides"—particularly either "pro-immigrant" Democrat or "anti-immigrant" Republican. In fact, immigration reform doesn't split politically along a horizontal line between liberal left and conservative right. That doesn't explain the Kennedy/Bush partnership. That doesn't explain why many Republicans want what Democrats want: to expand the number of new immigrant workers and to legalize the millions working and living in the country illegally. That doesn't explain support by other Democrats and Republicans for increased immigration enforcement and even limiting the total number of new immigrants.

It's more realistic to picture immigration reform as a vertical issue that cuts the middle of the horizontal left/right line. Take the two ends of that line and bring them down together making a horseshoe with an open end. At the bottom of the horseshoe are the civil libertarians on the left (Kennedy) and the corporate libertarians on the right (President Bush). Both wanted deregulation of immigrants but for different reasons—Kennedy on the left for civil humanitarian reasons to give refuge to the poor of the world; Bush on the right to have unregulated labor,the best and cheapest possible. At the top of the horseshoe are the "Economic Nationalists"—Americans who wanted to control immigration so it did not negatively impact the country. On the top left are many conservative Democratic Blue Dogs, highly concerned about the cost of immigrants on community resources, especially hospitals and schools; also on the left are some environmentalists, most of them former Zero Population Growth members who feel increased population in the United States, mainly due to immigration, is bad for the environment. On the right are Republican "American Firsters" if you will, concerned that strict enforcement of immigration laws will ensure that unregulated waves of immigrants do not overwhelm job, educational, and other opportunities for Americans.

These splits are easy to hear in the arguments about immigration reform made by various interest groups and politicians at hearings and panel discussions in think tanks and semipublic conclaves that reflect their beliefs. But the press doesn't usually cover them.

The press also generally misses the real battle going on in Congress between the Democrats and the Republicans. It's not over whether or not there should be immigration reform. Everyone seems to agree that "our present immigration system is broken." The real battle is *how* it should be "reformed." Options include fixing basic assumptions to favor specific interest groups (Latinos? High-skilled workers?); throw it out and start completely anew? Update pieces of it? Should it be done Ted Kennedy–style with bipartisan deals and compromises, or through the hardball, winner-take-all politics of filibuster threats and executive actions? Should it be done comprehensively in a big omnibus bill or should it be done in pieces—piecemeal?

The balance of power between the parties in Congress and the White House and how that has affected the passage of immigration bills is another element of politics to consider. Over the course of 50 years, the House and Senate and the balance of power between them and the White House has changed continuously. There have only been a few years when the president and both chambers of Congress were held by the same party. Has split control (as it was in 1965 and 1986 when the INA and the amnesty bill passed) actually benefited immigration reform or impeded it (as in 2006 and 2007)?

Democrats

Democrats are sometimes called the "mommy party" by MSNBC pundit Chris Matthews due to their conciliatory attitude toward misbehavior and their reluctance to blame or punish an individual for wrongdoing that they mainly see as being caused by societal and environmental factors beyond the "victim"/perpetrator's control. Democrats generally are seen as being compassionate, not punitive—especially toward the poor, children and young adults, minorities, and illegal immigrants. It may surprise some people to learn that Democrats weren't historically like that. It's hard to remember that the Teddy Roosevelt Progressives were Republicans, and that it was the Democratic Party that controlled the South and passed and supported the separatist Jim Crow laws until the Civil Rights Act made them illegal and the feds moved in in the 1960s.

In 1965, after the "fabulous 89th" Congress of strong liberal Democrats with its historic achievements that passed most of President Johnson Great Society legislation, one would think that the Democratic Party would have dominated national politics for the next several decades. After all, most of the Great Society policies like those of the New Deal have endured for well over 50 years. But only two years later, by 1967, the Democrats' and even President Johnson's influence was over. In 1968, Democrats lost the presidency to Richard Nixon, a moderate conservative (compared to Barry Goldwater) Republican.

The election seemed to expose 1965 as more of an aberration. "The pro civil rights coalition which had operated so effectively in previous years— Republican and Northern liberal Democrat, some Southern religious Democrats, civil rights, labor and liberal church groups—fell apart in 1966," according to the *Congressional Quarterly*.[16] That coalition is similar to what Democrats have tried to assemble to pass comprehensive immigration reform.

Democrats at the time (1965) had thought that (moderate) Democratic Southerners anxious to remove the taint of racism, would take over the traditional Southern Democratic seats in the House and Senate after the Civil Rights Act had passed. Instead a new generation of conservative Republicans gradually took over the political seats of the South, not only in the House and the Senate, but in state offices as well. The Democrats for the next five decades were committed to the belief that the federal government could and should do more, especially to help the less fortunate. They organized around issues of poverty and inequality. This viewpoint was often labeled "big government," "tax and spend" governing and was constantly at odds with Republican beliefs.

In the dawn of the twenty-first century, however, Democrats seem to have become organized mainly around identity/"minority" group politics. They battle over what the government can do for ever-newly identified groups with compelling stories of unequal treatment and discrimination.

In 2008, the first serious black Democratic presidential candidate won the "identity politics" sweepstakes by beating the first serious Democratic woman presidential candidate, Hillary Clinton. Black delegates for Hillary were called Uncle Toms if they voted for Hillary in the primaries (this was told to me off the record by black delegates from Florida at the contentious Democratic National Committee meeting in Washington, D.C., July 2008, to determine if Florida should be punished for splitting their primary votes between Barack and Hillary). After the success of Barack Obama, the Democratic Party seemed to decide that its future lay in targeting focused, single-message, identity groups.

During the 2012 Democratic nomination, "caucuses" of separate identity groups with specific issues that the Democratic National Committee had decided were their prime single-message voting blocs, met every day. They included: women (universal abortion and equal pay); blacks: (racism and civil rights); Latinos: (immigration reform); gays: (same-sex marriage), and so forth.

In the midterm congressional elections of 2014, the Democratic Party in each state selected *the* target group and issue that strategists decided would tip the election in that state in favor of the Democrats. Comprehensive immigration reform, with the "must have" section granting a pathway to citizenship for all or most of the some 12 million illegal immigrants currently living in the country, was always one of the top focus issues. It was believed that that legalization section was required in order "to win the Latino vote." But the problem with that particular strategy in the 2014 midterm elections was that Hispanic voters comprised less than 3 percent of the total electorate in each of the 12 or so target states that Democrats were fighting to keep from being flipped Republican. In Colorado (the only potential flip state that had close to 8 percent Latino electorate), Democratic senator Mark Udall's campaign decided to focus on winning the "women's vote" as well. He concentrated on abortion rights so exclusively however, that the press began calling him "Mr. Uterus." He lost. As did all the major Democrats who ran on identity-group focus messages. The Senate fell to the Republicans.

Democrats used to be more inclusive and diverse—even in the twenty-first century.

In 2007, the Democratic Blue Dog caucus was almost as big as the Progressive caucus. In fact the Democrats would not have won the House back in 2006 without the Blue Dog Democrats. It was the strategy of Democratic Congressional Campaign chairman Rahm Emanuel that Democrats could win the House by "whistling past Dixie" (a book by that name by Thomas F. Schaller reveals the strategy).[17] The idea was not to worry about losing the South because the Democrats could afford to lose Southern state votes (for which they would have to struggle anyway) by gaining instead the votes of Blue Dog Democrats who lived in the red "mountain states" of the Midwest. They were fiscal conservatives, extremely worried about the debt. Each Blue Dog Congressional Caucus member kept a chart in front of their main office door in the House Office buildings showing the growing debt; the number was raised every day.) Blue Dogs also were socially liberal. The only issue on which mainstream Democrats had to compromise with them was about gun control—Blue Mountain Dogs in the West liked their guns and opposed gun control. So Democrats under the leadership of Rahm Emanuel stopped talking about it from 2006 until the tragedy of Newtown, Connecticut, on December 14, 2012.

But in 2010 the Democrats lost the Blue Dogs and the House of Representatives because Rahm was no longer there to protect them from congressional liberals (known now as Progressives). In 2008, Rahm became Obama's Chief of Staff (before he became mayor of Chicago in 2012). In 2009 during a midnight House session, House Speaker Nancy Pelosi forced the Blue Dogs to vote for the Affordable Care Act (which came to be known as "Obamacare") that most Blue Dogs knew their conservative constituents did not want. The payback came the next year when their voters kicked them out of office and replaced them with Republicans.

Since Obama's reelection in 2012, Democratic leaders became even more nonnegotiable single-issue oriented. Democratic Senate leader Harry Reid's management of the Senate has reflected this. After the Republicans took over the House in 2010 and with a vulnerable Senate, Reid would not allow any bills to come to the floor for a vote that could split his party or might have Democrats speaking up against the positions of the president (such as on trade deals or energy development including the Keystone Pipeline). On those few bills when he allowed a vote, Reid prevented any amendments to be added, even from Democrats. As a result, most Democratic senators— including those from red states—had an almost 100 percent voting-with-the-president track record, a statistic that was well exploited by their Republican opponents in the 2014 midterm elections and one of a number of reasons why so many Democratic senators lost their races.

President Obama also stubbornly promoted nonnegotiable single issues with no compromises, such as "comprehensive" immigration reform. When he didn't get his way, increasingly he chose to go around Congress rather than compromising with them as Johnson would have done. Obama was increasingly making executive actions to get his way.

Democrats say it works; that they won the reelection of 2012 because of the presidential executive order to defer deportation of DREAMers, thus getting a historic percentage of the Latino vote. Single issues, they say, fire up their base. But it also can be said that the Democrats lost the Senate in 2014 because they too narrowly focused on identity groups single issues. In 2014, targeted populations such as Latinos, millennials, and women did not turn out to vote in the total numbers expected and more than expected voted Republican.

In 2015, one has to wonder how far a Democrat is allowed to stray from the core party, liberal narratives and remain a Democrat? Does any Democrat dare mention they may not be for same-sex marriage (such as the many African American and Latino churchgoers who voted in favor of state laws—including in California—that banned it)? What about questioning free abortions or even comprehensive immigration reform; can lifelong Democrats say they question the party stance on these issues and not be drummed out of the party? A 90-year-old Democratic woman's club in Washington, D.C., that for decades opened their biweekly meetings with "This is a place where Democrats *of all points of view* can meet and talk about the issues of the day," since 2009 now usually leaves out the "all points of view" bit.

On immigration reform, the Democrats are obsessively stuck on "comprehensive" immigration reform. Even when pieces are offered in the House and even by Democrats such as a separate AgJOBs Bill or a separate bill for investors, E-Verify and even to legalize DREAMers (or KIDS as the Republicans call them), the Democrats refused to consider it. It has to be comprehensive meaning including the legalization and eventual green cards for millions of illegal immigrants, or they won't support it. They absolutely will not consider piecemeal reform. In fact, Democrats have been very effective in spreading the narrative that when Republicans are against comprehensive immigration reform, then they are therefore against immigration reform all together. Which means Republicans are "anti-immigrant" and even "anti-Latino." It is common to hear media reporters and anchors repeat the Democratic mantra that by not supporting comprehensive immigration reform, the Republicans will lose any chance of getting the Latino vote and ever winning the presidency again because of their lack of diversity.

Yet it is rare to hear a Democratic elected official or spokesperson speak in favor of a piecemeal approach. Can it really be true that not a single Democrat in Congress opposes comprehensive immigration reform or is concerned about the impact of eager immigrant workers has on wage stagnation and African American unemployment that were described in chapter 4? As long as the Democrats are up, the single approach, comprehensive policy works. But what happens when they're down?

The comprehensive immigration reform bill that was passed in the Senate in June 2013 was an unusual attempt in the 113th Congress to try for bipartisanship. It was done soon after the 2012 reelection of Barack Obama and when Democrats were up and Republicans down. The bill was "comprehensive" in that it included a 13-year "pathway to citizenship for some eight million (not all) illegal immigrants. It was sponsored by a "Gang of Eight" including four Republicans who (true to growing diversity in the Republican Party) were willing to consider this mini comprehensive measure. There were fluent Spanish-speaking senators on each side—both of Cuban heritage:

Democrat Robert Menendez of New Jersey and Republican Marco Rubio of Florida.

The Senate Judiciary Committee scheduled two weeks of full committee bill "mark-up" meetings—not hearings with witnesses but meetings where all committee members gather around a half-moon table—Republicans to the left, Democrats to the right—to debate the details of a proposed bill. Judiciary Committee chairman Patrick Leahy of Vermont promised to hear every amendment and there were over 200 proposed by both Republicans and Democrats. The discussions on the amendments, while at times passionate, were always civil (much to the surprise and for some, disappointment, of the congressional press corps filling half the room). But in the end, no significant Republican amendment was passed.

Harry Reid ordered that for the vote in the Senate, the members had to file in quietly (almost single file), sit at their desks, and vote when their name was called—the official voting procedure that is almost never ever followed in the Senate (the only other time recently was when the Senate passed the health-care bill on Christmas Eve in an almost solemn sit-down vote when nearly all the members wore red or green accessories to mark the missed holiday evening). At the immigration hearing, Reid also allowed a large contingent of DREAMers (by definition illegal immigrants) to pack one of the galleries and after the vote, to cheer and chant loudly without being removed—against a protocol that is almost never violated. Every Democratic senator and 13 Republicans voted for the bill; while 32 Republicans voted against it. It was sent to the House with high hopes they would be forced to vote on it in the fall.

But the Democratic mojo ended drastically in October. The much-feted launch of the Affordable Care Act completely crashed. It tainted not only the glow of the Democratic agenda and the Obama administration's competence, but it also ended the idea of "comprehensive" anything passing in the 113th Congress. The Democrats could not overcome the downturn. In the 2014 midterm elections, the Republicans gained large majorities in both houses.

President Obama, an avid sports competitor who does not like to lose, took the Democratic losses hard. But as he said, he doesn't have to run again. Some say that is why he suddenly implemented his end-of-November executive action to grant deportation deferment and temporary job permits to some five million illegal immigrants just weeks after the disastrous midterm elections. It was essentially unnecessary: the beneficiaries—mainly illegal immigrants who had been in the country at least five years and have spouses or children who are American citizens—are already protected from deportation by DHS orders of 2012 to only detain and prosecute serious felon aliens. Similarly, the prosecutorial discretion for DREAMers had already been extended without too much furor and the Republicans were thinking of legalizing them anyway. Neither group was threatened by deportation, despite advocates' continual heartrending stories to the contrary (see *New York Times* lead op-ed of March 2, 2015 "A Life without Papers"). But what the five million beneficiaries of executive action didn't have before, and what the Obama's action order be given them, were open work permits and state driver's licenses—the latter a long-standing unquestionable state prerogative. Republicans immediately accused the president of going over the line of prosecutorial discretion and of violating the U.S. Constitution.

It seems clear that the executive action taken by the president after the disastrous 2014 midterm election results for the Democrats was a brilliant political Democratic move to provoke Republicans. It leaves them with few options. If it is unconstitutional, Republicans will have to wait for the case to move slowly through the federal courts, culminating in the U.S. Supreme Court. The other constitutional option, impeachment of the president, obviously would never be proposed by Republicans (as much as media anchors try to get Republican leaders to say they are considering it, as on CNN's Sunday show *State of the Union* on March 1).

The only power Congress has against a president's executive action is the funding of executive branch agencies, in this case the Department of Homeland Security. But that agency ironically is the one department that supposedly addresses Republican's core concern about illegal immigration—national security. It is awkward politically to say the least, for Republicans to consider defunding even a part of that department. Democrats have of course taken great advantage to malign Republicans on that move, reminding everyone who will listen that Republican "closed down the government" in 2013. (Note: another option Congress has is to change the jurisdiction of an agency or department to a more favorable one for the party in power. Democratic leader Manny Celler did it in 1947 when he switched immigration from a Labor Department jurisdiction to the Judiciary Committee, of which he was the chair, and could then steer the eventual replacement of the 1964 National Quota Act. Today, Republicans could switch the bureau of Citizenship and Immigration Services (CIS)—which administers the most contentious part of the November immigration executive action by distributing the work permits and other beneficiaries to the millions of immigrants who qualify— out of DHS and into a less vital agency like the Department of Labor, for instance, an option Democrats might not be able to oppose.

In January 2015 when the Republican House bill to delay Department of Homeland Security funding in order to block implementation of President Obama's November executive orders was sent to the Senate, the now minority Senate Democrats turned to filibuster threats to keep the bill from coming onto the floor. Senate Harry Reid seemed to feel justified, even as minority leader, to block any bill opposing the president from even being discussed on the floor. It's legal. Any one senator can use the filibuster threat to stop discussion of a bill. Democrats complained bitterly when Republicans used it in 2014 enough to "use the nuclear option"—they voted down use of the filibuster for administration appointments. Now in the minority himself, Reid apparently plans to use it for every bill that is not exactly what the Democrats want.

But it is a risky policy. The Democrats may get their way short term. In early 2014, the media continued to repeat the Democratic talking point that it was Republicans to blame for the "do nothing Congress" and governmental shutdown of 2013. But obviously not all voters are convinced. The Democrat's narrow, single-stance policy is no doubt a major reason why the Democrats lost the Senate in 2014 and why Americans are so disgusted with congressional gridlock. Now in the 114th Congress, while there is little chance that Republicans can garner the 60 votes needed to overcome a filibuster in the short term, the gotcha politics game may not bode well for Democrats in the long term.

It all depends on how Republicans react to Democratic provocations.

Republicans

Republicans are sometimes called by MSNBC pundit Chris Matthews the "daddy" party in that they tend to prefer punitive enforcement options as a solution for threats and challenges. Some may see Republicans as Congress's "wait-till-your-daddy-gets-home" fallback plan, to let the more punitive party do the hard part of enforcement.

It's been interesting watching the Republican Party since 2008, after the Democrats won the presidency and both chambers of Congress, change from being a strict, one-message cultural-warrior party (against abortions and gay marriages) whose next presidential candidate needed only to be coroneted at the next nomination convention. In the past seven years they have become a party rich with new, younger, and socioeconomic-education-and-racially diverse elected officials who are not shy to share the stage and to voice their differences with the leadership. There are many ideological groups with a say in the Republican Party today:

- Tea Party conservatives
- Ron and Rand Paul libertarians
- American (Pat Buchanan) Conservatives
- Neo (Cheney family) Conservatives
- Establishment Republicans (McCain, McConnell, Boehner)
- Evangelicals
- Moderate and centrist Susan Collins Republicans

In Congress, the Republicans' new "minority"-elected representatives and senators are especially visible and becoming political stars—young, vocal, multi-issue, handsome, male and female—like Marco Rubio, Ted Cruz, Raul Labrador, and Ileana Ros-Lehtinen, the first Latina ever elected to Congress and the first woman to chair the powerful Foreign Relations Committee. Republicans in 2014 elected the first Mormon, African American woman to serve in Congress and the only new black senator. They came in with a new solid voting block of working-class, white men—a demographic they are gaining from Democrats more every day; they have double the number of Hispanic-heritage senators than the Democrats (two to one). They also have the first Latina governor—Suzanne Martinez of New Mexico, a growing power that even Democratic pundit Bill Galston at Brookings Institute claimed at a post-2014 mid-election panel "Republicans would be foolish not to nominate her to be their vice presidential candidate in 2016."

In some ways the Republicans are beginning to look more diverse ideologically than the Democrats—though the media often describes that as being "split," "rent apart," "flailing," and other adverbs and adjectives of self-destruction. But their new diversity has the Republicans now struggling for party messages and stands on issues and even a presidential candidate that will please everyone.

No issue better illustrates the Republicans' struggle with their own diversity than immigration reform, about which each of the above-named groups have a different idea. There is no one "Republican" position on immigration (i.e., "anti-immigrant") despite the press efforts to make it seem so. Republican stances on immigration reform issues are across the board, including legalizing DREAMers (Ileana Ros-Lehtinen).

But Republicans generally agree on one priority: national security. Once the "borders are secure"—which includes interior enforcement that significantly reduces the number of new illegal immigrants coming into the country—then all Republicans agree the other parts of immigration reform can be discussed. That includes who and how many new legal immigration visas to give out for categories such as investors, highly skilled techies, trained agricultural and construction workers, and the like. It includes questions about whether or not new visas should be temporary or permanent or more easily adjusted to a green card. Some Republicans feel that very few new laws should be implemented or enforced: just allow free market forces to regulate immigrant labor. But most feel that those major decisions should be voted on in single bills or packets of bills after a process of committee debate and voting—piecemeal, not comprehensive.

National Security and Enforcement

Several pieces of legislation signed into law in 1996 marked a turn toward harsher policies for both legal and illegal immigrants. The Antiterrorism and Effective Death Penalty Act (AEDPA) and Illegal Immigration Reform and

Immigrant Responsibility Act (IIRIRA) vastly increased the categories of criminal activity for which immigrants, including green card holders, can be deported and imposed mandatory detention for certain types of deportation cases. As a result, well over two million individuals have been deported since 1996.[18]

There has been much objection to this. As was described in chapter 4, the deportation process has been variously used since 1965. Generally, almost all immigration laws pertaining to immigrants living and working in the country—from using false documents to overstaying a temporary visa to knowingly employing them—were pretty much ignored until the terrorist attack of 9/11. The modus operandi of immigration enforcement on the borders was "only OTMs—Other than Mexicans—would be detained" and almost all of them were "caught and released" since there were almost no detention facilities to hold them. Inside the country it was pretty much "if you get here you can stay." As Mark Krikorian often says: "there is nothing more permanent than a temporary visa."

But when the Bush administration in the midst of the Iraq war, created the Department of Homeland Security and its entirely new bureau of Customs and Immigration Enforcement (ICE), the idea of enforcement changed. All the secretaries of the DHS to date—two Republicans, two Democrats—have stated that they are committed to their constituents' broad and specific mission of law enforcement to protect national security. That includes terrorist threats, cyber security, and many other areas as well as immigration.

It was Michael Chertoff, the second DHS secretary under President Bush, who publicly announced in 2007 that he was making his top priority at the department the enforcement of the 1986 amnesty law that made it illegal for employers to hire immigrants without a work permit (including many on temporary spousal visas). Even President Obama's first DHS secretary, Janet Napolitano, perhaps the most liberal of all the Homeland Security secretaries and currently the president of the University of California system, constantly reminded Democrats who yowled as she continued to deport criminal immigrants, that she "had to enforce the laws; she did not make them." She resigned in 2012 after Obama's reelection and the implementation of deferred action on deportation for DREAMers—a group that now she has to deal with constantly in California, one of 13 states who have ordered their state universities and colleges to give in-state tuition subsidies to immigrants who are illegally in the country.

But Republicans are conflicted about enforcement as well. In 2007, when the comprehensive immigration bill pushed so hard by Ted Kennedy and President Bush failed to pass, its other major Senate advocate, Republican John McCain (Arizona) who was soon to be nominated the Republican presidential candidate, sat stunned in his chair shaking his head. But like Ted Kennedy, he soon expressed the "lesson learned." The press was to later constantly slander him as a "flip flop" when he deliberately stated that he had had to change his mind about comprehensive immigration reform: that it couldn't pass until enforcement measures both on the border and in the interior had effectively stopped the continual increase of illegal immigration. From then on he said he would only support bills that put "enforcement *first*" (a statement that got quickly spun by Janet Murguia, president and CEO of La Raza into "enforcement only," then "deportation only," then "deportation only in box cars"—a vile inference that immigration enforcement was equivalent to genocide and the Holocaust).

No politician can stand that kind of rhetoric no matter how false.

Republicans refocused their stand on enforcement from punishment of illegal workers to helping employers make sure they were not hiring immigrants without work permits. That meant strengthening the E-Verify system—an electronic database that employers could easily connect to (like a credit card check) to ascertain if an applicant for employment had a legal permit to work. The system was developed by the DHS in conjunction with the social security system and was offered as a voluntary aid for employers who did not want to break national immigration laws by hiring illegal workers. In 2008, Arizona made it mandatory for all employers wanting a business license in the state (upheld by SCOTUS).

In 2010, it was widely believed that the House would pass legislation making E-Verify a national requirement but that didn't happen; Republicans tried to make an E-Verify national requirement in the 2013 Senate Comprehensive immigration bill but it was rejected by the Democratic-majority judiciary committee. It is a very possible that an E-Verify national requirement piecemeal, stand-alone bill will be among those that Republicans may put on President Obama's desk to sign in 2015 or 2016.

Balance of Power

Democrats won back the presidency in 1977 with Jimmy Carter, lost it again in 1981 to Ronald Reagan and George H. W. Bush until 1993 with Bill Clinton, lost it again in 2001 to George W. Bush, and won it with Barack Obama in 2009. They controlled the White House for various 20 years, compared with 30 for the Republicans.

It was different for elections to Congress. Control of the House and Senate went back and forth. Contrary to popular belief, most of the time (in modern political history) Congress and the president are at odds; that is, most of the time the same political party does not control the White House, the Senate, and the House of Representatives. Only 13 times (26 years) since 1945 have both branches of Congress and the presidency been controlled by the same party; the Democrats have held this advantage more often than Republicans (11 to 2).

At the same time, Congress has usually been controlled by the same party. The "odd man out" has literally been the president. Since 1945, the House and Senate have been controlled by different parties only seven times (14 years)—but three of those have been since the 2000 elections, which makes this "seem" more normal than it is, historically. And there have been only two complete turnovers of Congress since 1949: one in 1995 and the other in 2007. Americans seem to prefer that the checks and balances envisioned by the founders be facilitated by having different parties control Congress and the White House.[19]

Similarly, control of the House and Senate between Republicans and Democrats went back and forth, especially in the midterm elections when the lack of a presidential race always meant a lower turnout of voters and often a repudiation of the White House party.

Increasingly, however, there were fewer and fewer competitive races for Congress. The reason has been said to be largely because of the gerrymandering of congressional districts—the reformatting of districts after every national census—every 10 years—to reflect a balanced number of voters. The redistricting is done usually by the party that holds the state governorship and/or the majority in the state legislature. Obviously, whoever does it will shape the district in favor of the party that controls the state government in that year. As Republicans increasingly win control of state governments, congressional districts, especially in rural states, favor Republicans. If the pattern of the past 15 years continues, it seems that the House may be a Republican lock.

But don't fret about unfairness. In the same way, one can say that the electoral college that officially elects the president and is based on the plurality of votes in a state, inherently favors a Democrat. Urban areas tend to vote Democratic. Votes in states dominated by large urban centers will favor Democrats even if the rest of the state votes Republican. In 2012, for instance, Republican candidate Mitt Romney was leading in Virginia throughout the night until the votes from northern Virginia cities were counted and Obama won the plurality and hence the electoral vote. The White House is almost a lock for Democrats if they choose a candidate that is not too extreme.

Both parties complain bitterly about these biases. But they do nothing to change the one that favors them. As for voters, as was said above, Americans seem to prefer that the checks and balances envisioned by the founders be facilitated by having different parties control Congress and the White House. Maybe the only real fight about party dominance in the next 20 years will be about control of the Senate.

It's unclear if the balance between control of Congress and control of the White House of Congress affects the passage of immigration laws or not.

- In 1965 when the INA passed, both houses were famously liberal Democratic along with President Johnson.
- In 1986, however, when Congress passed the amnesty bill under Republican President Reagan, the 99th Congress was divided: the Senate was Republican and the House was Democratic.
- In 1988, the Republicans lost the Senate and for his last two years, Reagan faced both chambers that were Democratic. Republicans did not want this to happen again.
- After Clinton's midterm election in 1995, the chambers went from both Democratic dominated to both Republican dominated for the next six years. No immigration reform bills were passed, but there was movement, including especially among Texas Republicans "pandering to Latino votes with a promise of a more liberal border policy with Mexico."[20]
- In 2001, President George W. Bush started his first term with a promise to Mexican President Vicente Fox for a more open border policy with that country. Congress was split with a Democratic Senate and a Republican House and seemed favorable to the new president's bill—but 9/11 sucked the air out of any initiative other than national security.
- After the midterms and for the next four years, Bush had both chambers of Congress Republican dominated. In 2006, the House passed a large immigration bill that focused on enforcement including making it a felony to be in the country illegally. That didn't pass the Senate.
- In 2007, with both chambers now Democratic, President Bush, Senator John McCain, together with the popular and powerful Democratic Lion of the Senate Edward Kennedy, put together a comprehensive immigration reform bill at the White House. Senate leader Democratic Nevadan Harry Reid agreed to let it be debated for two weeks on the floor of the Senate. It failed—twice.
- President Obama started his first term with both chambers Democratic but in the 2010 midterms, the House switched to Republican leadership. No immigration bills were entertained much to the fury of Latino activists who felt Obama had promised them a bill and had missed an opportunity with Dems in both houses.
- In 2013, after Obama's reelection with some help supposedly from his June 2012 executive order deferring deportation for DREAMers (illegal immigrants who had come into the country before the age of 16), a comprehensive immigration bill passed in the Democratic Senate with some Republican support from a bipartisan "Gang of Eight," but the Republican House refused to pass it, saying they wanted to consider only piecemeal bills not an omnibus one
- In 2014, the Senate turned Republican—both Houses now were led by Republican leaders who proclaimed they were committed to utilizing the

traditional congressional committee process and to eventually passing piecemeal immigration reform.

KEY PLAYERS IN IMMIGRATION REFORM IN THE TWENTY-FIRST CENTURY

The importance of powerful individuals to move major legislation is increasingly of interest in U.S. history. Certainly a significant part of the story of how the 1965 INA passed and was implemented and its impact the past 50 years is due to the individuals who were dedicated to its passage. The same is true of immigration reform into the twenty-first century. Three individuals stand out: Ted Kennedy again, who until the day he died continued his legacy-making commitment to an immigration system without discrimination. Also key as the fiftieth anniversary of the bill approaches are the two twenty-first-century presidents George W. Bush and Barack Obama.

Ted Kennedy

Almost until the day he died at age 77 in August 2009, Ted Kennedy was an active, respected, almost venerated senator. Immigration reform along with education were Ted Kennedy's top priorities. "The INA was Ted Kennedy's biggest legacy" John Bicknell a former CQ editor and coeditor of *Politics in America* said in 2014 at his book launch, that Ted Kennedy ceded his long-time chairmanship of the Senate Judiciary Subcommittee on Immigration to New York senate leader Chuck Schumer in 2008 after being diagnosed with a brain tumor, and turned to helping President Obama pass his health care bill.

Kennedy's was a tumultuous history as the youngest brother of a famous family of whom he was always in competition and tested by his three older brothers. But at 36, he found himself the lone survivor of the four and "the champion of a generation's dreams and ambitions." He failed spectacularly for a period, and then rose to be the most honored of senators by all who knew him on all sides of the political spectrum. In their comprehensive, dramatic history of Ted in *Last Lion: the Fall and Rise of Ted Kennedy*, the team of writers at the Boston Globe organized the book into three parts: "The Rise," "Trials and Tribulations," and "The Redemption."

Kennedy's successful landmark fight for passage of the Immigration and Nationality Act of 1965 happened in the first period: The Rise. Four years later after being involved in a fatal automobile accident and the death of a young campaign worker of his brother's, Teddy moved into a dark period of some two decades. As he battled the court cases and the negative press from the accident, and the traumatic cancer of his young son that eventually resulted in his leg being amputated, Kennedy struggled to keep his leadership on liberal causes in the Republican-dominated Congress and White House. In 1975, he was victorious in passing an overhaul of sentencing guidelines to make them limited by regulated mandates and less arbitrary. In 1975, he began a years-long battle to advance the Foreign Intelligence Surveillance Act to regulate the use of electronic surveillance for national security.

Today, these may seem like almost conservative-Republican issues, but at the time, they were unregulated and arbitrary systems than threatened freedom and equality. Kennedy's success in imposing regulation was a result of his growing ability to work with both sides of the aisle, to form bipartisan compromises and agreements. "He was tenacious and practical; a passionate legislator," former Republican attorney general Ken Feinberg said of him. "The perfect is the enemy of the good" was his philosophy. He'd make deals offering to yield on some elements of a policy if the other side would yield on voters. His view was "let's get a package and we can improve it later."[21] (This in many ways echoes the philosophy of the Democratic Party leadership today to pass 1,000-page-plus comprehensive bills without worrying about all the details. Nancy Pelosi, the first female Speaker of the House, famously said in 2009 at the passage of the huge omnibus health care bill that no one had had time to read in total—"the bill has to pass before they—and the rest of us 'can find out what's in it,'" she said in urging the passage of the Obamacare bill in March 2010.)[22]

But it wasn't until after Ted Kennedy's unsuccessful run for the presidency in 1991 and the end of his marriage that he was "finally liberated" from the expectations of others and felt free to become his own man.[23] He transformed himself into a symbol of wisdom and perseverance. His life is a lesson in moving forward. He just doesn't sit.

Returning to the Senate in 1982, Kennedy found that many of his closest friends and colleagues were no longer there. "He knew he would have to make a fierce defense of his liberal principles in a Senate controlled by the opposite party for the first time in his career of over two decades—and with a popular conservative Republican president. The civil rights era had defined him as a senator and a leader, and he "was determined to be the firewall against President Reagan's efforts to roll back some of the hard-won victories of the previous twenty years."[24]

But times were changing and some of his positions were to change the base of the Democratic Party. Kennedy supported court-ordered school bussing in order to have less segregated schools, but he was at times viciously attacked by Irish, blue-collar, working families in South Boston. He was angry because "he was always championing civil fights and here I was in his own backyard" said Robert Bates his former aide.[25] The rift between Kennedy and his blue collar base would have lasting impact on him. It taught him not to take the Boston Irish for granted and it spurred him to cultivate support elsewhere, especially among African Americans.

His first big fight with President Reagan was over the reauthorization of the Voting Rights Act—Kennedy's signature civil rights issue in 1964. He reached across the aisle to liberal Republicans such as Robert Dole of Kansas to craft a veto-proof renewal bill. Republican Orin Hatch of Utah became one of his closest friends and colleagues after Kennedy voluntarily gave up heading the Judiciary Committee for a time when the Republicans took over the Senate. He joined Hatch's Labor Committee as a minority member. Kennedy and Hatch subsequently "teamed up on some of the most significant public health legislation of the era—baffling and sometimes infuriating Hatch's Republican colleagues. It was some said an attraction of opposites and at times a mutual benefit partnership."[26] The same partnership developed between him and John McCain of Arizona, one of his closest colleagues, especially on immigration reform in 2007.

"Ted's success in picking Republican colleagues to support his causes enabled him to continue to generate legislation rather than simply block Republican initiatives." He partnered with various Republicans on a variety of issues including on immigration. When he wanted something done, he would tell his staff to do whatever it took to cobble together a majority. "Work it out!" he'd say to his staff. The Republicans came onboard because they liked and trusted their colleague from Massachusetts. He was fun and energetic and generous in giving them credit. They also knew he could deliver. He had found his way around the most painful part of life in the minority.

But he was also ambitious about his causes to help disadvantaged people. Among his bipartisan accomplishments were Title IX to give women in college equal access to athletic resources as men had (although that soon expanded beyond athletics).

He came eventually to work closely with two Republican presidents on immigration issues: in particular with Reagan on the 1986 Amnesty Act that did pass, and with President George W. Bush on a comprehensive immigration reform package in 2007 that did not.

"Most people didn't know this, but my husband . . . and Ted Kennedy were terrific friends" Nancy Reagan said in 2009 at news of Ted's death.[27] "An example of Kennedy's great skill was that he persuaded Ronald Reagan to enthusiastically support the amnesty bill," wrote Roy Beck, Director of NumbersUSA.

Ted's relationship with George W Bush was more practical. Bush had campaigned on education reform and though he had opposite views about the role of government in education, he knew he would need Kennedy who was the senior Democrat on the Senate Health, Education, Labor, and Pensions (HELP) Committee to pass his signature legislation No Child Left Behind.

When Kennedy and Bush met, each was surprised to find things to like in each other. . . . Both saw a bipartisan opportunity at the dawn of one of the most partisan eras that Washington had seen in many decades. They agreed to emphasize in front of the press, what policies they agreed on and not what separated them (perhaps one of the things they shared in common was that both had had close relatives who had occupied the Oval Office). In the end though, the alliance of Kennedy on Bush was based less on a genuine friendship than on hardheaded political calculation. Bush was practical and both he and Kennedy were in their legacy building years. They agreed on and famously were together at the passing of No Child Left Behind. (Interestingly, Laura Bush was in Kennedy's office when 9/11 happened.)[28]

In 2007, Kennedy focused on another group of "discriminated"-against workers with the hopes of passing in his dotage, a landmark bill. He wanted to pass an immigration bill that would be "comprehensive" in that it would give temporary legal status and work permits to 12–20 million illegal immigrants who would "come out of the shadows," pay a fine, and, if they passed a background check, could enter a process that would eventually lead to a green card, permanent legal residency, and if they chose, citizenship.

It was a year before he was diagnosed with a brain tumor, but Kennedy was energetic and vigorous, speaking in the enthusiastic hearty tone at his desk about the need for loosening immigration regulations, especially for those in the country illegally. In a booming voice, I heard him say several times in the Senate that "immigration is the civil rights issue of the day." He was wrong of course, but he believed it and so did many civil rights advocates (including many of his elderly, black, congressional colleagues) who filled the crowds at immigration rallies.

Kennedy put together an "improbable" team of Democratic and Republican senators to negotiate a bill. They included Lindsey Graham (R-South Carolina, then in his first term), Diane Feinstein (D-California), Mel Martinez (R-Florida), Ken Salazar (D-Colorado), Jon Kyl (R-Arizona), and Trent Lott (R-Mississippi). John McCain was active as well, but as his own man. The negotiations were contentious but in the end, President Bush enthusiastically supported the bill and Harry Reid allowed two weeks during the summer for debate on the Senate floor. But it failed—twice.

After the second loss, on June 28, 2007, Kennedy sat for a time at his desk looking stunned. Finally, his youngest son, Congressman Patrick Kennedy, came to his desk and leaning heavily on his arm, Kennedy slowly left the room. Less than a year later he was diagnosed with a brain tumor and died in August of 2009; he never gave up his advocacy, however, for comprehensive immigration reform. "Less than an hour after the loss in the Senate Ted had adopted a philosophical view about it. It always took an average of three Congresses—at least six years—to develop the necessary momentum for any kind of civil rights legislation he declared. Immigration

Kennedy vowed would be back. He always had the long view and the big picture in mind."[29]

What has to be noted, however, is that in the 50 years since his successfully fighting to end immigration selection based on preference and favoritism for certain national origins, Kennedy seems to have abandoned that concern for nationality preference and diversity. Even though he blamed the unexpected massive immigration numbers and changes to the American demographic—that he and Johnson had assured the public would not happen when they signed the bill under the Statue of Liberty that October day in 1965—Kennedy seemed to have changed his mind about nationality diversity.

His solution to taking care of the problem of illegal immigration was to legalize all those who were illegally in the country. The fact that the majority came from one country—Mexico—didn't appear to bother him. Discrimination no longer meant preference or favoritism toward the national origin of an immigrant. Nationality diversity was never mentioned by Kennedy in the twenty-first century. He was even considering a special legalization bill for the Irish.

It is obvious that the success of that exciting 89th Congress to pass so many bills to end discrimination became the dream of Kennedy later in life and his focus on immigration reform. He saw illegal immigrants as the new civil rights cause. He seemed to believe that immigrants were people discriminated against because they did not have equal rights of citizens. Discrimination and equal rights are the rallying cries for civil rights activists. For Kennedy and his ageing civil rights supporters looking for one last big landmark bill that would carry Kennedy's name, comprehensive immigration reform that would give equal rights to millions of immigrants who were "hiding in the shadows" was his next big civil rights goal.

The Twenty-First-Century Presidents: Bush and Obama

Immigration reform has been a contentious issue in both of the two presidential terms of Republican George W. Bush and Democrat Barack Obama. But both approached and dealt with immigration reform and with the opponents and advocates of reform in very different ways—and not in ways that might be expected.

Of the two presidents, George W. Bush was by far more enthusiastic and interested in passing comprehensive immigration reform than Obama. During his 2000 campaign against Al Gore, Bush made it clear that immigration reform would be one of his first year's priorities after he was elected. He made various approaches to his friend President Vicente Fox of Mexico and it seemed that a deal was pending at least with Mexico. But after the terrorist attack in September 2011, nine months into his presidency, his priorities obviously changed.

With a focus on national security now the top concern, President Bush significantly changed the way immigration was administered and enforced in the new Department of Homeland Security. It wasn't until 2007, the second half of his second term, that he turned once again to comprehensive immigration reform. He worked closely with Ted Kennedy and John McCain on the bill and left for a summit meeting that June expecting it to pass the Senate easily. When it failed he sent several cabinet secretaries to the Hill to lobby for its being reconsidered. Senate Leader Harry Reid gave it another two weeks on the floor for debate, but on June 28, the bill failed to pass cloture. Bush didn't try again but Democrats appreciated his advocacy. "It's the only thing that he was right about" some Democratic women would grumble.

President Obama by contrast showed little interest in immigration reform, even as a senator when it was a big issue in 2007. Already a Democratic candidate for president in 2007 after having been elected the senator from Illinois in 2004, he occasionally joined in the talks on comprehensive immigration reform that Senator Kennedy put together with a bipartisan team of senior senators. His presence impressed Kennedy, who knew the immigration issue was politically explosive and risky for a presidential aspirant.

In 2008, Ted Kennedy and his niece Carolyn Kennedy, the daughter of President John Kennedy, appeared at an American University campaign rally for Obama and endorsed him for president. They implied that he was "another John Kennedy." It was the turning point in Obama's intense, competitive race against Hillary Clinton (who until then had had the support of the majority of polled Latinos), and made it seem as if Obama shared Kennedy's commitment on issues including immigration reform—something Hillary was very cautious about. (She was the only Democratic candidate of a dozen during a 2008 presidential debate who came out against giving drivers' licenses to illegal immigrants.)

Obama avoided talking about immigration reform during his first presidential campaign on the strong advise of his future chief of staff, then chair of the Democratic Congressional Campaign Committee Rahm Emanuel. Mostly it was because they were counting on fiscally conservative Blue Dog Democrats to carry the election for them without the South, as they had done for Emanuel in 2006 when he turned the House blue. Most Blue Dogs were openly concerned about the fiscal impact of illegal immigrants on local town and city resources like hospitals, and did not generally vote for comprehensive immigration reform measures that would legalize millions of illegal immigrants.

After the 2008 election, Obama promised in his detached way "to address" immigration reform in his first term. (Note: after continuous research I have not found where he promised to pass, push for, prioritize, or any other verb except his favorite "to address.") He fulfilled that promise by giving a speech addressing immigration reform in early July 2009 at the American University. It was followed immediately by a vociferous rally of black civil rights leaders and Latino activists demanding the rights of illegal immigrants and the end to their discrimination.

But Obama refused to put his presidential muscle or even to commit any lobbying efforts from his cabinet to a comprehensive bill during the first half of his first term. Instead he focused all his efforts on passing a nonuniversal health care plan while both houses of Congress were Democratic (in 2014, several politicos including Senator Chuck Schumer—to whom Ted Kennedy had ceded his Senate leadership on immigration in early 2009—said that "the Obama administration had made a big mistake by prioritizing health care at the expense of other issues like immigration reform in 2009–2010.)"[30]

After losing the House to Republicans in 2010, Obama publicly told an audience of 10,000 people (I was one of them) at the Omni Shorham Hotel in Washington, D.C., at the La Raza annual conference, that he could not, would not go around Congress to make an executive order to defer deportation and give work permits to some two million DREAMers. The front rows were full of DREAMers screaming, "Yes you can," and he looked them straight on and said "No I can't." But he changed his mind a year later when his campaign for reelection was in trouble. In the summer of 2012 he made an executive order called Deferred Action for Childhood Arrivals (DACA) that would give some two million illegal immigrants who claimed to have come to the United States before the age of 16 a waiver from deportation and a work permit. When Obama won reelection in 2012, most of the media claimed—even claim today—that DACA won him the Hispanic vote and hence the reelection. (See Latino Vote below.)

But despite his big reelection win, President Obama again in 2013 refused to lobby for comprehensive immigration reform, even after supposedly heated lobbying by White House staffer Cecilia Muñoz and her former employers La Raza. It took a "Gang of Eight" consisting of four Democratic and four Republican senators, to put together and eventually pass a mini comprehensive immigration reform bill in June 2013. Obama did not openly lobby for it however, and the House (predictably) refused to bring it to the floor, their priority being to pass pieces of immigration reform, not a comprehensive omnibus bill.

In 2014, before the midterm elections, as the Republicans began to appear they would win back the Senate, Obama backed down on two specific promises he had made to order another executive action by October, to expand the deferment of deportation for DREAMers and to legalize and give work permits to their millions of parents and siblings. It was only after the Senate fell to the Republicans in the November midterms that Obama then ordered the extension of DACA, plus deferred action for some 3–4 million illegal immigrants who had family ties to close relatives who are American citizens or hold green cards—but not to the parents and family of DREAMers.

Some Republicans say he crossed the line constitutionally, but by January of 2015 they still weren't sure what to do about it. Some say Obama did it as a brilliant political move to provoke Republicans into an extreme action they would not stomach and would hurt them in the 2016 presidential elections (like defunding the DHS or starting impeachment proceedings against him). It was a clever political move; but it's not clear he really did it because of his commitment to immigration reform or the DREAMers. There was actually no urgency to do it; deportation for all but violent criminal aliens has been suspended and no one was in jeopardy of being deported immediately— certainly not DREAMers. He could have done it just for spite at Republicans who beat the Democrats so badly in the midterm elections. Obama is after all a clever politician as well as an intense athletic competitor who hates to lose.

Personal Immigration Experiences of the Presidents and Ted Kennedy

When it comes to immigration reform, it is clear that Obama's enthusiasm, effort, and commitment, is not even close to that of President Bush, much less President Lyndon Johnson or Senator Ted Kennedy. In this way it is notable that neither of the twenty-first-century presidents fit the stereotype touted constantly in the press of the "anti-immigrant" Republican and the "pro-immigrant" Democrat. Why are they that way?

Part of the explanation certainly lies in their different personal experiences and backgrounds with immigrants and immigration. Like everyone, personal immigrant experiences and family immigrant stories shape one's attitude toward immigrants and immigration law. That is equally true of presidents and legislators. Knowing a bit about each—President Bush and President Obama's personal history with immigration in his life—helps to understand their actions toward reform of immigration policy.

President Bush was raised in and identifies mostly with Texas where as a young child he reportedly had loving relationships with Mexican caretakers; as a young adult he worked shoulder to shoulder with Mexicans in the Texas oil fields and ranchlands. His wife Laura, even more, was a teacher and librarian in a rural Texas school with many Mexican and Central American immigrant students and had great sympathy for them and their often-difficult lives, including as illegal immigrants. In addition, brother Jeb married a Mexican national and raised their children in Spanish.

President Bush's sympathy and closeness to especially Mexico (one of the few countries he ever visited until he was president), his close relationship with Mexico's President Fox, and the plight of immigrants in Texas have made some call him "our first Latino president" (in the same sense that the sympathy and understanding President Clinton had for African Americans growing up poor in Arkansas gave him the (now ironic) moniker for a while as "our first black president"). President Bush mainly saw immigration as a Mexican issue.[31] He is particularly sympathetic to their plight as unauthorized immigrants.

President Obama on the other hand has a worldwide, infinitely broader experience and view of immigration than does President Bush. He is himself a second-generation immigrant, whose birth father was from Kenya, where close family relatives still live. In addition, his adopted father was from Indonesia where he lived (and spoke some Indonesian) as a boy. Both of his fathers were students persuing graduate studies at the University of Hawaii on foreign student visas when they met his mother. Both requested extensions of their visas on the basis of marriage with Obama's mother, both were denied, and both voluntarily returned home (or "self deported" if you will). Obama's mother remained in Indonesia most of her life and his half- sister was born and raised there. Obama attended secondary school in Hawaii at a very elite private middle and high school where he was one of the few African Americans students. Among his closest friends at his Hawaiian high school and in the private colleges he attended—Occidental outside of Los Angeles, California, and Columbia University in New York City—were Pakistani students with whom he studied and traveled.[32]

Obama placed several second-generation immigrants (at least one parent was an immigrant and spoke a heritage language at home) in the top tiers of his White House, including Rahm Emanuel (Israel) and Cecilia Muñoz (Bolivia). His top advisor Valerie Jarrett was born in Shiraz, Iran, where her African American father was a visiting physician. Obama is very comfortable with immigrants of many nationalities, but mainly he knows highly educated immigrants. Throughout his life, Obama has had relative little personal contact with Latinos, even in Chicago where as a community organizer he mainly worked with African Americans and for the first time got to know that part of his heritage.

It can be said that for Obama, immigration is not just about Latinos or illegal immigrants. His experience and knowledge of immigration is much broader than that narrow focus. In every State of the Union speech he has given, when he talks about immigration reform, he mentions the need to give green cards to advanced-degree foreign students—like his fathers. In addition, almost every time he meets with the Congressional Hispanic Caucus (and hears about the need to legalize millions of illegal immigrant workers), he almost always meets with the Congressional Black Caucus at about the same time (where he hears about the plight of millions of unemployed blacks).

It is interesting then to compare President Lyndon B. Johnson's background to that of President Bush. LBJ was also born, raised, and identified himself as a Texan. Like Bush, he worked with, was personally involved with, and very sympathetic to the immigrant Mexican families whose children he taught. He lobbied hard for their vote.

So, too, Ted Kennedy had strong ties to his Irish immigrant background and identified strongly with Boston's numerous Irish Catholics, who shared his family heritage. He felt closely related to them, extremely sympathetic to their problems (especially with discrimination), and expected their votes and support.

Even into the twenty-first century, Ted was always especially sympathetic to the plight of the tens of thousands of illegal Irish immigrants in the United States and open to discussions about legislation that might help them. Maybe he felt somewhat personally responsible for their plight. His successful repeal of the National Origins Act of 1924 took away their special privilege of no quota, since their nationality was considered part of the original national founders. (Any guilt Kennedy might have felt, however, certainly would have been constrained by the knowledge that setting a precedent to favor unauthorized Irish citizens living in the United States illegally with a special visa, would then be challenged by other significant immigrant groups to America—including Spanish, Germans, Italians, Chinese, and Africans, to name just a few—falling back into the trap of national origin preferences that Kennedy so fervently helped to end in the first place.)

Lobbying and Interest Groups

As the 50-year commemorations of the Civil Rights Act and the Voting Rights Act take place in 2015, the focus has also turned to the groups who propelled the civil rights movement itself. Even as journalist Julian Zelizer reminds us in his book *Fierce Urgency* that it was grassroots movements that enabled individuals like President Johnson and Senator Ted Kennedy to achieve their historic legislative successes in 1965. Yale professor Edward Rugemer, an associate professor of history and African American studies at Yale University, makes the same point in a *New York Times* letter to the editor, "In Ending Slavery, the Abolitionists Came First" about President Lincoln's ability to end slavery 100 years before. He wrote that the central significance of the abolitionist movement in American history is that

> beginning in the late 1820s, it fostered the creation of an antislavery constituency in the Northern states that grew over time. White Northerners may have been racists, but most became antislavery in their political views.
>
> One did not have to be an abolitionist to be against slavery.
>
> By the presidential election of 1860, the antislavery North was a sizable constituency that the Republicans captured. . . .
>
> Yes, the [civil] war [and President Abraham Lincoln] abolished slavery, but the abolitionist movement brought the war. [33]

There are some startling similarities between the periods leading to the ending of slavery (1820s to 1865) and those ending discrimination of immigration laws based on national origin exactly 100 years later (1920s and 1965). That includes the elections of uniquely powerful presidents in 1860 and 1960. Similarly, 50 years after the historic events, not all discrimination and racism has disappeared despite almost universal agreement that it should.

But what is different about immigration reform in 2015 and the passage of the Immigration and Nationality Act in 1965 (and the ending of slavery in 1865 for that matter), is that today there is simply no groundswell, sweeping, universal, grassroots movement or massive public momentum to reform immigration law. Today, while there are a wide range of interest groups and lobbyists that support all sides of immigration reform, there is no massive movement. Only once in a while do immigration lobbyists manage to put on a public demonstration and garner front-page news.

Ironically, the biggest national rally on immigration reform was in 2006—to *protest* the comprehensive immigration reform bill making its way through the House at the time. On March 6, tens of thousands of mainly Latino families marched to city centers throughout the nation to protest the Republican proposal to make illegal immigration a felony offense instead of a misdemeanor. The turnout was impressive in Washington, D.C.—thousands of Latino men, women, and children dressed in white and carrying flags (not only American, but also from their homelands—mainly Mexico and El Salvador) and signs (many in Spanish saying "*no somos criminals*"— we are not criminals). They were met on the mall by civil rights leaders (although it was notable that few African American demonstrators were in the crowd). The protest was effective. Republican congressmen hastened to remove the felony clause from the bill, but Democrats in the House wouldn't let them until the entire bill had been voted down in moral outrage against Republicans (a stain they couldn't erase in the 2008 presidential elections).

There have been really no other massive grass roots demonstrations since, certainly none that would propel widespread public outcry and urgency for comprehensive immigration reform. Most demonstrations since 2007 involve representatives of illegal immigrants and their families—mostly Latinos and some elderly African American civil rights leaders such as the Reverends Jessie Jackson Sr. and Al Sharpton. Their turnout numbers in the hundreds if not double digits—certainly not like the tens and hundreds of thousands of demonstrators who provided the overwhelming momentum for civil rights that propelled everyone but the most extreme Southern segregationist to vote for it.

Lobbyists and interest groups around immigration reform can be categorized basically in three groups:

- Latino activists who overwhelmingly advocate for "comprehensive" immigration reform, not piecemeal;
- Commercial interests who basically want fewer regulation on foreign labor; and
- "Restrictionists" who want generally more enforcement of immigration laws.

Members of all these groups cross party lines and all of them are split into subgroups that can differ widely about their views on immigration reform—most especially Latinos. The interest groups backing different forms of immigration reform are far more complicated, nuanced, and intermingled than that.

None of them self-identity or can be truthfully labeled "anti-immigrant"—even those who want more enforcement or fewer immigrants, and certainly those who want to stop illegal immigration and not support anything (like massive amnesties) that might encourage it. There is not even one congressional member who self-describes as "anti-immigrant." That designation has been applied exclusively by advocates for illegal immigrants and by the unquestioning media. Even Senator Chuck Schumer, when he replaced Ted Kennedy as chairman of the Senate Immigration Subcommittee in 2009 said, "Americans are not anti-immigrant. They are very pro-immigrant and pro-immigration. They just don't want illegal immigration."[34]

Latinos

The most vocal and most covered of the immigration reform support lobbyists are simply called "Latinos." Latinos or Hispanics (terms now used interchangeably) denote people with a Spanish-speaking/Latin American national origin, living in the United States. They include a wide spectrum of individuals and families from those who have been citizens for over 10 generations, to recently arrived immigrants—permanent, temporary, or unauthorized. According to 2014 census data, there are a historic 52 million individuals who self-describe as Latino presently living in the United States. They differ in terms of race, religion, creed, and national origin, socioeconomic background, and politics. The one thing they have in common is that most of them, at sometime in their family history, came from a Spanish-speaking country in or near the American continents.

Despite their huge diversity, Latinos as a group have become so identified with the comprehensive immigration debate that much of the press seems to think that immigration is only about Latinos. Some seem to believe that only Latinos (and then the majority) are illegally in the country; therefore to be against illegal immigration is to be "anti-Latino."

Yet "Latinos" were not recognized or labeled as an identity group in the first half of the century. In fact, the National Origins Act of 1924 did not have a quota for immigrants from Mexico, Central America, or Latin America; agricultural workers and ranch hands were welcome to cross the southern border in unlimited numbers to work in the popular *bracero* program until the 1965 Immigration and Nationality Act was passed. When the INA included immigrants from the Americas in an overall cap of 120,000 per year, it was the most contentious issue of the debate for passage (see history chapter 3) precisely because Mexican and Central American nationals had never been regulated before. The cap was ordered in order to assure that no nationality anywhere was to be given preferential treatment. The cap on immigrants from Mexico and the Central and South American countries was done in the commitment to nationality diversity and against discrimination based on national origin. After all, one can't say there are to be no stated preferences for any nationality, but then allow all Mexicans to come in who want to.

"Latinos" did not become a political identity until the 1960s and 1970s. They were undoubtedly inspired by budding African American organizations that had been involved in the civil rights movement and then evolved into more narrow ethnic identity/issue politics. The first impetus for Latino activism was in 1965 when Cesar Chavez's United Farm Workers in Delano, California, joined the Filipino grape strikers. As a pacifist, Chavez employed tactics such as hunger strikes and spiritual crusades, and enlisted and received the support of national politicians, the Catholic Conference of Bishops, and eventually, big, organized labor. He was always against illegal immigration, however, and saw it as a threat to Latino farmworkers who already were established in the country. When Chavez died in 1993 he was mourned as a national hero.[35] Many other Latino civil rights activist organizations were founded in the 1970s and 1980s, often by Latino students in Southern California. A movement of "Chicanos" basically representing immigrants from northern Mexico who had settled in the Southwest of the United States, was particularly active in the liberal political movements of the time. By the twenty-first century they had evolved into an ethnic studies subgroup on various university campuses in California and Texas.

The largest organization representing Latinos today is the National Council of La Raza (the Race, NCLR) based in Washington, D.C., with regional offices throughout the United States. The NCLR was founded in the 1960s originally to study and represent Mexican Americans, but expanded with the help of major foundations to include counseling and support programs in education, health care, housing, home ownership, business development, and citizenship preparation for all Latinos. But it is mostly known for its highly visible advocacy for comprehensive immigration reform, including the legalization of all illegal immigrants. In 2008, La Raza's long-time vice president and immigration political advocate Cecilia Muñoz was appointed as White House intergovernmental liaison officer, the highest ranking Latino/a in Obama's executive suite and his point person on immigration reform. None of the many other Hispanic organizations in the United States—including outstanding ones offering college education support like Excelencia in Education—have the political clout and access to the White House that La Raza has.

But the biggest missed, uncovered, biased "story" of immigration reform in the press is the seemingly inability of the media to grasp the idea of the immense diversity of America's Latino-heritage population. Even Latino journalists give most of the non-Hispanic media an F when it comes to covering immigration—including NPR in a special show about covering Latinos:

> Popular Hispanic news blogger Julio Ravela says he cringes at the coverage of Hispanics in most of the mainstream media (MSM). During an interview July 4, 2014 aired on NPR's *On the Media*, he had a major piece of advice for most mainstream news people:
> "Don't assume all Latinos are the same! They didn't all grow up eating tacos; and while immigration is an important issue, most Hispanics are here legally and concerned more about health, education and jobs so go beyond immigration," he said. "Like all Americans, Hispanics have divergent opinions and on many social issues, are more Republican than Democratic (when speaking about gays in Spanish, he says he is always sensitive to the Catholic viewpoint)."
> Ravela and Jorge Ramos of UNIVISION both agree that the Hispanic demographic is highly diverse and don't think of themselves first as "Latinos" as the press tends to depict them. Spanish-speaking first generation Hispanics, who are interviewed disproportionately by the press, usually identify themselves first as their homeland nationality: Peruvians, Nicaraguans, Mexicans, etc., not Latino. Ravela and Ramos are concerned that the MSM is causing racial barrio-ization in the news by focusing so narrowly on the mainly first-generation Spanish-speaking Hispanic immigrant population. Ravela gave NPR only a "C" even for this broadcast—but an A for effort to at least covering the subject. [36]

Especially annoying is the general media's failure to report that:

- the majority of the Latino population are citizens;
- almost all of the country's Hispanic population's growth now comes from U.S.-born children, not new immigrants;
- most American Latinos (especially citizens) do not speak, read, and write Spanish fluently, if at all;
- most Latinos work in, manage, or own small businesses; and

- there are more Latinos in the army than African Americans, and in the Border Patrol than "non-Hispanic" whites.

The "Latino Vote"

During the Barack Obama presidential campaigns of 2008 and 2012, large Latino organizations like La Raza focused on trying to get more Latinos to become naturalized, to register, and to vote. Their goal was one million more voting Latino citizens—most of that coming from citizens who had never registered. Their second priority was to help long-time, permanent residents or green-card holders to naturalize, to go through the process to become U.S. citizens. The reasoning for Democrats was that Latinos would automatically vote Democratic.

But only a small proportion of the million citizens that La Raza was able to sign up in 2008 and 2012 were Mexicans, although that was the target population. Their lack of success may be because this population has "'a comparatively lower tendency to become U.S. citizens than other national-ities' according to [the Pew Hispanic Center]. Certainly proximity of their homelands has much to do with this."[37]

The premise of the Latino as an automatic Democratic voter may also be wrong, despite it's being repeated constantly by Democrats and in the media. The sloppiest, laziest mistake the media makes constantly about Latino vot-ers is to equate their population numbers with the electorate. It's the "demog-raphy is destiny" spin that claims that as a state's population becomes more Hispanic, it inevitably will become a blue state. Somehow even good, senior reporters such as Susan Page of *USA Today*, repeat without question this mantra and the one about "Latinos are the fastest-growing demographic."

The truth lies in the numbers.

- Latinos are not the fastest-growing demographic in the United States to-day; since the 2009 census, Asians have moved ahead and remain the fastest.
- In 2012, Hispanics residing in the United States numbered 52 million—a historic number.
- Of these, 23 million (less than half) were citizens over the age of 18 and eligible to vote.
- In 2012, 14 million eligible Latino voters registered to vote.
- In 2012, 11 million Latinos cast votes—about 48 percent of the electorate (in 2008, 52 percent of the Hispanic electorate voted).
- The "Latino vote" made up 8.4 percent of all votes cast in the 2012 election.
- In 2012, 8 million Latinos, 67 percent of the total, voted for President Obama. (Clinton got 74 percent in 1984; 95 percent of African Americans,

over 15 million voters, voted for Obama in 2012, over 60 percent of their electorate.)

- In 2012, 3 million Latinos voted for the Republican ticket, about 27 percent (44 percent of Latinos voted for Republican governors in Texas and Colorado—states that Democrats had predicted the Latino demographic would turn blue).
- Latino voters made up more than 10 percent of the total electorate in only 11 states in 2012, all but two (Florida and New York) are located in the Southwest.
- Southwest states votes came in *after* Obama had won the requisite number of needed electoral votes in 2012; Latino voters in the most populous Latino states did not win the election for Obama in 2012, though the win of Florida was a significant help. Of the 11 Latino heavy states, only two (California and New York) are solidly blue.
- Voters in New Mexico and Nevada, large Latino-demographic states, voted in Republican Latino governors and for a Republican senator over a Democratic Latino candidate in 2012.
- It was found that the majority of Hispanic-heritage voters did not understand Spanish and many ads in Spanish had to be hastily retranslated into English.

These facts show clearly that Democrats and the media need to be careful about taking the Latino vote for granted—as being slam-dunk Democratic. They need to factor in that almost a quarter of millennials—who tend to be apolitical and nonpartisan—are of Hispanic heritage; that many military and law enforcement officers as well as many older Latino-heritage citizens (especially women), are conservatives who predictably vote Republican. In fact, Ronald Reagan famously said that "Latinos are really conservative Republicans—they just don't all know it."

The veracity of the mantra "demography is destiny" must be questioned as well as the assumption that all Latinos are liberal, civil rights activists urging politicians to pass comprehensive immigration reform. While most Latinos, like most Americans who all are from immigrant stock, are sympathetic about the plight of illegal immigrants, the issue of immigration reform was rarely rated higher than five in continual polls of Latino voters of their top issues in 2012. Even Democratic Party chairman Debbie Wasserman-Schultz from Florida told a National Press Club in 2013, after the 2012 elections briefing, that "Latinos in my district never rate immigration reform as their top issue; but they are sensitive to it; it is a gateway issue for them."

In fact, Hispanic Republican members of Congress are growing in number and as a whole, are younger, fresher, more visible, and more multi-issue oriented than Democrats. What frustrates Democratic activists most about the Republican Hispanics is that they "don't act Latino." Hispanic Republicans do not tend to play the ethnic identity politics card. Hispanic Republican congressional members like Ileana Ros-Lehtinen (Florida), Raul Labrador (Idaho, the first Mormon Hispanic in Congress), and Mario Diaz Balart (Florida), do not tend to become members of or be active with the Congressional Hispanic Caucus. But they were all advisors of the Senate and House "Gang of Eight" that had hopes of formulating and passing a bipartisan, kinda-sorta comprehensive immigration bills until the Obamacare blowup in November 2013.

Hispanic Republicans have a multitude of political interests, however, and don't obsess about immigration reform. In 2014, almost all of them supported the Republican leadership's strategy that immigration enforcement enhancement must come first; then subsequent reform bills should be done in well-debated, stand-alone pieces—not in an omnibus comprehensive package. They mostly favored securing enforcement measures that would increase the number of border patrol, detention centers, and speedy removal of most new illegal immigrants trying to cross the border illegally.

Most Republican Hispanics also favor stronger interior enforcement like E-Verify, before expanding the numbers of legal immigrants (especially investors and highly skilled workers and foreign students with advanced degrees). Most of them also favor legalization of some of the illegal immigrant population, including young children who came in at an early age with their parents and have stayed a number of years (they call them KIDS not DREAMers), agricultural workers, families of military service personnel, and some long-time residents with successful businesses that employ American workers.

But the press rarely, if ever, cover the pieces of immigration reform that Republican Hispanics and other Republicans (such as Senator Jeff Flake [Arizona] and Senator Lindsey Graham [South Carolina]) favor. The media's sole source for positive immigration reform articles seems to be exclusively Democratic Latinos—especially Luis Gutierrez, the 12-term (as of 2015) loquacious, and charming Puerto-Rican-heritage congressman from Chicago. Gutierrez has been the comprehensive immigration reform spokesman and voice for the Democratic Congressional Hispanic Caucus for almost a decade.

It has certainly been an excruciating journey for him. In 2007, after Blue Dog Democrats took over the House (including Hispanic Caucus leader Xavier Becerra of California), Gutierrez was able to defeat what came to be labeled by the press as the "draconian" immigration bill Republicans had been floating that would have made being in the country illegally a felony. By 2007, Luis was so sure that the comprehensive immigration bill then being formed in the White House with Ted Kennedy would pass, that he was openly considering not running again for Congress by 2010. He dropped hints that he was interested in running for the mayor of Chicago.

But then disaster.

The Senate bill did not pass and Gutierrez's hometown colleague (nemesis perhaps?) Rahm Emanuel made it clear that comprehensive immigration reform would not be an issue for Democrats during the 2008 presidential and congressional races. At one point, Gutierrez threatened that CHC members would not pay their Democratic Party dues or help in the presidential campaign if immigration reform wasn't pushed, but Rahm's tightly controlled congressional campaigns did not change its strategy: immigration reform was not to be a campaign issue by anyone.

After Obama won the presidency and Democrats maintained control of both the House and the Senate, Rahm became the White House chief of staff. But Gutierrez found that against all expectations, the White House was even less friendly about comprehensive immigration reform than the Bush White House had been. Obama, America's first black president, met only rarely with the Congressional Hispanic and Black Caucuses—and then usually on the same day or two. He made it clear that he expected them to fully support his major priority, the Affordable Care Act. Gutierrez could only wait until 2010 to try to push comprehensive immigration reform again, so he gave up his plans to retire and ran again.

Then, another disaster.

The Democrats were "shellacked" (Obama's words) in the 2010 midterm elections and so was the Blue Dog caucus. In the last desperate days of the 112th Congress, Gutierrez tried to pass at least one important piece of immigration reform—the DREAM Act. He loaded it up as much as he could to make it as comprehensive as possible, but although it passed the House, it did not pass the Senate. The expanded bill turned off Republican senators like Texan Kay Bailey Hutchinson, who had planned to vote for the original: "It wasn't what I had been told" she indicated in interviews.

In 2011, Republicans took over the House by such a margin that the Judiciary Committee was allotted only five Democratic members—none of them Hispanic except for the Puerto Rican resident commissioner (who was an official member but did not have a vote on the floor). But immigration reform is not a big issue for Puerto Rico; their citizens are considered to be full U.S. citizens if they reside in the states. In 2011, Luis Gutierrez was not even on the Judiciary Committee.

The dawn of 2011 delivered another blow for Gutierrez's ambition. Rahm announced he would leave the White House in the fall to run for the mayor of Chicago (which he won). So despite being in the minority in the House and not even being on the committee, Gutierrez decided to stay on in Congress to fight for immigration reform. In 2012, after Obama's reelection and the beginning of the 113th Congress, Gutierrez asked to be secundered to the Judiciary Committee and its subcommittee on immigration. He was his usual confident, accessible, animated talkative self, pushing always for the moral case of comprehensive immigration reform. He was so open to talking to the press in his lively way at great lengths and at high volume and velocity (often mixing sentences in Spanish and English) that even reporters who had crowded around him in the congressional lobby would gradually drift away with no more questions to ask. Gutierrez would organize spontaneous press briefings mainly featuring very sympathetic illegal-immigrant DREAMers and unaccompanied minors; but the briefings were sparsely attended by the print media and rarely covered by the electronic media.

None of that seems to discourage Gutierrez. He is by far Congress's most persistent voice for comprehensive immigration reform and the Latino vote. It is most often the talking point of the amiable Illinois congressman that the media repeats so often that even some renowned Republican strategists like Karl Roe have come to believe them.

One of Gutierrez's mantras is that Republicans will be a marginal party of old white men if it continues to refuse to vote for comprehensive immigration reform. Another is that Republican's insistence to have "border control" first and to expand the enforcement of immigration laws tears families apart and makes Republicans anti-immigrant, anti-Latino, and wholly out of touch with America. Gutierrez maintains, and the press continually repeats his vision, that by 2050 (more than 35 years hence), when the U.S. Latino heritage population will have grown to close to 20 percent of the total population, the Republican Party will be almost dead.

But Gutierrez's and the medias' narrative does not take into account the reality of the growth of American-born Latinos, their great diversity, and the natural proclivity of the descendants of immigrants to identify less and less with their parents' and grandparents' homeland—especially when their parents hail from dozens of different nationalities and cultures. It also doesn't take into account (although Gutierrez is certainly aware of it) how much young Latinos are intermarrying with other cultures—not only Anglo, but also Asian.

The mantras like "demography is destiny" and the "monolithic Latino voting bloc will be liberal Democratic in perpetuity" really smell more like old twentieth-century stories—not twenty-first-century ones. It is more than likely that by the second half of the twenty-first century, the "Latino vote" will become as dispersed and meaningless as the "Italian vote" is today.

Other Latino Interest Groups

There are many other Latino organizations, some of them with broad national reach, that actively help Hispanics take a growing, solid place in the American middle class. Many support immigration reform, but it's not their main issue. They include large national organizations of Hispanic legislators, engineers, chambers of commerce, educators, cultural groups, and the Spanish-language media (which increasingly are either becoming bilingual or have switched to English-language dominance).

Above all there is the Catholic Church—bishops and deans, deacons and priests who gratefully welcome the many new Catholic immigrants not only from Latin America, but also from Africa and Eastern Europe (especially Poland) who can fill the church pews that native Americans are leaving. Maybe because of this, Catholic leaders tend to be very active promoting comprehensive immigration reform and the legalization of almost all illegal immigrants. In fact they vigorously deny that category. "There is no such thing as an illegal person!" they often say. "We obey the laws of a higher authority," they will actually say in public as well as often "the Bible says we must welcome the stranger" (implying it seems that that means giving illegal immigrants citizenship along with refuge).

The presence of some of these Latino-specific interest groups in immigration rallies has contributed to the perception that there is a public movement and support for immigration reform. But their message is naturally Latino-centric. It smacks of exclusiveness. It leaves out the great diversity and the very raison d'etre of the 1965 Immigration and Nationality Act to welcome immigrants from all cultures and nations of the world without preference for any one culture (i.e., Latino) or any one country (i.e., Mexico).

But in all the demands of Latino interest groups to legalize millions of mainly illegal workers from Mexico and Central America (about nine million), there is never any mention, no recognition at all, of the unemployment and wage stagnation of American workers. There is no empathy especially toward unemployed African Americans, even though in some cities like Washington, D.C., the unemployment rate of blacks is almost six times that of Latinos (including thousands working illegally). A 2013 report by the DC Fiscal Policy Institute found that in 2012, blacks in Washington, D.C., had an unemployment rate of 17.8 percent; Latinos, 2.9 percent; and whites, 2 percent.[38] African Americans have all but disappeared in some occupations like construction and hospitality and driving taxis in Washington, D.C., which are all dominated by immigrants—especially from El Salvador and Ethiopia.

After the Kennedy/Bush bill failed in 2007 and immigration was declared off the table by the Obama campaign strategists, enthusiasm for the immigration issue was visibly waning. Maybe it was compassion fatigue, but Latino activists' demands for comprehensive immigration reform for Latino workers who were doing better across the nation than African Americans seem to be eliciting less and less public sympathy.

That is, until the DREAMers were created.

Dreamers

Americans love children—from infants to young adults. Minors in most countries are considered adults by around age 18; but in Mexico and Central America it's 15—the *quincinera* birthday. In the United States, Obamacare gives dependent-child-rate insurance to those under the age of 26; it's an example how Americans are particularly sympathetic to young people. Poor, struggling, innocent, illegal immigrant children especially are seen very sympathetically. In 1983, schools in America were ordered by the U.S. Supreme Court to offer free public education K–12 to all children regardless of immigration status. The order was aimed specifically at children who were illegally in the country.

Now college students who are illegally in the country have become the new focus of sympathy. The belief that all children in America should be able to go to college, that that is an inherent part of the American Dream, has now become a primary immigration-reform issue. In fact, the rights of college-age, illegal immigrants is the hottest issue in immigration reform politics today. It has Congress in a quandary. Political parties are split over the issue. The president has become highly involved. So have the states. In the past six years, 15 states have decided (sometimes by voter initiative) to grant in-state tuition subsidies to illegal immigrant students. For supporters of comprehensive immigration reform, especially Latinos, the new focus on college-age, illegal immigrants dreaming of a college education suddenly gave them a new story, new life, a new compassionate, heartrending reason for legalizing millions of unauthorized immigrants.

The object of all this sympathy and action soon became known as DREAMers. Senator Orin Hatch, the amiable Mormon Republican from Utah who was one of Ted Kennedy's best friends and colleagues, is said to have been the first legislator to come up with the idea of legalizing children who had been brought into the country by their parents illegally through no fault of their own. The story that is told and marketed is that these children are innocent of any wrongdoing, have no idea that they are not legally in the country, and only dream of going to college and developing their talents to contribute to the only country they have ever known.

The story of DREAMers is compelling. It speaks of fairness and compassion, flexibility and the American Dream. It is reasonable to argue for this particular group of illegal immigrants to have a special pathway to citizenship. Legislation in 2010 established the requirements of DREAM (Development, Relief, and Education for Alien Minors) Act proposals; they were imbedded unchanged in the 2013 Senate bipartisan comprehensive immigration reform bill. The basic requirements to become a DREAMer in the legislation were expected to be met by some two million children. These are basically the same requirements used for applicants for President Obama's executive action called DACA—Deferred Action for Childhood Arrivals. They include that for anyone to qualify as a "DREAMer" they must have

1. come into the United States before the age of 16;
2. resided in the United States for five consecutive years;
3. earned a high school diploma or a GED;
4. attended or intend to attend a four-year college for at least two years or served in the military for two years;
5. not been convicted of any serious felonies;
6. not reached the age of 30 (decreased from 35 in 2010);
7. kept documents to prove all of the above; and
8. paid the fee (around $500 and going up).

And if any of the statements are untrue or documents are fraudulent, the applicant may be fined.

DREAMers by definition are not children, even though they are often referred to as such. They are actually millennials, young adults, since they must have graduated from high school, which means they are at least 18 years old. It is notable what is *not* included in the DREAM Act requirements, even though the marketing often makes it sound as if these elements are basic.

1. There is no requirement that an applicant actually came in with their parents or anyone else for that matter.
2. There is no requirement that they came in illegally.
3. There is no requirement that they were innocent about entering the country illegally (tens of thousands of teenagers from Mexico and Central America knowingly cross the U.S. southern border continually).
4. There is no English language requirement at all. "They can learn English once they apply for citizenship," Audrey Singer, a Senior Fellow at the left-of-center Brookings Institute explained.
5. The GED, which is universally acknowledged not to be the equivalent of a high school diploma, can be earned at any age, in another language, and on the Internet;
6. There is no minimum high school grade average required.
7. Minimum military service for Americans is three years, but DREAMers need only complete two years, even though few if any will qualify since illegal immigrants are not allowed to be recruited in the armed services.
8. Multiple convictions of misdemeanors and "minor" felonies (such as knowingly using false identity documents) do not exclude DREAMer status.

9. DREAM status, along with full job benefits and eventual green cards, is only for college students illegally in the country—not for those on legal temporary visas.

About two million illegal immigrants were expected to apply for DREAMer status, but in reality far fewer would actually be able to obtain the documents and have the qualifications and interest to get the benefit. To date and despite a lot of outreach by support groups, about 700,000 have qualified for DACA initially, but the applications after three years have leveled off. About 30 percent of the qualified applicants are from Asia (usually having overstayed a legal temporary visa); the majority of the rest are from Mexico.

The DREAMer legislation immediately became political. Since the basic premise is reasonable, there was also much sympathy by legislators on both sides of the aisle to pass this happy exception for legalization. The problem was exactly how. Democrats, especially in the Obama White House, insisted that it be an essential unseparable part of comprehensive immigration reform; it was universally acknowledged that DREAMers could be *the* driver of comprehensive immigration reform. The warning was that, if it were separated out, it might pass by itself, but the rest of the package, including legalizing millions of other illegal immigrants, wouldn't pass—not for years or decades.

That DREAMers had become the bait and switch for comprehensive immigration reform was clear when on July 23, 2013, the House Judiciary Immigration subcommittee called a hearing to propose a Republican dream act called "the KIDS Act." It was essentially the same as the Democratic proposal (except some advocates suggested lowering the entry date to around 10 and requiring at least six years in an American elementary or secondary school). During the hearing Democratic Representative Gutierrez left the congressional dais to be a hostile witness against the bill. He said it was "un-American" to specify any particular group for legalization and it had to be part of a comprehensive bill or he would lobby against it. DREAMers who were on the witness panel (most of them in their mid-20s) begged emotionally (even cried) that the bill must include their parents and family members, including those who had already been deported.

The KIDS proposal died with the 113th Congress. It could well be resubmitted in the 114th as a stand-alone bill

Hispanic Serving Institutions (HSIs)

One other key Hispanic lobbying group must be mentioned especially in the context of the DREAMers. That is the group of colleges known as HSIs or Hispanic Serving Institutions. Their excellently organized and highly effective, bipartisan, congressional lobby organization is HACU—the Hispanic

Association of Colleges and Universities. HSIs and HACU are major players in the high-pressure though not-so-visible movement to legalize DREAMers.

The reason is existential. In the first year of the Obama administration, Secretary of Education Arne Duncan dedicated a ten-year, $1 billion dollar fund for HSIs (a similar fund was established for HBCU—Historic Black Colleges and Universities) to be used to support the institutions' programs geared to Hispanic-heritage students. Unlike HBCUs, HSIs do not have to have a historic location and history of serving Latinos. Any public or private institution of higher education can become an HSI if it can document a threshold enrollment of 25 percent of it undergraduates as of Hispanic heritage.

The designation was coined in 1986 by the newly founded Hispanic Association of Colleges and Universities. The concept became official federal policy in 1992 under President Clinton and reauthorized in 2008 under an amendment of the Higher Education Act. For revenue-starved universities, becoming an HSI could be the proverbial gold mine to Title V diversity and MSI (Minority Serving Institution) program funding. For the U.S. Department of Education, it was an obvious and marvelous incentive to recruit and retain their top target students—minorities, especially Hispanics.

That 25 percent threshold can make for some strange introductory greeting between educators. It's not uncommon when attending a meeting of university and college administrators to be greeted with:

"Oh, you're with an Hispanic publication? We're 22.4 percent."

"Oh we're 23 percent."

"Oh we're 24.6 percent—about 50 students to go!"—followed by grins and even high fives.

Of course we all know what everyone is referring to: how close their institution is to having 25 percent of their full-time undergraduate students who self-identify as ethnic "Latinos/Hispanics."[39]

There is no official, federal list of HSIs, but based on the criteria, HACU—which has become a superbly well-organized lobbying organization for HSIs—reports that 370 four-year, two-year, nonprofit, and for-profit colleges in the 50 states, Washington, D.C., and Puerto Rico qualify for the designation. This is up from 268 in 2010. Of the additional colleges, 70 percent are public institutions, 49 percent are two-year degree granting colleges. HSIs also include 10 research universities including HSI medical schools.

"Hispanics will make up 74 percent of new workers by 2020. HACU bipartisan initiatives are oriented especially to growing workforce needs in STEM fields and agricultural management. HSIs can only strengthen those initiatives," said Davila Serena, HACU's Executive Director for Legislative Affairs at the 2014 HACU annual capital legislative forum in Washington, D.C. The HSI funds provide great incentive and competition for universities and colleges across the nation to recruit a large number of Latino college students. A huge potential source of HSI-qualifying Hispanic students are DREAMers.

The legalization of DREAMers has become one of HACU's top legislative goals. Their stance for the past eight years is that the DREAM Act is so important to Hispanic families (and to HSIs) that it must be passed as soon as possible—if not part of a comprehensive package, then piecemeal; if not a Democratic DREAM bill, then perhaps a Republican KIDS Act. "We'd definitely consider (a Republican stand-alone "KIDS" bill) if it allows young people to help their families," said Antonio R Flores, the long-time president of HACU in a phone interview in 2014.

This has placed HACU at odds with the White House, particularly with Cecilia Muñoz, and with legislators such as Luis Gutierrez. But the fate of HSIs is changing, too; it depends on the comprehensive Higher Education Act's reauthorization, which is supposed to happen in 2015. But that, like everything else in the new Republican Congress, will also happen piecemeal.

Commercial Interests

Of course there are major organizations that are not particularly Latino oriented that both support and oppose the comprehensive reform of the 1965 INA. Some of them have obvious commercial interests for advocating for the legalization and amnesty of illegal immigrant workers, an expansion and easement of visas for needed skills workers, and the elimination or softening of enforcement of laws that restrict employers and immigrants no matter what their status, from working in the United States and eventually obtaining a pathway to citizenship—a green card, permanent legal residency status. Of course in all cases, this looser policy toward immigration is good for the bottom line of these organizations, especially in terms of increasing membership, revenue, and political clout.

Labor Unions

It may be surprising to realize, even as it maybe makes sense, that the Great Society and the globalization of commerce and labor mobility was not good for labor unions. After the 1960s, the strength of the once most-powerful lobbying group in turn-of-the century American politics was starting to wane. In the 1950s, 40 percent of workers in the private sector belonged to a labor union; by 2013, less than 7 percent did. By 2015, public sector unions for once-untouchable workers like teachers and firemen are now under attack.

Some blame McCarthyism and the Cold War's fight against communism, which tainted the ideals of the "worker state" in America. Some blame America's success with a relatively free market economy now emulated throughout the world. Many blame globalization and foreign competition. "The role of organized labor has changed for two simple reasons," writes labor journalist Philip M. Dine in his 2007 book *State of the Union*. "First, some employers have become more enlightened and treat workers better without a union. Second, a combination of [employer-friendly] labor laws . . . discourage workers from voting for unions."[40]

The SEIU (Service Employees International Union) is one of the country's most powerful service sector unions today. It played a major role in the election and reelection of President Obama. But its policies are somewhat confused toward immigration: it organizes illegal immigrant workers, encourages them to demand minimum wage and be accorded all the rights of American and legal immigrant workers, and at the same time it lobbies against temporary visas and claims to be against open borders.

"Labor's self-interest involves representing American workers and their jobs and wages, while also protecting (illegal) immigrant workers from exploitation," writes Dine.[41] Focusing on the confusing issue of immigration is not a big win for labor. It is even more perplexing since protecting and encouraging illegal immigrant workers places labor unions in a strange partnership with organizations such as the Chamber of Commerce and corporate libertarians who do not want labor to be regulated.

Others

Other commercial supporters of comprehensive immigration reform are obvious and some need only be listed here as examples. They include the following:

- The U.S. Chamber of Commerce, a major organization with a breathtaking headquarters overlooking the White House, with affiliates in hundreds of U.S. cities and towns, one of the largest and most active being the U.S. Hispanic Chambers of Commerce (which meets in Washington, D.C., every year). During the George W. Bush administration, the president would deliver a keynote speech almost every year—including several sentences in Spanish that it was claimed "he spoke bravely." Hillary Clinton also spoke to the group numerous times, as has Cecilia Muñoz and other from the Obama White House. As the prime voice for free-market economies, including a globally available labor force, the Chambers of Commerce understandably have a major interest in the deregulation of labor, including immigrant labor.
- The CEOs of Microsoft, Google, and many other high-tech industries have met often with legislators since 2010 in support of comprehensive immigration reform—but mainly to be sure that it includes an increase in visas for H-1B high-tech workers. It is not clear that the legalization of millions

of low-wage, illegal immigrants is really the priority of these CEOs who tend to avoid an ostentatious lifestyle that includes high-maintenance MacMansions, but seem to have been sold on the Democratic message that immigration reform has to be comprehensive or nothing. That may change in 2015.

- Civil and corporate libertarians as represented by the Koch CATO institute in Washington, D.C., proclaim a seductive message of liberty from regulations; they famously advocate for the deregulation of commerce, drugs, trade, and immigrants. Many Democrats and Republicans are attracted to their message.
- Globalists, sometimes known as "flat landers," after *New York Times* columnist Tom Friedman's book *The World Is Flat*, seem to believe that the globalization of commerce, corporations, and social media have made national borders and sovereign nation-states obsolete. They are wrong of course, but "globalization" is often used as an excuse for relaxing immigration regulations in the same way that the U.S. motto, "A Nation of Immigrants," is—as a policy that, as Friedman puts it, "leaves open a wide front gate."
- Universities: despite their nonprofit status, the higher education industry along with its immigration partner, the foreign-student industry, is highly supportive of comprehensive immigration reform; some of the top political issues in immigration today involve the institutions of higher education—especially DREAMers, expanding "optional practical training" (OPT) periods for post-graduate foreign students (from 12 months to 36 months in some cases), eliminating caps for foreign students in public colleges' undergraduate programs, and granting green cards to foreign students graduating with advanced degrees in STEM fields.

All of these issues are very sympathetic to Americans in general for whom not only going to college is essential to the American identity and the "American Dream," but who also firmly believe that all of the hundreds of thousands of foreign nationals studying in the United States on foreign student visas are not only "the best and brightest in the world" (that is to imply, far better and brighter than American kids), but also confirm that our universities and colleges are the best in the world. (Some are, but mainly they are the most wonderfully diverse in the world; literally anyone can go to some college or other in America if they only want to and can come up with the time and the money.) Higher education is a growing and lucrative industry in the United States and counted as one of America's top five exports; foreign students contribute over a billion dollars a year to the U.S. economy.

Most Americans and certainly most members of the press do not know that over 450,000 foreign (aka, "international" students in politically correct speech, despite the fact they are studying on F visas—as in "foreign") students, mostly at public universities, are graduate students, and the majority are studying for advanced degrees in the STEM fields and come from mainly two countries: India and China. At present, the foreign student visa is unlimited in number—because it is temporary and specifically "a nonimmigration visa." If it becomes an immigration visa, as many universities hope in order to increase recruitment, then foreign students will be counted in the immigration numbers game and may end up being capped. Universities pushing for foreign student immigration visas (which could happen as a stand-alone bill in 2015–2016) should probably think about what they're wishing for.

The interesting thing about all of these organizations and politicians who support comprehensive immigration reform is what a broad spectrum they cover. Maybe the reason they haven't become a marching, public momentum, however, is that together they make a really strange bunch of bedfellows. It is still a bit startling to go to a panel discussion on the rights of illegal immigrants at a far-left think tank such as the Center for American Progress and NDN, and find on the stage executives of the U.S. Chamber of Commerce, corporate CEOs, and the libertarian home ship, the CATO Institute. They all are mostly solid Republicans who oppose Democrats on almost all of their core issues such as equal pay, minimum wage, labor union membership, and business, banking, and commercial regulations. Something seems out of whack with these strange bedfellows of liberals and corporate libertarians and the silence of the media about it. That may be due to the increasingly officious suffocation of political correctness.

Restrictionists

There are a number of organizations that want to restrict immigration either by cutting back on the number of legal immigrants or more usually, by stopping illegal immigration altogether. Many if not most Americans, including Democrats, are truly uncomfortable with the growing number of illegal immigrants in the country and the tendency by libertarians to protect them from U.S. laws (labor, education, driving licenses, immigration, and so on). Many Americans throughout the country (even in California) also are concerned about the "offshoring" of American jobs inside America by employers who hire growing number of legal immigrants and foreign students. But there are only a small number of organizations and congressmen who publicly express these concerns. As in 1965, it is difficult to come up with an American grassroots message for restricting immigration that can't be accused of being racist, xenophobic, nativist and of course, Nazi.

The handful of organizations that do have a national voice to restrict immigration, however, have been surprising effective.

- CAPS—Californians for Population Stabilization has produced and shown on prime-time cable TV and in major newspapers, especially on Capital Hill, some gut-wrenching ads that focus on jobs.
- NumbersUSA, a Spartan organization run by Roy Beck, a formal environmentalist journalist, has such an effective grassroots phone, fax, and e-mail response network that in 2007 it literally shutdown the entire communications system of the U.S. Congress with a deluge of electronic protests against the comprehensive immigration bill on the floor of the Senate. That sparked its highly responsive grassroots system of electronic protests for every comprehensive initiative being considered in Congress ever since.
- Center for Immigration Studies, founded by a mix of liberal and conservative scholars, is a font of breaking-news, deep, irrefutable, data-based studies on immigration that support their goal of limiting immigration. The charming and often witty director Mark Krikorian was called "the provocateur standing in the way of immigration reform" in a cover story in the Style section of the *Washington Post* on June 17, 2013, by Manuel Roig-Franzia. "A Washington question of the moment—Can immigration reform pass?—might be reframed this way: Can Mark Krikorian be stopped?" concludes the article.

Environmentalists

Even as the GREENs in Europe gained such popularity that they have won legislative seats in various national parliaments such as Germany, they have never coalesced into a political force on their own in the United States. They have increasingly become a faction of the Democratic Party and a contentious one at that, mainly over the issue of the Keystone Pipeline, favored by many Midwest Democrats—legislators extremely important to the party since losing the House in 2010 and the Senate in 2014.

Environmentalists' major issue "climate change," also known as "global warming," also has had a hard time gaining credibility: it is very complex with very slow outcomes, despite hype of cities like San Francisco being underwater in a few centuries. Even naming the issue is an obstacle. Skeptics of their cause can agree that climate change is happening, but they question if man has made it worse, and if anything that what the environmentalists urge government to do, will really make any difference since climate change is a global problem. It's an issue that may be better worked out through international agreements that are then enforced.

By 2015, the biggest energy issue for Americans also has incredibly made a complete turnaround—from oil dependency on foreign nations to independence. This thanks to new technologies that concern environmentalists, with the discovery of fracking; clean oil, gas, and coal production; and pipelines that can carry crude oil from Canada for thousands of miles. By 2015, Americans are suddenly looking at plunging gasoline prices as a huge boon to working Americans and especially immigrants and their families who increasingly live in the suburbs and must use an automobile to survive. Plus all Americans (though maybe not our foreign policy) should benefit from the incredible freedom (and leverage) we'll have being energy independent.

It may however hurt nations like Mexico who the past few years have become more prosperous thanks to their oil industry. In the past few years, net migration from Mexico is zero; as many nationals have returned to Mexico as have come in. One reason is the "broadening economy" of Mexico, according to a 2012 Pew Hispanic Center Hispanic Trends report.[42]

Environmentalists also play an unexpected role (albeit small) and have had a voice in immigration policy since the 1960s—if not a unified voice. A certain segment of them have supported limiting immigration because they believe population growth—which has been driven mainly by immigration in the United States—harms the environment. Professor Cafaro has suggested in writing that immigration be halted altogether by a moratorium for a few years, and then cut back substantially. He expected some pushback from the right and corporate libertarians, but he was shocked at the virulence of criticism from the left, especially colleagues at the university.[43]

American Economic Nationalists

Republican Congressman Tom Tancredo of Colorado (now retired), Congressman Steven King of Iowa, and their legislative assistant George Fishman have been the congressional point men for restricting immigration for over a decade. King is a soft-spoken but often tart commentator about immigration and especially illegal immigrants, from Storm Lake, Iowa. He ran a local contracting and construction company, where he became outraged about the unenforcement of immigration laws in his community when he found himself and his associates constantly being underbid and his American workers and their families losing their skilled jobs to illegally imported workers.

King ran for Congress in 2002. There he has become the unremitting voice against comprehensive immigration reform. But he often also opposes many of the stand-alone bills favored by the Republican leadership on the basis that they would hurt American workers. Some of the impolitic remarks by this highly religious congressman (such as "many of the kids coming illegally over the Mexican border have calves the size of melons because of the heavy bags of drugs they must carry") are met with outrage and labels of racist and "Latino hater" by sensitive mainstream journalists and journalism professors, always on the lookout especially for politically incorrect, insensitive remarks. King's comments do distract from many of the valid points that he makes.

In the first days of the new Congress in 2010 when the House flipped Republican, King introduced a bill to change the precedent of birthright citizenship for children born to illegal immigrants and birth tourists. It was bad timing. His passion and focus on this controversial proposal probably was the reason that King was not given the chairmanship of the House Immigration subcommittee, as had been widely expected.

Republican Senator Jeff Sessions of Alabama speaks in the low, soft drawl of an endearing Southern gentleman from the old school, even when he's passionate. On the floor of the Senate and in the Committee, he speaks often in opposition to comprehensive immigration reform. His many well-researched and reasonable amendments to the Senate comprehensive immigration reform bill of 2013 were met with civil debate and very calm respect by his Democratic colleagues who are always polite to him. But none of his proposals passed in the democratically controlled 113th Senate. Sessions undoubtedly will be a strong voice for new piecemeal immigration proposals that come before the 114th Congress just as he had been a strong opponent of omnibus packages. He was adamantly against the president's "unconstitutional overreach" with executive orders in November 2014 to legalize millions of illegal immigrants; but it is unclear what Sessions will be able to propose to block them.

IMMIGRATION REFORM TIMELINE 2000–2015

Even with all the hype about immigration reform in the media since the beginning of the new millennium, nevertheless immigration was a rather tepid election issue in 2004, 2008, and 2012. During the past twelve years, even Hispanic voters never rated it more than fifth in priority in polls listing their top issues. Topping immigration were concerns about jobs, the economy, education, and health care.

Immigration reform started out in the new millennium to be one of the highest priorities on President Bush's agenda. But it was usurped nine months later by the war on terror. President Obama in turn, never showed much interest in the issue. It could be that it surprised even him to suddenly find the press labeling immigration reform as one of his top "legacy" issues (this after Obamacare got into so much trouble).

Despite the distractions however, a number of very important legislative and administrative actions involving immigration have been implemented between 2000 and 2015. A brief timeline includes the following:

2001   President Bush promises comprehensive immigration
                reform will be a top and first priority of his new presidency.

He invites President Fox to his ranch, celebrates the first Cinco de Mayo ever in the White House, and prepares to open up wider border agreements with Mexico. But then on 9/11 the terrorist attack on New York and the Pentagon is perpetrated by foreign nationals mainly from Saudi Arabia, many of them in the country illegally or with unvetted student visas or expired temporary visas, and possessing multiple driver licenses from multiple states.

2002   The SEVIS system is revived and becomes a nonnegotiable electronic tracking system required of universities and colleges to maintain as a condition of being able to give out unlimited numbers of foreign student visas.

2004   Democratic House leader Rahm Emanuel declares immigration reform to be a nontopic for Democratic 2008 election candidates.

2005   The Department of Homeland Security is created out of over 100 duplicating enforcement and intelligence agencies as well as newly developed ones. The old Immigration and Naturalization Service (INS) that housed all immigration agencies for almost 100 years, is broken up into two main bureaus: CIS and ICE, with a newly expanded mission on border security and a new focus on interior enforcement—especially work sites hiring immigrants without work permits. Development of the E-Verify system is initiated and more border detention facilities, manpower, and equipment are dedicated to the southern border.

2006   Mass demonstrations of Latinos saying "no somos criminals" protest a Republican immigration reform bill that would have made being in the country illegally a felony.

2007   A comprehensive immigration reform including a new mass amnesty is developed by President Bush and Senators Kennedy and McCain; it fails.

2008   Obama promises to address immigration reform if he is elected president.

2009   Obama fulfills his promise to address immigration reform at a lecture on immigration at America University attended by civil rights organization leaders. But the president puts his full negotiating powers and focus behind enacting a health care act, not comprehensive immigration reform. The Obama administration changes the DHS priority to cyber security and less on immigration violations except against "serious felonies involving violence."

2010   The DREAM Act passes as a stand-alone bill in the House in November by desperate Democratic majority leaders who had just lost the election to the Republicans; a frantic effort to pass it in the Senate fails in December.

2011   Obama tells a La Raza conference of over 10,000 people in Washington, D.C., that he cannot go around Congress and make an executive order to legalize DREAMers.

2012   With the campaign for second term going badly, Obama in June announces he will order a deferred action, called DACA (Deferred Action for Childhood Arrivals), of deportation for DREAMers.

2013   After Republicans shut down the government for six weeks and ruin their brand by enabling sequestration, the Senate in June passes a bipartisan kinda-sorta comprehensive immigration reform bill that would legalize some eight million of the estimated 12 million illegal immigrants living and working in the United States, as well as making E-Verify a national requirement for all employers, beefing up the border guard, and expanding H-1B, student, and investor visas. Expectations are that the House Republicans would pass a similar bill as the best and maybe only way to help their image in the coming midterm elections. But then in October the Obamacare roll-out was a complete disaster and suddenly the Democrats are seen as inept, out-of-touch, and weak. Republicans instead held numerous hearing and passed several stand-alone bills including E-Verify. On July 23, 2013, the House Judiciary Subcommittee on Immigration considers passing a KIDS bill that follows much of the lines of the DREAM Act, but all the Democrats on the panel oppose it on the basis that it is not comprehensive.

2014   DREAMer activists decide to become more aggressive by demonstrations at homes of officials, including handcuffing themselves to the White House fence. They end up not only causing the only sympathetic Republican leader of their cause, Eric Cantor, to lose his primary election, but also enabling an unknown Tea Party conservative economics professor who is solidly against comprehensive immigration reform to win Cantor's Virginia seat.

Despite media hype about the Latino vote and immigration being crucial for Democrat to keep the Senate in 2014, in fact the Republicans make a sweep of the Senate and the House in the midterm elections, confirming that there is no significant Latino Democratic vote in any of the key states to stop Republicans.

After the election wipeout for Democrats, President Obama implements an executive action to defer deportation and give working permits to some five million illegal immigrants, mostly adults in mixed families of American citizens, but not the parents of DREAMers per se. It is called DAPA—Deterred Action for the Parents of Americans. It also expands DACA by easing the upper age limit.

2015   The 2016 elections season begins immediately with the press again hyping the Latino vote and the importance for Republicans to back comprehensive immigration reform. In the first two months of the year the immigration battle plays out over whether or not to defund the CIS in the Department of Homeland Security to block it from carrying out Obama's November executive action. The press covers it minutely, but there is no public outcry. The constitutionality of the president's actions to give benefits, including state driver's licenses and temporary job permits, to those for whom he has deferred prosecution, appears to be headed to the Supreme Court after a federal court in Texas puts a hold on the action.

Comprehensive vs. Piecemeal Immigration Reform

The core battle that has been going on between the Senate and House, the Democrats, and the Republicans over immigration reform is over procedure, not just content; it is over "comprehensive" vs. "piecemeal" reform. Now that the Republicans control both houses until 2016 at least, it is very clear that the "comprehensive" approach to anything is pretty much DOA. Republicans openly oppose these favored Democratic omnibus bills that number thousands of pages that no congressman has time to read. They are offended when Democratic leader Nancy Pelosi states that they can "find out what is in it once it's passed."

Republican lawmakers insist that immigration reform (and other issues as well) must be debated, decided, and voted on in small pieces—piecemeal, not comprehensive. They have much more control over them. Various committees can get in on the debate. This is a much more complex, nuanced, and wonky process for the instant—something the 24/7, instant, electronic media devoted to headlines hates to cover.

Democratic activists continue to insist on comprehensive reform that includes the legalization of millions of illegal immigrants—the majority of whom are Mexican nationals. This is their red line—what Republicans call "blanket amnesty."

But 2016 is an election year. Both parties are hoping to win the presidency. Both parties hope to win the Senate. Both parties want to be seen as being able to govern. That means being open to compromise and be positive about immigration and immigrants.

Such compromise is possible. It has already been seen. The 2013 Senate bill legalized some eight million of the 12 million illegal immigrants in the country. There were many pieces in it that both parties agreed to. History shows that often more compromises are reached when government is divided, especially in a president's last year of his last term.

In 2015, in a Republican-dominated Congress, it is very likely that many of the pieces and stand-alone bills that the Republican House has already considered and passed in the last four years may come up for a vote again in the 114th Congress. Many of those pieces are elements that Democrats including the president support—especially giving green cards to foreign students graduating with advanced degrees in the STEM fields. They include programs to legalize or make it easier to come in legally for some particular immigrant populations such as agriculture workers, high-skilled techies, and investors—all groups Democrats also want to see given pathways to citizenship. It is very possible that some of these fairly significant pieces of immigration reform will be debated in committee, passed (possibly in small packages) by both chambers, and set on the president's desk to sign.

Such a piecemeal approach would obviously benefit Republicans. It will be hard for the press and the Democrats to keep chaining them down with the moniker of being "anti-immigrant" and "anti-immigration-reform" if good pieces of immigration legislation are being passed and sent to the president to sign. It could also help Republicans win over some more Hispanic and immigrant groups—especially Asians who tend to be highly educated in the sciences. Passing piecemeal immigration legislation would also put the issue in the president's court, so to speak. After all, it will be difficult for the president to veto every piece of immigration reform Republicans send to him and try to make them seem "anti-immigrant."

Democrats could also benefit, however, by a piecemeal approach. It helps the immigrants whom they claim are a core Democratic constituency, especially if Republicans are forced to compromise on granting legal status to DREAMers and such. In fact, probably most of the groups that would in the end be legalized by a piecemeal approach are exactly those that the president already has separated out by giving them the possibility to apply for temporary prosecutorial discretion (on a case-by-case basis) through DACA and DAPA. Democrats also could win further if a number of these pieces of immigration reform would be wrapped up in a kinda-sorta "comprehensive" immigration reform package.

The piecemeal approach would allow the many complicated issues of immigration to be truly discussed and debated. The press might not be pleased in general—too much in the weeds for entertaining consumption! But it could be the way to make immigration reform the civil debate it needs to be instead of a gotcha political game between identity groups.

Chapter Six

Lessons Learned

The history of over 140 years of evolving national immigration law that led to the "law that changed the face of America" and to the intense politics of immigration today, has been presented in the five chapters of this book. The economic, demographic, technological, and political changes in the country have been reviewed that drove the first comprehensive immigration law to be passed in 1924—a law that severely limited immigration to specifically preferred groups based on national origin. Then those tumultuous changes of the Depression, war, leadership, and redemption were highlighted that led to the civil rights movement, the Great Society, and the historic Immigration and Nationality Act of 1965—the most liberal immigration law in the world. Finally, the impact and unintended consequences of that law over the next 50 years were examined, along with the changing economic and social environment of America that brought us to the present intense congressional politics over reform of the 1965 INA.

Detectible patterns and trends can be observed in this history. Some questions can be addressed. Some lessons and foresights can be learned that might help to develop future immigration laws in the United States. These are the ones that stand out.

IMMIGRATION LAWS WILL NEVER BE DONE "ONCE AND FOR ALL"

It must be obvious to any reader by now, after observing how national immigration law has evolved in this country over the past 140 years, that it is a constant work in progress. Clearly, no immigration law will ever be chiseled in stone (as a poem may be). It will never "be fixed" "once and for all" as President Obama has been heard to say.

Immigration laws obviously respond to dynamic forces—drivers—in the nation and outside, which are constantly changing: economic, demographic, technological, and political. In this century and those to come, a fifth driver may well be added: climate calamity (for lack of a better term). We may see entire countries become uninhabitable necessitating an entire evacuation of their populations and demanding an internationally agreed-upon environmental refugee policy.

But whatever the causes, these drivers of immigration affect the opportunities immigrants and citizens alike have to work and to make a good life for themselves and their families in a sovereign nation. The drivers not only change global migration patterns, but also the attitudes and abilities of sovereign nation-states to welcome, host, and integrate immigrants, including refugees. Immigration laws will continue to be a prime domestic policy issue that every nation-state continually will have to deal with.

To be a successful "nation of immigrants," immigration laws have to balance the interests of the nation-state and the interests of immigrants. They have to be flexible, not rigid, and change with the times. Expectations about assimilation have to be made clear. The laws and principles of each nation's immigration policy need to be constantly updated, tweaked, and refocused.

Such changes for the INA have been the topics of heated discussions in the immigration reform debate of the past eight years. As they age, aspects of immigration law that were important decades ago, become obsolete and unnecessary. Accepting the fact that immigration reform is a continual work in progress is a more positive and realistic way—a less dramatic, vilifying, sky-is-falling way—to approach the necessity to periodically change immigration laws in the future.

IMMIGRATION IS AN ESSENTIAL DOMESTIC ISSUE

It has been said that all nations are "nations of immigrants" now. The importance of attracting and retaining the "right" immigrants to help a nation prosper is increasingly recognized in the Western world. It is a national decision about who, how many, and how.

Despite what some libertarian globalists say, belonging to a nation-state with defined borders, centuries of history and traditions, and recognized national citizenship is important to almost everyone. National identity is one of the basic identities a person has that doesn't change over time. The predicted death of nation-states and national identity by obsolescence, their replacement by a globalized citizenship is clearly not happening. Even within a strong union like the EU, Swedes are still Swedes, French still French. While the "globalization" of business, communication, transportation, and problem confrontation (like health epidemics) through electronic media and international organizations continues to expand throughout the world, sovereign nation-states still are not only surviving and not facing extinction, but are also actually growing in number.

Perhaps the continued popularity of nation-states and national citizenship is because as multi-everything democracies homogenize elite cultures, citizens long for and embrace the uniqueness of their nations' core identities and heritages that make these citizens not only stand out, but also belong to something definable. Perhaps the freedom of global mobilization and communication makes it safe to be "nationalistic." Whatever the reason, in the now second decade of the twenty-first century, the concept and viability of sovereign nation-states even within multi-national organizations such as the EU and the United Nations, are still solid and supported.

It seems that in the twenty-first century, sovereign nation-states will still have defined borders. National governments will still be responsible for the national security of their citizens—which includes access to good jobs within the nation-state. They will continue to be uniquely responsible for deciding and choosing who can come over their borders, stay, and work, and how they might become a citizen in the sovereign nation-state. Citizens will actively seek and encourage immigrants who they feel will contribute to the future prosperity and security of the country. As immigration laws are national laws, nation-states' law enforcement officials still will have the duty to enforce them. There is really no doubt that as long as sovereign nation-states exist, they will continue to have immigration laws that spell out the parameters of immigration decisions and how they are to be enforced.

IMPORTANCE (OR NOT) OF MOVEMENTS FOR IMMIGRATION REFORM

Immigration reform never has enjoyed massive grass-roots national support in the United States. It has always been part of another movement, of a surge of a popular political passion of the day led by strong, politically leaning media and interest groups. We have seen how concern about massive surges of Chinese workers after the gold rush in California led to the first national immigration law—the Chinese Exclusionary Act of 1882; how the first comprehensive immigration law, the Nationality Origins Quota Act of 1924 was passed because of the threat labor unions saw by the increasingly uncontrolled historic surge of immigrants between 1880 and 1920. The 1965 INA was passed because of the civil rights movement and public (some say liberal) guilt and horror over the Holocaust before and during World War II when the United States turned away Jewish families fleeing Eastern Europe because of our restrictions on immigrants from their countries of origin.

So what compelling, grassroots movement now underlies comprehensive immigration in the twenty-first century? Not unions—they have all but vanished. Not outrage over immigration discrimination based on national origin. In fact ironically, now many nationality representative groups are demanding that their particular nationality (like Mexican or Irish or Southeast Asian) be allowed more visas than others for a variety of reasons. Perhaps the hardest case to make for green card preference is the one that is the most loudly advocated in Congress—for immigrants who knowingly came into the country illegally or knowingly overstayed their temporary visas. Their case based on civil rights discrimination is weak. You know it when advocates have to resort to moral and religion reasons: "It's the right thing to do," and "The bible says so."

So what is the movement behind immigration reform in the twenty-first century? So far in the new millennium, it is driven by two dramatic events: the terrorist attack of 9/11 by mostly unvetted immigrants, an event that focused immigration control now onto national security, and the election of the first black president, Barack Obama, followed by the death of the twentieth century's most liberal icon, Senator Ted Kennedy. Both represent the success of the civil rights movement of the 1960s and its turning point into a splintering movement of ever-growing numbers of highly distinct identity groups all demanding their rights.

The point is that since the beginning of the twenty-first century, there are multiple and good reasons for changing, updating, fixing, adding to, and/or eliminating pieces of immigration law. But there is no public unified "fierce urgency" to do so for any one fix, such as stopping illegal immigration, or granting blanket amnesty to all who are here illegally, or closing the borders and deporting all unauthorized immigrants. Instead, there are on the table a large variety of options, proposals, ideas, suggestions, and demands on how and what to do by an equal number of diverse interest groups advocating for them.

But most Americans understand that immigration is complicated. They know and are proud that we have been a successful nation of immigrants over time and that immigration is a vital part of our domestic life. Most Americans are interested in and can handle complex and passionate arguments about the various aspects of immigration, as long as those discussions are civil. Most understand that to balance the interests of the nation-state and of the local community and of the immigrants from every country in the world takes time to consider, debate, and legislate. But there is no broad public urgency for one fixed way—only from lobbyists with vested interests. And even those vested interests are across the spectrum.

IMMIGRATION ISSUES SPLIT BOTH POLITICAL PARTIES

Put aside the media's constant proclivity to reduce all issues including immigration to two sides (as if everything they cover has to be reported like a sports match or a shootout with a clear winner and a clear loser, a good guy and a bad guy). But immigration issues are much more complicated and nuanced than that. The history of our evolving immigration laws and immigration reform politics today show clearly that there are both Democrats and Republicans who want fewer restrictions on immigrant labor (call them corporate and civil Libertarians); just as there are both Republicans and Democrats who want to better control the number of immigrants who come into the country and base that selection mainly on their work skills. There are religious Democrats and Republicans who really in their hearts don't think immigrants should ever be deported; just as there are Republican and Democratic military and law-enforcement officers and legislators who firmly insist that our nation must respect and enforce our immigration laws as we do all our other laws.

What most Americans know and agree on however, is that if a plurality of the citizens don't like a law or even a constitutional amendment (like prohibition for instance), then they must make the legislators (not the enforcers or the executives) change it.

What also is clear is that there is broad consensus among most every Republican and Democrat that the assimilation of immigrants has been one of the best characteristics of the United States. Most American politicians and citizens are proud that we have set the world standard of what a successful nation of immigrants looks and acts like. Now in the twenty-first century it is normal to honor our diverse family cultural heritages (especially the food), as well as our American one. Most everyone in the United States now recognizes that immigration is one of our greatest legacies—as individuals, families, and as a nation-state. Most unusually among nations, Americans truly assume that almost everyone in the world would like to immigrate to the United States and to become an American citizen—to become one of us and like us.

What splits members in our two major political parties are the details of immigration management. The choices that must be made are many: the who, the how, the what, how many, and how much enforcement. Immigration, like infrastructure and so many other domestic issues, is bipartisan and not owned by one party or the other. All the media and lobbyist-advocacy hype that makes it seem as if there are just two sides to immigration and that the two political parties are lined up unwaveringly on either side—the anti-immigrant Republicans vs. the pro-immigrant Democrats—is disingenuous, uninformed, and simplistic to the point of insulting. (Perhaps the lesson learned here is that in the end, the bipolar-oriented press should be given the Jon Stewart treatment—exposure with gentle mockery.)

It's pretty clear, looking at the history of immigration politics, that party affiliation doesn't matter for the success of immigration reform. As was pointed out in chapter 5, most of the time in modern political history Congress and the president have been "unbalanced" and at odds. That is, most of the time the same political party does not control the White House, the Senate, and the House of Representatives. President Johnson's "fabulous 89th" was an aberration. But Americans seem to prefer that the checks and balances envisioned by the founders be facilitated by having different parties control Congress and the White House. The lesson is that most legislation passes when the balance of power between president and Congress is mixed.

LEADERS WHO CAN COMPROMISE ARE CRUCIAL

The historic Immigration and Nationality Act of 1965 passed in part because of the alignment of a powerful social movement (civil rights) that elected and supported a majority Democratic House and Senate that passed a historic number of the liberal Democratic president's agenda including the replacement of the 1964 national origins immigration law.

But arguably the INA might not have been included in all that Great Society legislation if it hadn't been for the intense engagement of three political leaders: President Johnson, Senator Ted Kennedy, and Senator Philip Hart. All were personally and passionately involved in the immigration issue, had life-stories that made them particularly sympathetic to recent immigrants—including those residing illegally in the country and to those who had been discriminated against by the 1924 National Origins Quota Act.

But what made them key to the successful passage of the INA was not only that they were personally committed to immigration reform and sat in powerful positions. They were also very charismatic, outgoing men who were respected by people of vastly different points of view. They knew how, enjoyed, even relished making deals and compromises.

In the many stories that Robert A. Caro, Lyndon B. Johnson's prolific biographer, relates about how the "Master of the Senate" worked what always stands out is how Johnson would humble himself, would make the other person in the negotiation feel essential and crucial to the deal, would always let the other person get the credit. He would also spend hours on the phone, hosting key legislators from both parties at the White House, working with his once opponents in the Senate relentlessly to get a bill—most remarkably to open the way for the civil rights bill in 1964 by getting a discharge petition to pass with a majority vote in the House, bypassing the committee procedures. The time and effort Johnson spent over Christmas 1963 at his home in Texas and in early January is almost unbelievable. It was barely two months after he had been given the reins of president when JFK was assassinated on November 22. How he succeeded in managing this extraordinarily rare legislative move is dramatically told in *The Passage of Power: The Years of Lyndon Johnson*, by Robert A. Caro.[1] It is extremely hard to pass a discharge petition and maybe only the intense support of a fully engaged political leader like President Johnson can make it happen. (Note: for an amusing, although not wholly accurate, portrayal of the work it takes to pass a discharge petition, curl up on your TV couch with Reese Witherspoon in her movie, *Legally Blond 2*.)

Ted Kennedy's skills in bipartisan negotiating were also key to not only the passage of the INA in 1965, but also to subsequent add-ons. As related in chapter 5, Kennedy, the liberal lion, partnered with conservative icon President Ronald Reagan to pass the amnesty bill of 1986. He did it again with who the POTUS liberals hated most, President George W. Bush. With Bush and Senator John McCain in 2007, Kennedy wrote the comprehensive immigration reform bill in the White House and lobbied intensely for it in the Senate. Despite its failure, Kennedy remained an enthusiastic partner with McCain and others, preparing for the next comprehensive immigration reform bill that he was sure would come again in the next Congress.

Even in Kennedy's dark days of personal crisis, he was known and liked in the Senate for his civility, friendliness, and courtesy—his reaching out to the other side for partnership and bipartisanship. He was often passionate when he spoke, but always civil to his fellow members of Congress. Like Johnson he knew how to pull the levers of power, but mainly he used the leverage of friendship (and especially mutual Irish sociability) to make a deal with the other side.

Then there was Philip Hart, the senator whose name (not Kennedy's) adorns the official title of the 1965 Immigration and Nationality Act—the Hart-Celler Bill. A passionate civil rights Democrat, he was also a close friend and comrade in arms with Republican senator Robert Dole whom he met in a VA Hospital after having been severely wounded on Utah Beach in Normandy on the first day of the Allied invasion. He was elected to the U.S. Senate in 1958 and would be reelected by overwhelming majorities in the 1964 and 1970 elections. Hart came to be known as the "Conscience of the Senate" working tirelessly for passage of the civil rights laws. The Hart Senate Office Building was named in his honor in August 1976, shortly before he died of cancer; the vote was 99–0.

"He was not known for fiery words or sensational headlines, but was a man held in great esteem by his colleagues—Republican or Democrat, Liberal or Conservative for his moral and ethical standards. . . . To him, politics was the noble art of governing and governing was about building a better future for our children and our children's children.[2] On a plaque on the building is this tribute: "A man of incorruptible integrity and personal courage strengthened by inner grace and outer gentleness. . . . He advanced the cause of human justice, promoted the welfare of the common man and improved the quality of life. His humility and ethics earned him his place as the conscience of the Senate."

This is the kind of bipartisan leadership upon which the INA was built.

In the past seven years this conviviality has waned in Congress. There is no one like Kennedy, Johnson, or Hart in the present Congress or White House. Many journalists, lobbyists, and politicians who have been there for decades say that the raw partisanship and stalemate in Congress and unwillingness to work with the other side is the worst in their memory. Some of the reasons are analyzed by experts such as Thomas Mann of the Brookings Institute and Norm Ornstein of the American Enterprise Institute. In their book with the rather startling title: *It's Even Worse than It Looks: How the American Constitutional System Collided with the New Politics of Extremism*, the authors point to the fact that most congressmen and women now do not live in Washington, D.C., with their families any more but return home every weekend, usually on a Thursday night, coming back on Monday.[3]

The little time that American legislators do spend in Congress, is taken up with partisan caucus and committee meetings and fundraising events to raise the millions of dollars it now takes to win an elected office. There is little time to meet those on the other side of the aisle in Congress, much less in the family-life sites and evening and weekend social events where Washington, D.C., politicians and lobbyists from all sides used to meet. There is little time to build a social or common relationship among congressmen from the other party except in adversarial confrontations in committee meetings or on the floor, where even there the members sit grouped together by party affiliation, their actions continuously scrutinized by their party whips.

The complete overuse of the filibuster (or even the threat of one) in the Senate now dictates that any bill that cannot garner 60 votes in support be withdrawn or not even introduced on the floor altogether. Legislative maneuvers that would not allow any amendments on bills became the modus operandi of Senate Leader Harry Reid. They very well may have contributed to the Democratic Party's losing the chamber in 2014.

This decade of impasse may have peaked however. The 113th Congress was the most unproductive in congressional history and even the public who are partisan supporters expressed fury at the polls. Voters of both parties demanded that their representatives get something done—at least discuss legislation and vote on it. By 2015, it was obvious that politicians on both sides of the aisle were hearing from many constituents and journalists that they have to be more "bipartisan." Both parties in the beginnings of the 2016 presidential election race are hearing from their friends and foes alike, "Show that you can govern."

That means showing they can make a deal, compromise, and agree on bipartisan legislation—like Johnson, Kennedy, and Hart.

CONFRONTING RELUCTANCE TO ENFORCE IMMIGRATION LAWS

Increasingly, the public has become aware of how difficult it is to pass major legislation or just about any legislation. It's almost a miracle that everything comes together even in the ideal cases when there is a social movement, the political parties are aligned or have a monopoly, and there is a strong leader. But finally some bills do get passed in both chambers, the president signs them, and they become laws.

Now they have to be budgeted and the funds allocated to the agencies to implement them. And they have to be enforced if they are broken.

The enforcement of immigration laws is a conundrum for most Americans, especially officials on the front line who have to physically do it—have to physically detain and "remove" young men, women, and children who, as is almost always said in the press, "just are trying to make a better life for themselves and their families." Most illegal immigrants are peaceful and hardworking. Some experts argue that they contribute more to the economy than they cost in benefits, and that they all create jobs for Americans—many economists including David Dyssegaard Kallick of the Fiscal Policy Institute make the argument that even those who take work on the bottom ladder of employment "free up" Americans who had those jobs and force them to move onto better ones, hence improving their economic futures."[4]

Of course none of that is an excuse for breaking the law. (Many convicted felons say they stole and broke the law because they wanted to make a better life financially for themselves and their families if they had them.) Most apologists for illegal immigrants won't even talk about the numerous misdemeanors and felonies that most unauthorized immigrants commit by just being in the country illegally—driving without a driver's license (misdemeanors) or by knowingly showing employers fraudulent identification documents or ignoring a deportation order or reentering the country illegally after having been involuntarily deported (all felonies, the latter not excusable even for DACA applicants, though advocates are trying to have that one waived as well). Passionate legislators like Luis Gutierrez and other advocates for illegal immigrants argue that it is "un-American" not to legalize everyone who is in the country illegally[5]

Yet laws by definition define what is an illegal action and what is not and how that illegal action should be punished. Elected legislators pass the laws; the executive branch signs them into law and is required to enforce them; the U.S. Supreme Court decides if the laws are constitutional if they are brought up for adjudication in the lower federal district and there is disagreement among them. Immigration law is no different. It is hard to argue that any law can be valid and obeyed if it is not enforced.

Still there is a core disconnect in federal laws regarding illegal immigrant workers. While it is illegal for an employer to "knowingly" hire employees without valid work permits and documents, and it is definitely legal for employers to ask workers for documents proving they have the right to work in the United States, employers are not required to ascertain if the documents are valid or correctly identify the individual presenting them. Furthermore, it is *not* illegal or unlawful for immigrants without legal authority to be in the United Stated to *seek* employment and to work. In 2010, Arizona voters approved a state proposition making it illegal for illegal immigrants to seek work in the state; that was declared unconstitutional by the Supreme Court in June of 2012—although SCOTUS upheld other aspects of the law including the "show me your papers" provisions.

Here is where a strange but true realty surfaces about immigration laws. There is in the land a moral conundrum about the enforcement of immigration laws—especially inside the borders. Most Americans, including most Democrats, accept the fact that our nation's borders should be "controlled"—at least they should be policed enough to keep out the "bad" guys trafficking drugs and "slaves" and wanting to do harm to the country. But traditionally there has been a different feeling about stopping people looking for jobs—not labor crossing the borders. For decades there was an unspoken rule among border patrol agents—the majority of whom are Latino-heritage males, especially Mexican males. It was "detain OTMs only"—Other than Mexicans. The Mexican agricultural laborers and cowboys who crossed the border—some of them for generations—were known and accepted by most border patrol agents who, like most law enforcement officials, normally practice daily an informal prosecutorial discretion. As such, most illegal border crossers when "caught," were given a notice to appear in court for an immigration hearing at a future date and let go. There were few detention facilities, so few border crossers were arrested. It was called "catch and release." Few if any of those given notice appeared in court—a felony offense that was rarely enforced until the immigrant was detained again.

That all ended after 9/11 and the establishment of the DHS. The border patrol was enlarged; sophisticated tracking equipment was bought; a double, ten-foot fence along the California/Tijuana border was built; and the number of detention facilities were increased (and continue to be) many fold. The unspoken OTM process continued at a certain level (for well-known Mexican citizens who crossed over regularly), but was tightened during the Bush administration with a documented increase in detentions of non-Mexicans.

But the real difference came in the establishment of the Immigration and Customs Enforcement bureau or ICE—the first agency in our history charged with enforcement of immigration laws *inside* the United States. We had never had a tradition of internal enforcement. Many Americans have a gut rejection about internal enforcement. It sounds almost *Nazi*. Internal enforcement of immigration law can be safely said to be generally repugnant, especially to many residents in cities and towns. It is the personal, hard-working/family aspect of illegal immigration that makes it so hard to punish.

In many ways immigrants, and maybe especially illegal immigrants, are often seen and portrayed as the epitome of the America Dream—independent, courageous, hard-working individuals who will defy laws to earn a better life for their family. Liberal, independent people especially in the Southwest and the Mountain States, respect, admire and even are in awe of the struggles and determination of illegal immigrants, and many admit they would do it themselves if they were in their shoes. Most Americans are very compassionate, understanding, and sympathetic toward illegal immigration and illegal immigrants in general.

This general attitude puts especially local authorities such as mayors in a conundrum (see "Unenforced Laws and Sanctuary Cities" in chapter 4). Mayors at a January 20, 2015, panel "The Next America" sponsored by the National Journal in Washington, D.C., which the author covered agreed, "We don't have the power or the resources to enforce immigration laws. We just deal with everyone equally in the community the best we can." "I feel no responsibility to uphold the rule of law when it comes to immigrants in my community," a mayor from Colorado admitted in a personal interview. Same panel on January 20; see chapter four "Unenforced Laws and Sanctuary Cities"

Enforcing national immigration law is obviously a distant concern for these mayors (who by the way were all Republicans). In the rush of all the daily affairs and interactions with all of their residents, their problems, and their demands, upholding national immigration policy understandably seems to be only a matter of geeky "political philosophy."

That is probably true for many if not most of the American cities' busy residents, concerned and even often overwhelmed with their daily lives. Most want to be neighborly, want others to like them, admire those who work hard and are good family people, are good role models. They don't want to think that they might be illegally in the country. In 2007, when Michael Chertoff, President Bush's second Secretary of Homeland Security, decided to go after immigration labor violations as a top priority, immigrant advocates and the press whipped up public outrage at the sight of workers being marched out of their work sites in handcuffs. Human rights groups sued the government on behalf of the workers, public demonstrations were held in protest in many Latino communities. Chertoff soon after announced that workplace enforcement would be confined to employers, not to the employees.

The Obama administration has focused on detaining and deporting only violent convicted felons as well as those who have defied deportation orders and actual removal multiple times. Still, that is met with fury by most advocates. That criticism has obviously driven President Obama's executive actions in 2012 and 2014 to defer deportation at least during his administration for over seven million unauthorized immigrants—more than half of the total estimated illegal immigrant population in the United States today.

It is clear that one of the biggest problems about immigration laws in the United States (and Europe as well) is their enforcement—not their existence or their reform. Almost nobody today except a few extremist, globalist libertarians, support the idea of open borders and global citizenship; most citizens accept and support the idea and even the necessity of having immigration laws. But public support is temporal for enforcing immigration laws vigorously or even for using the ultimate measure of deporting even for a small proportion of those who have broken immigration laws.

Demands for more strenuous immigration enforcement only comes when the public perceives immigration or particular kinds of immigrants as dangerous to their security or that of their communities, including physical security, economic and job security, and at times (what is happening in France and Sweden for instance) threats to the national cultural identity and core values. These times of danger usually peak at a particular event (9/11, the massacre of the magazine editors in France). But most of the time citizens of liberal, prosperous, Western countries are comfortable with having spelled out in legal codes and on paper, immigration laws that are specific and punitive if broken, but are generally not enforced.

It's a lazy way of handling difficult immigration enforcement. It could lead, in fact most probably does lead, to increased illegal immigration, something few libertarian and free-market advocates ever talk about. Instead of stopping illegal immigration, their main focus seems to be on legalizing those already here—a good way to eliminate illegal immigration for the time being, but not for the future.

But even more worrysome is that the protection of certain groups from law enforcement (i.e., illegal immigrants in this case and almost always identified as "Latinos") could lead—may be leading—to a precedent that enforcement and penalties for "minor" misdemeanors and felonies crimes should not be enforced for other particular ethnic or identity groups. It encourages the idea that every particular identity group can complain that selection of who is punished for committing crimes is "discrimination" and "racial profiling."

President Obama often says, "We are not only a nation of immigrants, but also a nation of laws." It is assumed he is including immigration laws. But what if in your gut, you don't like the law? Many advocates for illegal immigrants seem to feel that the 1965 law that changed the face of the nation is so unacceptable to them that it should just be ignored with civil rights disobedience tactics.

But just as children cannot be raised without behavioral "borders" and appropriate incentives for obeying basic rules (including appropriate punishment if they break them), so too must our national borders and immigration laws be upheld. There has to be consequences for breaking a law or the law is meaningless. It's difficult to punish people whom you like, even love, especially if the "crime" doesn't seem to be individually so bad. You end up being flexible, giving them "byes," trying to find excuses not to punish their open and obvious law-breaking.

But justice also has to be fair. If some people in the community are punished for committing misdemeanors and felonies, then all should be. Even when you love them.

It's called "tough love."

NEED TO TONE DOWN THE RHETORIC

Even though for most Americans at this time there is no fierce urgency for a huge overhaul of the 1965 INA, still, in the past ten years, efforts to "reform" it have become an intense, contentious political battle that seems likely to become a presidential electoral issue in 2016 and beyond. The harshness of political rhetoric has gone way beyond the rational issues of national immigration policy. The debate has become moralistic, ideological, and personal with unhelpful labels and emotions that are only too eagerly covered by a news media with increasingly obvious political agendas of their own.

Civil rights liberals and libertarians, especially the professional lobbyists, who have made immigration into a civil rights, racial issue need to look around them. It may surprise them to see that most people in the United States think that being together with people of all races, cultures, nationalities, and religions in every situation in their lives is absolutely normal. The lack of diversity in the everyday life of most Americans is becoming now more one of ideology and socioeconomic factors, not race, gender, creed, and national origin. The Supreme Court itself has made some decisions to redefine affirmative action programs to either be terminated, or at the most, be based not on race but on socioeconomic diversity.

The new concern about clustering of like-minded people in American neighborhoods also is not so much one of race but of educational background, political ideology, and religious faith. Even Democrats seem to require that their new top leaders, including minorities, attend an Ivy League college in order to be a viable candidate for national office, just like President Obama and the Castro twins. (Joaquin Castro was elected to Congress from San Antonio Texas in 2012 and Julian, the mayor of San Antonio, was appointed by President Obama to be the Secretary of HUD (Housing and Urban Development) in 2014. They were born in San Antonio Texas in 1974 to a single mother who was a Chicano activist. Both are very personable, outgoing, and charismatic; both attended Stanford University and Harvard Law School and do not speak fluent Spanish.)

The fact is that the majority (over 70 percent) of American Latinos and blacks today are middle class, including some 10 percent of blacks residing in the United States today who are highly educated, foreign-born immigrants. Americans throughout the United States increasingly intermarry and move out of their birth neighborhoods. The millennials, their siblings, and all the next generations of Americans will be growing up with "global world" expectations, whose close friends will be diverse in every traditional way (race, religion, creed, and nationality), and increasingly so in educational attainment, economic ambition, and political ideology as millennials turn away from the Wall Street ambitions of the earlier generation.

In the past 50 years, African Americans especially have succeeded in obtaining and becoming role models in every level of every field of endeavor, especially politics. They have their own elite and highly wealthy 1 percent who are part of a very exclusive Washington, D.C., "A" List. A most enlightening book on the diversity of African Americans since the 1970s is *Washington Post*, Pulitzer Prize–winning columnist Eugene Robinson's 2010 book *Disintegration: The Splintering of Black America* (the title was his wife's idea).[6]

Immigration discrimination based on national origins is now a thing of the past. Immigrants from every nation in the world, every background language and culture, are welcomed—even recruited and encouraged (diversity lottery) to apply for a green card—into the United States. The problem now is more first-generation immigration's clustering in various skills and jobs. But even that will dissipate by the second generation. The number of illegal immigrants over the southern border is declining due to increased enforcement, decreasing job opportunities in the United States, and rising economic well-being in Mexico. Their children who were born in the states are citizens, increasingly go to college, intermarry, and become globalized Americans whose dominant language is unquestionably English.

Civil rights leaders (especially blacks) need to rethink their focus on illegal immigrants as a civil rights cause. Republican leaders need to stop listening to immigrant activists who proclaim all illegal immigrants are Latinos and that all Latinos in the electorate will be Democratic activists 40 years hence. No group is monolithic, as many demographers including Paul Taylor in his latest book "*The Next America*" conclude.[7] Both parties are struggling to find themes that bridge differences. "Middle class economics" of 2015 is Democrats' latest effort. But as the new generations intermarry, one has to wonder if any ethnic identity will matter particularly in a majority-minority society.

Leaders of both parties need to address the impact of Americans' enthusiasm to hire immigrants with or without work permits on the continual rising unemployment rates of African Americans in cities with high immigrant populations. Especially Democrats will need to talk about the negative impact of unenforced immigration laws on American citizens (including whites) and legal immigrants, as well as the benefits.

The press needs to call out the spin of well-intentioned advocates for illegal immigrants for instance. They have been very successful in personifying the behavior of illegal immigration. First they turn the choice of coming and staying in the country illegally into a personhood (an illegal immigrant) but with a less officious moniker like "undocumented person." Then they imply that being for or against that behavior (of illegally entering and staying in the nation) is to be for or against the person or the group of people who does that behavior (as in "there's so such thing as an illegal person"). So if one is against illegal immigration, for instance, then that means one is against immigrants, one is anti-immigrant. Many activists spin it further by insisting that if one is against illegal immigration, and since a majority of illegal immigrants are Latinos, then one must be against Latinos or anti-Latino. And that leads to accusations of racial profiling (even though Latinos are not a race), which is against civil and human rights (ignoring that immigration is neither a civil nor a human right in the first place). With such rhetoric and spin, the whole process and duty of a nation-state to choose who can (and who can't) immigrate into it and to enforce that choice, suddenly becomes an issue of racism.

Hypersensitivity on race has dangerous consequences. It certainly has deterred civil debate about immigration in the public sphere in the past ten years. "By the 2012 campaign, anything said by any conservatives on the subject of either immigration or benefits was ipso facto racist," wrote columnist Dan Hannon in the February 9, 2015, edition of the *Washington Examiner*.

"We have to deracialize everything, take race out of everything," said Andrew Young, the former U.S. Ambassador to the United Nations, a Georgia congressman and friend of Dr. Martin Luther King. "Seeing racism in everything must not be a legacy of the civil rights movement," Young, an original member of the SCLC (Southern Christian Leadership Conference) during the 1960s civil rights movement, said at a panel on the anniversary of the Civil Rights Act in April 2014 at the LBJ Library in Austin, Texas. [8]

The bottom line is that immigration into the United States since the 1965 INA is not about race or racism. It's certainly not just about Latinos; immigrants come from every country in the world. And immigration policy certainly isn't just about illegal immigration either; very few pages (fewer than

100) in the thousand-page plus immigration bills are devoted to illegal entry and enforcement. In addition, immigration enforcement is not "discrimination," "racial profiling," or "racist." Even deportation is a common immigration enforcement measure; it can be said that without deportation as an ultimate punishment, immigration laws would have no validity.

The lesson is clear. Journalists need to point out in their articles and reports that racism and civil rights rhetoric by many advocates for illegal immigration and comprehensive immigration reform, is just that—hyped rhetoric to fire up supporters. The public they are trying to persuade eventually does understand that this kind of extreme language only prevents the civil debate they want and they turn away from it. In the end, repeating it unremittingly hurts the advocates and the media who don't make people aware of it.

Of course discrimination will never really end completely. It is natural for human beings to want to be with those who are like them. Eventually in life, everyone is discriminated against in some way (those over 50 years old experience a particular, universally equal discrimination, especially in the job market; age discrimination is not based on any of the traditional biases of color, creed, etc., but is equal for all). It is right to try to end discrimination of all kinds, to make it known and demand justice? But it will never be perfectly done away with. In the end, everyone, every person, has to deal with the cards they were given—the good ones and the bad ones.

The diversity of America brought on by the INA is truly a unique world experience. Senator Ted Kennedy and President Johnson and the other leaders who worked so hard to pass the INA in 1965 with votes from Southern Democrats, many of whom were still openly racist and segregationists at the time, did not resort to the language of guilt, accusation, and racism to achieve their legislative successes. That kind of rhetoric won't help immigration reform in the twenty-first century either.

CONCLUSION—PROSPECTS FOR IMMIGRATION REFORM IN 2016 AND BEYOND

Clearly the environment in the second decade of the twenty-first century for passing a liberal comprehensive immigration reform package is nothing like 1965. Shall we count the ways it isn't?

1. No broad, public, fierce urgency movement like civil rights. Instead, the focus of immigration for some is on protecting national security; for others, the need for desirable highly educated and trained immigrants who will create prosperity and jobs, no matter if they originate from just a few countries; for others, mainly about legalizing millions

of illegal immigrants currently living and working in the country, some for decades, other who have only recently been deported.

2. Split government (not an eager, united, liberal Democrat Congress together with the president).
3. No strong presidential leadership for the issue as President Johnson gave.
4. No one in either party's leadership who are beloved and respected deal makers and compromisers as Johnson, Kennedy, and Hart were.
5. Continued pressure for more border security and more internal enforcement, and to stop illegal immigration and enforce the rule of law.

The economic environment and consequent immigration drivers are even more dissimilar today from 1965. In fact (scary to say) the economic factors today look more like 1924 than 1965.

1. Income inequality approaching the "Roaring Twenties"
2. Uncontrolled waves of new immigrants approaching that of the unregulated and historic surges of desperate immigrants fleeing war-torn Europe between1880–1920
3. Slow recovery from a recession (1921 and 2008) where low-wage, temporary jobs with few benefits offered to and taken eagerly by immigrants over Americans, especially African Americans
4. Middle-class wage stagnation and low rates of social upward mobility
5. Fear of pending job loss and economic depression
6. Fear of pending war and terrorism abroad that could envelop the United States and general public distaste for becoming involved in another foreign war.

These factors led not to the liberal immigration law of 1965 but to the highly restrictive immigration law of 1924 based on national origin preferences and quotas.

In sum, the historic drivers and predictors rather point to a more restrictive immigration policy than a liberal one in the next few years. That will be heavily fought over by the civil and corporate libertarians and the restrictionists in Congress. But that doesn't mean no immigration reform measures will be passed at all, nor does that mean that all illegal immigrants will be deported—some certainly will be legalized.

There are many reasons that some pieces of positive immigration reform that everyone agrees to could happen before the presidential elections in 2016 and certainly beyond. There is every indication that some, if not a good half, of the illegal immigrants in the country today will be legalized. Here's why:

1. While government is likely to remain mixed in the next decade (that is, at least one of the congressional chambers will be of a different party than the most likely politically centrist president of either party, but probably Democratic), which is not a bad thing. The "fabulous 89th" Congress of 1965 with a liberal strong president was unique—and short lived. What is truer is that passing legislation in a mixed Congress is much more usual, requires much more deal making and engagement, but can be very successful because that is the only way that something will get done.

2. Both parties really want to win the presidency in 2016 (possibly with a minority or a second- or third-generation immigrant on the ticket).

3. Both parties really want to win the Senate in 2016.

4. Both parties want to show they can "govern" and get things done (although in early 2015 the Republicans have more incentive to do so since they are in control of Congress, whereas Democrats may have more interest in showing that Republicans can't; but Democrats cannot count on the public always blaming Republicans for congressional inaction, especially if Obama decides to veto most every bill that the Republican Congress passes to him to sign).

5. There are reasonable people in both parties who know they will have to make some compromises and make some deals on some issues such as trade, energy, and even immigration. There are a number of legislators across the political spectrum who agree on a number of specific changes of immigration law including green cards for some foreign students in science, a national E-Verify and expanded investors visas, just to name a few. These issues can pass with bipartisan support if party members can get their extreme fringes to agree: (a) The Democrats are going to have to persuade their fringe to accept piecemeal legislation over a huge, omnibus, comprehensive bill that legalizes all or almost all of the unauthorized immigrants presently living and working in the country—especially those less than a decade here. (b) The Republicans are going to have to persuade their fringe to accept the legalization of some illegal immigrants—most likely many in the same groups whom President Obama has ordered legalized under DACA and DAPA (i.e., DREAMers, though at a lower entry age; and parents of American citizens who have been here at least ten years).

6. The Democratic president is near his last year of his last term; while he might hate in his gut to let Republicans win anything, still he is supposedly looking for a productive finish for his own legacy and a positive atmosphere in which to vote for a new Democratic president.

7. The electorate itself is becoming more diverse; Republicans are struggling to deal with their multitude of voices and moving away from their former, narrow base of social issues supported by faith groups;

while Democrats are beginning to realize that they too have moved to far to narrow, single-message, target groups that now, in the middle of the second decade of the twenty-first century, are diversifying rapidly within themselves.

8. Bipartisanship is in the air; the electorate is demanding it.
9. Americans want the government to work—literally and figuratively.

No one presently in Congress is a master at bipartisan deal making and compromise like Johnson, Kennedy, and Hart were. But that doesn't mean they can't learn the lessons of those grand leaders. Senator Orin Hatch, friend of all of them, could be a teacher.

Bipartisan deal making and compromise are the primary lessons of the Immigration and Nationality Act of 1965.

Bibliography

BOOKS

Peter S. Canellos, ed., *The Last Lion: The Fall and Rise of Ted Kennedy* by the team at *The Boston Globe*, with foreword statement by Senator John McCain (New York: Simon & Schuster, 2009).

Robert A. Caro, *The Passage of Power: The Years of Lyndon Johnson* (New York: Random House, 2013), chapter 20, "The Johnsons in Johnson City."

Roberta A. Caro, *Master of the Senate* (New York: Random House, 2010).

Aneesh Chopra, *Innovative State: How New Technologies Can Transform Government* (New York: Atlantic Monthly Press, 2014).

Henry G. Cisneros, ed., *Latinos and the Nation's Future*, "The Latino Presence: Some Historical Background," by Nicolas Kanellos (Houston: Arte Publico Press, 2008), pp. 15–25.

Philip M. Dine, *State of the Unions: How Labor Can Strengthen the Middle Class, Improve Our Economy, and Regain Political Influence* (New York: McGraw Hill, 2007).

Otis L. Graham Jr., *Unguarded Gates: A History of America's Immigration Crisis* (Lanham, MD: Rowman & Littlefield, 2004).

David Maraniss, *Barack Obama: The Story* (New York: Simon & Schuster, 2012).

Thomas Mann and Norman Ornstein, *It's Even Worse than It Looks: How the American Constitutional System Collided with the New Politics of Extremism* (New York: Basic Books, 2012).

Gary May, *Bending toward Justice: The Voting Rights Act and the Transformation of American Democracy* (Durham, NC: Duke University Press, 2015, paperback with new preface).

Margaret S. Orchowski, *Immigration and the American Dream: Battling the Political Hype and Hysteria* (Lanham, MD: Rowman & Littlefield, 2008).

Eugene Robinson, *Disintegration: The Splintering of Black America* (New York: Anchor Books of Random House, 2010).

Thomas F. Schaller, *Whistling Past Dixie: How Democrats Can Win without the South* (New York: Simon & Schuster, 2006).

Gene Smiley, Introduction "The U.S. Economy in the 1920s" Economic History Assn. EH.net eh.net/encyclopedia/the-u-s-economy-in-the-1920s.

Ira Stoll, "Introduction," in *JFK, Conservative* (New York: Houghton Mifflin Harcourt, 2013).

Paul Taylor and the Pew Research Center, *The Next America: Boomers, Millennials, and the Looming Generational Showdown* (New York: Public Affairs , 2014).

Mark K. Updegrove, *Indomitable Will: LBJ in the Presidency* (New York: Crown Publishers, 2012). Updegrove is the director of the LBJ Presidential Library and Museum in Austin and wrote *Baptism by Fire: Eight Presidents who Took Office in Times of Crisis*; and *Second Acts*. Includes lots of telephone conversations and admiring quotes.

Alan Wolf, *The Future of Liberalism* (New York: Alfred A. Knopf, 2009).

Colin Woodard, *American Nations: A History of the Eleven Rival Regional Cultures of North America* (New York: Penguin Books, 2011).

Julian E. Zelizer, *The Fierce Urgency of Now: Lyndon Johnson, Congress, and the Battle for the Great Society* (New York: Penguin Press, 2015).

John Zobgy and Joan Snyder Kuhl, *First Globals: Understanding, Managing, & Unleashing the Potential of Our Millennial Generation* (published by authors, 2013).

UNIVERSITY AND THINK TANK REPORTS, AND VARIOUS STUDIES

American Committee on Italian Migration, "Remarks by John F. Kennedy to Delegates of the American Committee on Italian Migration," June 11, 1963, The American Presidency Project, http://www.presidency.ucsb.edu/ws/?pid=9269,http://www.presidency.ucsb.edu.

DC Fiscal Policy Institute, "For Some DC Groups of DC Residents, Unemployment Remains High in the Wake of the Recession," by Marina Manganaris, March 7, 2013.

The Holocaust Memorial Museum, "Refugees." www.ush.org/wic/en/article.hp?Modueid+10005139.

International Institute of Education (IIE), "Open Doors Report," November 2014.

LBJ Presidential Library, "LBJ on Immigration," President Lyndon B. Johnson's Remarks at the Signing of the Immigration Bill, Liberty Island, New York, October 3, 1965, http://www.lbjlibrary.org/lyndon-baines-johnson/timeline/lbj-on-immigration#sthash.gxT4Fx8U.

LBJ Presidential Library, "Seeing Is Believing," by Joseph A. Califano, http://www.lbjlibrary.org/lyndon-baines-johnson/perspectives-and-essays/seeing-is-believing-the-enduring-legacy-of-lyndon-johnson#sthash.eXYL6ykY.dpuf.

The Miller Center, University of Virginia, American President Reference source, "Franklin Delano Roosevelt," online.

Migration Policy Institute, "Immigration Facts," February 2007, No. 18, "Immigration Fees Increases in Context," available online at MPI website.

Pew Research Center, "From Germany to Mexico: How America's Source of Immigrants Has Changed over a Century," includes map of German Heritage Population in 1900 by Jens Manuel Krogstad and Michael Keegan.

Pew Research Center: Hispanic Trends, "Hispanic Nativity Shift," report by Jens Manuel Krogstad and Mark Hugo Lopez, April 29, 2014, Immigration in America website, http://immigrationinamerica.org/590-immigration.

Pew Research Center: Hispanic Trends, "Net Migration from Mexico Falls to Zero—and Perhaps Less," by Jeffrey S. Passel, D'Vera Cohn, and Ana Gonzalez-Barrera, April 23, 2012.

Pew Research Center: Social & Demographic Trends, "Millennials in Adulthood: Detached from Institutions, Networked with Friends," March 7, 2014.

University of California at Santa Barbara, "The Politics of Immigration Reform" PhD thesis of Betty Koed, 1995.

ARTICLES AND OP EDS

ABC News, April 14, 2010, "A New Baby Boom? Foreign 'Birth Tourists' Seek U.S. Citizenship for Children," by Devin Dwyer.

Americans for Immigration Control Weekly News and Commentary, April 9, 2007, "Kennedy's Broken Promise."

Ars Tecnica, September 2, 2013. "How Can They Be So Good? The Strange Story of Skype," by Toivo Taenavsuu.

Chronicle of Higher Education, January 6, 2015 "Foreign Students Aren't Edging Out Locals, Numbers Show," by Karin Fischer and Lance Lambert.

Chronicle of Higher Education, January 23, 2015, "The Progressive Case for Reducing Immigration," by Philip Cafaro.

CQ Almanac, 1965, "National Quotas for Immigration to End."

Daily Mail, April 2014, "More People than Ever Living Outside Their Home Country."

Hispanic Outlook, October 21. 2013, "Dreamers Could Make or Break Immigration Reform in 2013," by Margaret Orchowski.

Hispanic Outlook, January 27, 2014, "Are Hispanic Millennials Leading Their Generation?" by Margret Orchowski.

Hispanic Outlook, April 7, 2014, "News Coverage of Hispanics Makes Some Cringe: Even NPR Gets a C" by Margaret Orchowski, UNCENSORED.

Hispanic Outlook in Higher Education, September 23, 2014, "State of HSIs 2014: Growing Fast," by Margaret S. Orchowski.

Jewish Virtual Library, "Emanuel Celler," http://www.jewishvirtuallibrary.org/jsource/biography/Celler.html.

Los Angeles Times, August 28, 2009, "The Gipper and Ted Kennedy Had 'Wonderful' Friendship," political commentary.

Migration News, March 2000, vol. 7, number 3, "Mexico: Dual Nationality, Politics."

March 31, 2006, "Ted Kennedy 'Reformed' Immigration in 1965," by Rush Limbaugh.

New York Times, September 23, 2013, "Number of Illegal Immigrants in U.S. May Be on Rise Again, Estimates Say," by Julia Preston.

New York Times, February 1, 2015, "The Only Baby Book You'll Ever Need," opinion piece by linguist Michael Erard.

New York Times, February 6, 2015, "In Ending Slavery, the Abolitionists Came First," letter to the editor by Edward B. Rugemer, associate professor of history and African American studies, Yale University, in response to an op-ed in the *New York Times* Sunday Review, February 1, 2015, "Was Abolitionism a Failure?" by John Grinspan.

New York Times Review, February 26, 2015 *"Muslims in America."*

NewsOne for Black America, April 8, 2014, "State of Black America 2014: Blacks and Latinos Remain Underemployed," by D. L. Chandler.

Politico, December 31, 2014, "How 'Selma' Diminishes Dr. King: MLK Was a Political Genius. Why Does the Film Obscure That?" by Josh Zeitz.

The Public Perspective, October/November 1998, "Immigration: The Real Kennedy Legacy," by Patrick Reddy, p. 19.

Reuters News Service, February 13, 2013, "Cuban Perks under Scrutiny," by David Adams and Tom Brown in Miami.

Slate, March 5, 2014, "NASA Budget 2015: More Cuts, More Politics," by Phil Pliat, http://www.slate.com/blogs/bad_astronomy/2014/03/05/nasa_budget_2015_more_cuts_more_politics.html.

Small Business Trends, May 8, 2013, "Complete History of Social Media: Then and Now" by Drew Hendricks, in Social Media section.

TIME magazine cover story "The Me Me Me Generation: Millennials are lazy, entitled narcissists who still live with their parents. Why they'll save us all. By Joel Stein. May 9, 2013.

U.S. News & World Report, opinion blog, March 9, 2010, "the bill has to pass before they—and the rest of us 'can find out what's in it,'" by Peter Roff.

USA Today, "U.S. population growth slows to just 0.71%," by Greg Toppo and Paul Overberg, October 7, 2014.

Wall Street Journal, Opinion, February 3, 2015, "Nevada's Right Choice on Immigration," by David B Rivkin Jr. and Lee A Casey.

Washington Examiner, February 9, 2015, "Hypersensitivity on Race Has Dangerous Consequences for All," by Dan Hannon.

Washington Post Opinions "Pelosi defends her infamous health care remark, by Jonathan Capehart, June 20, 2012.

Washington Post, January 29, 2015, "Do We Really Mean 'Never Again'?" by Charles Krauthammer.

Washington Post, January. 14, 2015, "Charles Lane: A country trapped in 1965 Ambitions," op-ed by Charles Lane.

Washington Post, Book World, January 18, 2015, "The Political Ordeal behind the Great Society," a review of Julian E. Zelizer's book *The Fierce Urgency of Now*, by Wendy Smith.

Washington Post, January 10, 2015, "The Lesson We Should Take from 'Selma,'" op-ed by Katrina vanden Heuvel, editor and publisher of *The Nation* magazine.

Washington Post, Style section, June 17, 2013, "Mark Krikorian: The Provocateur Standing in the Way of Immigration Reform," by Manuel Roig-Franzia.

Washington Post, March 2, 2015, "The Next America is Now," op-ed by Robert J. Samuelson, quoting a conference at the Brookings Institute on Paul Taylor and the PEW Research Center's book, *The Next America: Boomers, Millennials, and the Looming Generational Showdown*.

WiredPen, "Visual Guide: The Balance Of Power between Congress and The Presidency (1945–2015)," WiredPen.com.

RADIO AND TELEVISION REPORTS

C-SPAN 3, American History TV, "LBJ and Civil Rights—Immigration and the Great Society," January 10, 2015, from a panel on April 9, 2014, in Austin at the LBJ Presidential Library on the 50th anniversary of the Civil Rights Act.

National Public Radio, *All Things Considered*, "1965 Immigration Law Changed Face of America," interview hosted by Michele Norris and Robert Seigel interviewing Jennifer Ludden and Otis Graham, May 9, 2006.

Notes

1. WHY IMMIGRATION LAWS?

1. Article 13 (2) of the United Nations Declaration of Human Rights states, "Everyone has the right to leave any country, including his own, and to return to his country."
2. *Wall Street Journal Review*, January 17–18, 2015.

2. FROM STATES TO FEDS

1. Nathaniel Philbrick, *Mayflower: A Story of Courage, Community, and War* (New York: Viking, 2006). This is a quote taken from an interview the author had with Philbrook at the Library of Congress book fair in 2007.
2. Margaret Sands Orchowski, *Immigration and the American Dream: Battling the Political Hype and Hysteria* (Lanham, MD: Rowman & Littlefield, 2008), pp. 22–23.
3. Otis L. Graham Jr., *Unguarded Gates: A History of America's Immigration Crisis* (Lanham, MD: Rowman & Littlefield, 2004), p. 3.
4. Deanna Barker, Frontier Resources, "Indentured Servitude in Colonial America," online newsletter of the Cultural Interpretation and Living History Section of the National Associate for Interpretation, March 10, 2004.
5. Orchowski, *Immigration and the American Dream*, pp. 24–25.
6. Ibid., p. 27.
7. Ibid., p. 27.
8. William W. Freehling, *The Road to Disunion* (New York: Oxford University Press, 2007) as cited in *The New York Times Book Review*, April 8, 2007, "The Three Souths," by Eric Foner.
9. *New York Times*, January 2015, "Muslims in America."
10. "The Homestead Act of 1862," http://www.archives.gov/education/lessons/homestead-act/.
11. Graham, *Unguarded Gates*, p. 16.
12. Ibid.
13. Ibid., p. 17.
14. "Immigration in America," February 14, 2012, Immigration in America website, http://immigrationinamerica.org/590-immigration-act-of-1924.html.

15. Graham, *Unguarded Gates*, p. 50.
16. Gene Smiley, Introduction, "The U.S. Economy in the 1920s" Economic History Association. EH.net eh.net/encyclopedia/the-u-s-economy-in-the-1920s.
17. Graham, *Unguarded Gates*, p. 16.
18. Ibid., p. 32.
19. Ibid., p. 13.
20. Ibid., pp. 44–45.
21. Ibid., p. 46.
22. Upham-Bornstein, Lida "Immigration in Ameirca." From immigrationinamerica.org.
23. Ibid., p. 40.
24. Ibid., p. 48.
25. Ibid., p. 49.
26. Ibid., p. 21.
27. Ibid., p. 48.
28. Ibid.
29. Ibid., p. 50.
30. Edward Lewis, *America, Nation or Confusion?* (Harper and Brothers, 1928).
31. Graham, p. 50.
32. Ibid., p. 49.
33. Ibid., p. 50.
34. Ibid., p. 49.
35. Ibid.
36. Ibid, p. 19.
37. Ibid., p. 14.
38. "Immigration in America."
39. Graham, p. 40.
40. Graham, pp. 51–53.
41. U.S. Department of State, Office of the Historian, https://history.state.gov/milestones/1899-1913/japanese-relations.
42. Graham, p. 194.

3. MAKING THE LAW THAT CHANGED THE FACE OF AMERICA

1. Otis L. Graham Jr., *Unguarded Gates: A History of America's Immigration Crisis* (Lanham, MD: Rowman & Littlefield, 2004), p. 95.
2. "LBJ on Immigration," President Lyndon B. Johnson's Remarks at the Signing of the Immigration Bill, Liberty Island, New York, October 3, 1965, http://www.lbjlibrary.org/lyndon-baines-johnson/timeline/lbj-on-immigration#sthash.gxT4Fx8U.
3. Immigration and Nationality Act of 1965, Public Law 89–236, enacted June 30, 1968, http://legislink.org/us/pl-89-236; 79 Stat. 911, http://legislink.org/us/stat-79-911.
4. *Congressional Quarterly Almanac*, 1965, p. 479.
5. Julian E. Zelizer at a talk on his book *The Fierce Urgency of Now: Lyndon Johnson, Congress, and the Battle for the Great Society*, at Politics and Prose bookstore, January 12, 2015.
6. The Miller Center, University of Virginia, American President Reference source: "Franklin Delano Roosevelt."
7. *Congressional Quarterly Almanac*, 1965, p. 467.
8. Peace Corp, John F. Kennedy Presidential Library and Museum www.jfklibrary.org/JFK/JFK-in-history/Peace-Corps.aspx.
9. JFK Presidential Library and Museum.
10. Ibid.
11. *Congressional Quarterly Almanac*, 1965, p. 467.

12. The Holocaust Memorial Museum, "Refugees."

13. Pew Hispanic Research Center, May 27, 2014, "From Germany to Mexico: How America's Source of Immigrants Has Changed over a Century," http://www.pewresearch.org/fact-tank/2014/05/27/a-shift-from-germany-to-mexico-for-americas-immigrants/.

14. Emanuel Celler, *You Never Leave Brooklyn.* (New York: J. Day Company, 1953).

15. Pew Hispanic Research Center, May 27, 2014.

16. Ibid.

17. Jewish Virtual Library, "Emanuel Celler," http://www.jewishvirtuallibrary.org/jsource/biography/Celler.html.

18. Ira Stoll, *JFK, Conservative* (New York: Houghton Mifflin Harcourt, 2013), p. 34.

19. *Boston Post*, October 2, 1952.

20. Ralph Dungan, from an oral history, December 9, 1967.

21. Stoll, *JFK, Conservative*, p. 34.

22. Peter S. Canellos, editor, *The Last Lion: The Fall and Rise of Ted Kennedy* by the team at *The Boston Globe* (New York: Simon & Schuster, 2009) with foreword by Senator John McCain, pp. 12–13.

23. "John F. Kennedy and Ireland," John F. Kennedy Presidential Library and Museumwww.jfklibrary.org/JFK-in-History.

24. The American Presidency Project, June 11, 1963, "Remarks by John F. Kennedy to Delegates of the American Committee on Italian Migration," http://www.presidency.ucsb.edu/ws/?pid=9269.

25. Mark K. Updegrove, *Indomitable Will: LBJ in the Presidency* (New York: Crown Publishers, 2012), p. 168.

26. Canellos, *The Last Lion*, p. 29.

27. Ibid., 28–41.

28. Ibid., 24–26.

29. Ibid., 38–39.

30. Ibid., 72.

31. Ibid., 86.

32. Ibid., 86–89.

33. Ibid., 107.

34. Ibid.

35. Ibid., 107–12.

36. Ibid., 114.

37. U.S. Senate, Subcommittee on Immigration and Naturalization of the Committee on the Judiciary, Washington, DC, February 10, 1965, pp. 1–3.

38. Roberta A. Caro, *Master of the Senate* (New York: Random House, 2010).

39. Rowland Evans and Robert Novak, *Lyndon B. Johnson: The Exercise of Power* (New York: New American Library, 1966), p. 104.

40. Updegrove, *Indomitable Will*, p. 168.

41. http://www.lbjlibrary.org/lyndon-baines-johnson/perspectives-and-essays/seeing-is-believing-the-enduring-legacy-of-lyndon-johnson.

42. Updegrove, *Indomitble Will*.

43. Graham, *Unguarded Gates*, p. 93.

44. Updegrove, *Indomitable Will*, p. 168–69.

45. Lyndon B Johnson Presidential Recordings, Johnson Conversation with Edward Kennedy on March 8, 1965 (WH6503.4), Miller Center University of Virginia millercenter.org/presidentialrecordings/lbj-wh6503.04-7043).

46. C-SPAN 3, American History TV, "LBJ and Civil Rights—Immigration and the Great Society," broadcast on January 10, 2015, from a panel on April 9, 2014, in Austin, Texas, at the LBJ Presidential Library on the fiftieth anniversary of the Civil Rights Act (journalist) book on LBJ, and MLK, with Taylor Branch, Doris Kearns Goodman, Joseph A. Califano, Andrew Young.

47. This is general information that can be found online under Andrew Jackson Young in various sources including Wikkepedia. Andrew Jackson Young (born March 12, 1932) is an American politician, diplomat, activist, and pastor from Georgia. He has served as a congress-

man from Georgia's 5th congressional district, the United States ambassador to the United Nations, and mayor of Atlanta. He served as president of the National Council of Churches USA, was a member of the Southern Christian Leadership Conference (SCLC) during the 1960s civil rights movement, and was a supporter and friend of Dr. Martin Luther King, Jr.

48. Updegrove, *Indomitable Will.*

49. LBJ Presidential Library, "Seeing Is Believing," by Joseph A. Califano, on LBJ library website. See more at http://www.lbjlibrary.org/lyndon-baines-johnson/perspectives-and-essays/seeing-is-believing-the-enduring-legacy-of-lyndon-johnson#sthash.eXYL6ykY.dpuf.

50. *Politico*, December 31, 2014, "How 'Selma' Diminishes Dr. King: MLK Was a Political Genius. Why Does the Film Obscure That?" by Josh Zeitz.

51. Ibid., p. 88.

52. *Congressional Quarterly Almanac*, p. 475.

53. Some references from Rush Limbaugh's piece from his radio show "Ted Kennedy 'Reformed' Immigration in 1965," March 31, 2006.

54. *Congressional Quarterly Almanac*, p. 475.

55. National Public Radio, *All Things Considered*, "1965 Immigration Law Changed Face of America," interview hosted by Michele Norris and Jennifer Ludden and interviewing Otis Graham. May 9, 2006.

56. *Congressional Quarterly Almanac*, 1965, p. 476.

57. Ibid., 475.

58. Graham, *Unguarded Gates*, p. 91.

59. Canellos, *The Last Lion*, p. 114.

60. *Congressional Quarterly Almanac*, p. 477.

61. Graham, *Unguarded Gates*, p. 89.

62. Julian E. Zelizer at a talk on his book, *The Fierce Urgency of Now.*

63. Graham, *Unguarded Gates*, p. 87, and PhD thesis of Betty Koed of University of California at Santa Barbara on "The Politics of Immigration Reform," 1995.

64. *Congressional Quarterly Almanac*, "National Quotas for Immigration to End," p. 462.

65. Ibid., 463.

66. *Washington Post*, January 29, 2015, "Do We Really Mean Never Again?" by Charles Krauthammer.

67. Julian E. Zelizer, *The Fierce Urgency of Now: Lyndon Johnson, Congress, and the Battle for the Great Society* (New York: Penguin Press, 2015), p. 214.

68. Updegrove, *Indomitable Will*, p. 133. Updegrove is the director of the LBJ Presidential Library and Museum in Austin; he wrote *Baptism by Fire: Eight Presidents Who Took Office in Times of Crisis*; and *Second Acts*, which includes a lot of telephone conversations and admiring quotes.

69. Zelitzer, *The Fierce Urgency of Now*, p. 163.

70. Ibid.

71. Updegrove, *Indomitable Will*, p. 170.

72. *Washington Post*, Book World, January 18, 2015, "The Political Ordeal behind the Great Society," a review of Zelizer's book *The Fierce Urgency of Now*, by Wendy Smith.

73. *Washington Post*, January 15, 2015, "Ghosts of the Great Society: Too Much of Our Government Is Confined by 1965 Ambitions," op-ed by Charles Lane.

4. IMPACT AND UNINTENDED CONSEQUENCES

1. Otis L. Graham, *Unguarded Gates: A History of America's Immigration Crisis* (Lanham, MD: Rowman & Littlefield, 2004), p. 92.

2. *Statistical Yearbook of the Immigration and Naturalization Service*, 2001, at www.ins.usdoj.gov/graphics/aboutins/statistics/IMMO1yrbk/IMM2001.list.htm from Graham, *Unguarded Gates*, p. 94.

3. National Public Radio (NPR), *All Things Considered*, "1965 Immigration Law Changed Face of America," interview hosted by Michele Norris and Robert Siegel interviewing Jennifer Ludden, Stephen Klineberg and Otis Graham, May 9, 2006.

4. NPR, *All Things Considered*, May 9, 2006.

5. Graham, *Unguarded Gates*, p. 91.

6. Ibid., 93.

7. Margaret S. Orchowski, *Immigration and the American Dream: Battling the Political Hype and Hysteria* (Lanham, MD: Rowman & Littlefield, 2008), p. 57.

8. *Migration News*, March 2000, vol. 7, number 3, "Mexico: Dual Nationality, Politics."

9. Ibid.

10. Ibid.

11. Pew Research Center: Hispanic Trends, "Hispanic Nativity Shift," report by Jens Manuel Krogstad and Mark Hugo Lopez, April 29, 2014.

12. Ibid.

13. Migration Policy Institute, "Immigration Facts," February 2007, No. 18, "Immigration Fees Increases in Context," available online at MPI website.

14. Pew Research Center: Hispanic Trends.

15. From a "Newsmakers" meeting "Immigration and the 2008 Elections: Are We Victims to Political Spin?" sponsored by the National Press Club and the International Center for Journalists on April 18, 2007.

16. Orchowski, *Immigration and the American Dream*, p., 57.

17. Ibid., 60-61.

18. Ibid., 61.

19. *ABC News*, April 14, 2010, "A New Baby Boom? Foreign 'Birth Tourists' Seek U.S. Citizenship for Children," by Devin Dwyer.

20. *Hispanic Outlook in Higher Education*, October 21, 2013, "Dreamers Could Make or Break Immigration Reform in 2013," by Margaret Orchowski.

21. Pew Research Center: Hispanic Trends.

22. Orchowski, *Immigration and the American Dream*, p. 62.

23. *New York Times*, September 23, 2013, "Number of Illegal Immigrants in U.S. May Be on Rise Again, Estimates Say," by Julia Preston.

24. Ibid.

25. Orchowski, *Immigration and the American Dream*, p. 59.

26. Graham, *Unguarded Gates*, p. 106.

27. *Congressional Record*, June 7, 2007, p. CRS7318.

28. Orchowski, *Immigration and the American Dream*, p. 37.

29. *Plyler v. Doe*, 457 U.S. 202, 1982.

30. John Willshire Carrera, Esq., *Immigrant Students: Their Legal Right of Access to Public Schools. A Guide for Advocates and Educators* (Boston: National Coalition of Advocates for Students, 1992).

31. Immigration Reform and Control Act (IRCA), 100 Stat. 3359, 8 U.S.C.A.§1101, 1986.

32. Americans for Immigration Control Weekly News and Commentary, April 9, 2007, "Kennedy's Broken Promise."

33. Tom Murse, "Executive Actions Versus Executive Or Definition of Executive Actions and List of Example." http://uspolitics.about.com/od/Gun-Control/a/Executive-Actions-Versus-Executive-Orders.htm.

34. "Executive Actions versus Executive Orders."

35. http://www.npr.org/sections/thetwo-way/2014/11/20/365467914/so-just-what-is-an-executive-action-anyway.

36. Ibid.

37. *Boston Globe, The Last Lion*, p. 377.

38. Alan Wolf, *The Future of Liberalism* (New York: Alfred A. Knopf, 2009).

39. Graham, *Unguarded Gates*, p. 88.

40. Hearing on government immigration statistics before the House Subcommittee on Immigration, on June 6, 2007.

41. *New York Times*, January 31, 2015, "Why Are Cubans So Special?" op-ed by Ann Louise Bardach.

42. Reuters News Service, February 13, 2013, "Cuban Perks under Scrutiny," by David Adams and Tom Brown.

43. Ibid.

44. Aneesh Chopa, *Innovative State: How New Technologies Can Transform Government* (New York: Atlantic Monthly Press, 2014).

45. Mark K. Updegrove, *Indomitable Will: LBJ in the Presidency* (New York: Crown Publishers, 2012), p. 170

46. *Washington Post*, Book World, January 18, 2015, "The political ordeal behind the Great Society," a review of Julian E. Zelizer's book *The Fierce Urgency of Now*, by Wendy Smith.

47. Ibid.

48. Julian E. Zelizer, *The Fierce Urgency of Now: Lyndon Johnson, Congress, and the Battle for the Great Society* (New York: Penguin Press, 2015), p. 323

5. REFORMING THE INA IN THE TWENTY-FIRST CENTURY

1. *Washington Post*, January 15, 2015, "Ghost of the Great Society: Too Much of Our Government Is Confined by 1965 Ambitions," op-ed by Charles Lane.

2. *Washington Post*, January 10, 2015, "The Lesson We Should Take from 'Selma,'" op-ed by Katrina vanden Heuvel, editor and publisher of *The Nation* magazine.

3. *NewsOne for Black America*, April 8, 2014, "State of Black America 2014: Blacks and Latinos Remain Underemployed," by D. L. Chandler.

4. USA Today "U.S. population growth slows to just 0.71%" by Greg Toppo and Paul Overberg, October 7, 2014.

5. "Hispanic Nativit Shift" *Hispanic Trends*, April 29, 2014, PEW Research Center.

6. Pew Research Center: Social & Demographic Trends, March 7, 2014, "Millennials in Adulthood: Detached from Institutions, Networked with Friends."

7. John Zogby and Joan Snyder Kuhl, *First Globals: Understanding, Managing and Unleashing the Potential of Our Millennial Generation* (ebook, published by the authors, 2013).

8. *TIME* magazine, "The Me Me Me Generation," May 9, 2013, by Joel Stein.

9. *Daily Mail*, April 2014, "More People than Ever Living Outside Their Home Country."

10. *Hispanic Outlook*, January 27, 2014, "Are Hispanic Millennials Leading Their Generation?," by Margaret Orchowski.

11. For more information, see "Apollo–Soyuz Test Project," Wikipedia, http://en.wikipedia.org/wiki/Apollo%E2%80%93Soyuz_Test_Project.

12. For more information, see "Space Shuttle," Wikipedia, http://en.wikipedia.org/wiki/Space_Shuttle.

13. *Slate*, March 5, 2014, "NASA budget 2015: More Cuts, More Politics,"by Phil Pliat, http://www.slate.com/blogs/bad_astronomy/2014/03/05/nasa_budget_2015_more_cuts_more_politics.html.

14. Small Business Trends, May 8, 2013, "Complete History of Social Media: Then and Now," by Drew Hendricks.

15. Ars Tecnica. September 2, 2013, "How Can They Be So Good?: The Strange Story of Skype," by Toivo Taenavsuu.

16. Julian E. Zelizer, *The Fierce Urgency of Now: Lyndon Johnson, Congress, and the Battle for the Great Society* (New York: Penguin Press, 2015), p. 259.

17. Thomas F. Schaller, *Whistling Past Dixie: How Democrats Can Win without the South* (New York: Simon & Schuster, 2006).

18. *Economist*, February 8, 2013, "The Great Expulsion," http://www.economist.com/news/briefing/21595892–barack-obama-has-presided-over-one-largest-peacetime-outflows-people-americas.

19. WiredPen, "Visual Guide: The Balance of Power between Congress and the Presidency (1945–2015)," WiredPen.com.

20. Otis L. Graham Jr., *Unguarded Gates: A History of America's Immigration Crisis* (Lanham, MD: Rowman & Littlefield, 2004), p. 163.

21. Peter S. Canellos, ed., *The Last Lion: The Fall and Rise of Ted Kennedy*, by the team at *The Boston Globe*, with foreword by Senator John McCain (New York: Simon & Schuster, 2009), p. 204.

22. *U.S. News & World Report*, Opinion blog, March 9, 2010, "the bill has to pass before they—and the rest of us "can find out what's in it," by Peter Roff.

23. Canellos, *The Last Lion*, p. 236.

24. Ibid., 233–36.

25. Ibid., 20.

26. Ibid., 331–37.

27. *Los Angeles Times*, August 8, 2009, "The Gipper and Ted Kennedy Had 'Wonderful' Friendship," political editorial.

28. Canellos, *The Last Lion*, pp. 353–55.

29. Ibid., 379.

30. "What Went Wrong for Democrats in 2014," remarks by Senator Chuck Schumer at the National Press Club on November 25, 2014.

31. Orchowski, p. 170.

32. David Maraniss, *Barack Obama: The Story* (New York: Simon & Schuster, 2012).

33. *New York Times*, February 6, 2015, "In Ending Slavery, the Abolitionists Came First," letter to the editor by Edward B. Rugemer, in response to an op-ed in the *New York Times* Sunday Review February, 1, 2015, "Was Abolitionism a Failure?" by John Grinspan.

34. A speech Chuck Scumer gave to the Migration Policy Institute in the winter of 2008 at Georgetown University Law School when he took over the Senate Immigration Subcommittee from Ted Kennedy.

35. Nicolas Kanellos, "The Latino Presence: Some Historical Background," in *Latinos and the Nation's Future*, edited by Henry G. Cisneros (Houston: Arte Publico Press, 2008).

36. *Hispanic Outlook*, April 7, 2014, "News Coverage of Hispanics Makes Some Cringe: Even NPR Gets a C," by Margaret Orchowski, UNCENSORED.

37. Margaret S. Orchowski, *Immigration and the American Dream: Battling the Political Hype and Hysteria* (Lanham, MD: Rowman & Littlefield, 2008), p. 57.

38. DC Fiscal Policy Institute, March 7, 2013, "For Some DC Groups of DC Residents, Unemployment Remains High in the Wake of the Recession," by Marina Manganaris.

39. *Hispanic Outlook in Higher Education*, September 23, 2014, "State of HSIs 2014: Growing Fast," by Margaret S. Orchowski.

40. Philip M. Dine, *State of the Unions: How Labor Can Strengthen the Middle Class, Improve Our Economy, and Regain Political Influence* (New York: McGraw Hill, 2007), pp. ix, x.

41. Ibid.

42. Pew Research Center, *Hispanic Trends*, April 23, 2012, "Net Migration from Mexico Falls to Zero—and Perhaps Less," by Jeffrey S. Passel, D'Vera Cohn, and Ana Gonzalez-Barrera.

43. *Chronicle of Higher Education Review*, Jananuary 23, 2015, "The Progressive Case for Reducing Immigration," by Philip Cafaro.

6. LESSONS LEARNED

1. Robert A. Caro, "The Johnsons in Johnson City," in *The Passage of Power: The Years of Lyndon Johnson* (New York: Random House ,2013), part V, chapter 20.

2. Lake Superior State University, Senator Philip A. Hart Memorial Scholarship, "Philip A. Hart biography."

3. Thomas Mann (Brookings Institute) and Norm Ornstein (American Enterprise Institute), *It's Even Worse than It Looks: How the American Constitutional System Collided with the New Politics of Extremism* (New York: Basic Books 2012).

4. Kallick made this argument most recently at a panel on May 21, 2015, in which the author attended at the Bipartisan Policy Center, Washington, DC.

5. Hearing of the Immigration Subcommittee of the House Judiciary Committee, July 23, 2013.

6. Eugene Robinson, *Disintegration: The Splintering of Black America* (New York: Anchor Books of Random House, 2010).

7. *Washington Post*, March 2, 2015, "The Next America is Now," op-ed by Robert J. Samuelson, quoting a conference at the Brookings Institute on Paul Taylor and the PEW Research Center's book, *The Next America: Boomers, Millennials, and the Looming Generational Showdown* (New York: BBS Publications.

8. Panel at the LBJ Presidential Library on the Civil Rights Act, recorded by CSPAN, April 10, 2014.

Index

219

About the Author

Margaret (Peggy) Sands Orchowski, PhD, is the credentialed Congressional Correspondent for the *Hispanic Outlook on Higher Education* magazine in Washington D.C.; she writes several feature stories a month plus a monthly column UNCENSORED covering higher education and immigration issues. She was BillAnalysis Editor at Congressional Quarterly in Washington D.C.; a reporter for Associated Press in Peru, an InterAmerican Press Association Fellow in Argentina, a press officer for the United States in Switzerland, and a staff reporter and feature writer for her hometown newspapers in Santa Barbara, California, among other journalism positions. In 2013, she received a grant from the Fund for Investigative Journalism; her story on the challenges facing American Hispanic engineering students from the foreign student industry was published April 9, 2014, in the *Hispanic Outlook* magazine. She obtained a BA in journalism and Latin American affairs from the University of California, Berkeley; a MA in political science and international relations from the University of California, Santa Barbara; a MA in urban affairs from Occidental College, Los Angeles, and a PhD in comparative public and education/finance administration from the University of California, Santa Barbara. She completed language and cultural immersion programs at Middlebury College, Vermont (Spanish); Unversidades de San Marcos, Lima, Peru, and de Buenos Aires, Argentina; and at les Universites de Grenoble in France and de Geneve in Switzerland (French).

Orchowski's book *Immigration and the American Dream: Battling the Political Hype and Hysteria* (Rowman & Littlefield, June 2008) was recommended by Governor Bill Richardson as a "must-read for everyone in Congress and in every D.C. think tank." She has given over 60 presentations at foreign affairs and public policy organizations, book fairs, and book stores (including Politics and Prose in Washington D.C.) and has appeared on television and public radio talk shows in 18 states. She was featured on C-SPAN's Washington Journal; her op eds have appeared in *The Hill* newspaper, *NewsHawk*, *American Prospect*, *USNews&World Report Opinion*, AOL.com, the *Indianapolis Star*, and the *Atlantic Journal Constitution* among others.

Peggy lived and worked for over ten years abroad, speaks and works in four languages easily and raised her two children in three.